Always pal
Jenn

With many blessings
and much LOVE
heading your way!
Mumma
Gee Gee
Yara ♡

From My Heart

To Yours

A 365 day inspirational guide

to help you find your way through life

Thomas and Lou Ann Bruck

Kindle Create

ISBN-978-1-7365383-0-2

Cover design by: Hank Yuloff

Back cover Photograph: Charles Ruscher

Mandala design: Rhianne Newlahnd

Printed in the United States of America

Epigraph

"Our greatest fear is not that we are inadequate. Our deepest fear is that we are powerful beyond measure. It is our light, not our darkness that most frightens us. We ask ourselves, who am I to be brilliant, gorgeous, talented, fabulous? Actually, who are you not to be? Your playing small does not serve the world. We were born to make manifest the glory of God that is within us. And as we let our own light shine, we unconsciously give other people permission to do the same."

Marianne Williamson

Acknowledgements

To all the people who read my blogs and encouraged me to put them in a book. This is for you!

To you who are reading this book today, right now, may your days be brighter and bring more love and caring into your life!

To all our children, Michael, Deborah, Chris, Uma and Jim who light up our lives with joy!

To all those who follow their heart and keep on creating their magnificent dreams!

Thomas and Lou Ann Bruck have written a must-read primer for anyone journeying toward heart-based living...Read this book - and learn from two people who, more than anyone I know, walk their walk." — *Danette Wolpert, Executive Director, ILLUMINATE Film Festival*

Thanks so much for writing this book. I have been down for quite a while because of my wife Nikki's passing. It was a very difficult three years leading up to it. I am taking it one step at a time. Some days are good and some days aren't. What you wrote inspired and lifted me. I will continue to read it again and again, to remind me of the truth and to rebuild my life. I am honored that you asked me to promote it. This book will be a blessing to anyone who reads it. - *Michael Byers has been on Broadway, in television, and concert. A talented singing artist; sings 'Music for more joyful living' find him at MichaelByersMusic.com*

In FROM MY HEART TO YOURS you will feel like you are reading the personal diary of a wise protector of the Earth. The Bruck's gently taking you through the steps to turn a small rivulet of interest to a raging storm of preservation and action. This is a love letter to the world in which we live, written by one of her most gentle caretakers. It isn't only about the most obvious tracks to become aware of our surroundings, but to change our point of view in how we perceive and act to preserve them. — *Hank Yuloff, best-selling author, award winning speaker and small business coach. Find him at YuloffCreativeMarketingSolutions.com*

Foreword

Thomas shares from his heart when he writes and speaks. His desire to help people live their happiest and most healthful life is so deeply ingrained in him, it's remarkable. He is also talking to himself as he writes; as we all are only human and need reminders to be our own best self.

Before I met Thomas forty years ago, I knew I wanted a long term relationship with someone who was in alignment with me in body, mind and spirit. I moved from Texas to Arizona in 1979 with my 13 year old daughter to be a pharmacist and massage therapist at the A.R.E Medical Clinic (Association for Research and Enlightenment) – based on Edgar Cayce's holistic teachings.

I knew my life was going to dramatically change as I loved helping people holistically – the pharmacist in me sold herbal products that Edgar Cayce recommended in his health readings (to learn more about Edgar Cayce, read 'There is a River' by Thomas Sugrue) and as a massage therapist at the clinic, connecting with people one on one with the element of touch.

The Clinic's Patient Care Director was Thomas Bruck back in the late 70's. I instantly felt a strong spiritual connection with him. Whenever he spoke at meetings or in other settings, I loved listening to his honesty, sense of humor and heartfelt caring for us all.

One day he had a dream to buy the clinic's pharmacy – coincidentally I had the same dream the same night. We did buy the pharmacy and were business partners for three years. Several of us had planned to go to Disneyland together, others cancelled and we fell in love under the red and white umbrella at Carnation Plaza while dancing together! Thirty-eight years later we still love, acknowledge and respect each other. What a great team we have been!

During the last few years Thomas has been sharing daily blogs on Facebook and our Positiveplace.com website. At his request I reviewed them before he published them. Sometimes it was simple typos or continuing the thought for more clarity. It was an honor to support him in this way.

One way to read it is to ask a question and then open it up to give a deeper meaning or insight and maybe even an answer! Reading from front to back cover is an option as well. We are grateful and blessed to share these with you! May you enJOY and let it enrich your life as it has many blog readers and ours!

As a result of a gift Thomas shared with me: The Listening Path by Julia Cameron that was newly published in January 2021, I began doing morning pages as I did many years ago. One idea I received while writing was to write quotes after each day's guide and so I did!

Lou Ann Maxwell Murillo Bruck

Introduction

Words are so important in our lives. They can heal, maim, encourage, discourage, inspire, denigrate and on and on. In June of 2017 I had a spiritual experience. I was going out on a solar sales call to the town of Cottonwood Arizona. I drove down winding rutted dirt roads with dust trails flowing behind me like some kind of super cape. When I arrived, I could see immediately that the house had an inferior roof on which to install solar panels.

The gentleman invited me inside his home and handed me an auburn colored glass of ice cold tea. We sat and chatted for a while. I gazed around the room. Many familiar well-worn and faded books lined several bookcases that surrounded us. There was a moment's pause in our conversation when he asked me "Do you know who Quan Yin is?" I replied that I did (Quan Yin is an East Asian Goddess of compassion).

His bright eyes narrowed a bit. He rubbed his well-lined, tan face and said *"Quan Yin has a message for you. 'You have many gifts and talents that you are not sharing with others. The world is in crisis. Many souls feel sad and their spirits are broken. You have the ability to help them rise from the ashes of their damaged lives'. I want you to go home and start a blog. Your message will inspire many."*

I left there on that fateful day and headed back to Sedona. I then started a blog that led to this book. As I shared our blog with many readers, some have encouraged me to put them together in a book. Here it is. I hope you receive some pleasure and inspiration from it.

My life partner and wonderful wife, Lou Ann, has been with me on many of these journeys and events. Each night, after I finished blogging, Lou Ann read the entry and suggested different ways of sharing. She also added some ideas of her own. Then she edited each blog for grammar and content.

I have been learning and sharing spiritual ideas and concepts for more than fifty years. I was fortunate to attend a wonderful metaphysical school in Washington DC in the early seventies. I was exposed to most of the major philosophies and religions of the world. After schooling, I attended dozens of seminars, workshops and intensives along my path. I have read hundreds of books on a wide spectrum of new thought and ancient learnings.

If I say things in the blogs and in this book and do not give credit to the originator of the information, it is unintentional and I apologize. As you will see, I have done my best to give credit to these wonderful wise people living or have lived! If for any reason, you find any information in this book needs to be credited, please let us know.

One more point: I have shared wonderful songs of hope and praise and magic and wonder by so many talented singers, songwriters in dozens of these blogs. I wanted to actually share the printed lyrics with you but that became too costly and sometimes impossible. So I have given you a YouTube link so that you can enjoy this music as much as Lou Ann and I do. Please take the time and find the music and let it fill you up to overflowing!

It has been clear to me for most of my life that when I follow my heart, my life flows. When I try to figure things out and get in a fear space, my life doesn't work so well. It is our hearts that connect us all. Most of all the differences we create are from the ego and the Monkey mind! So, thank you for taking this journey with me each day. We are lovers on a journey of the soul. Our spirits sing to us through our hearts!

Thank You, Life!

For all the love I feel inside. For all the laughs I shared with those I love. For every second of my life, every breath, thought, feeling, wink, sneeze, tear.

For all the things I have seen and done. All the games I lost and won, all the friends who shared their heart. All the dreams that gave me hope.

For all my children and their families, for my life partner who gave me strength. For all the books that taught me life. For every song that chilled my soul.

For being able to read, being able to learn, being able to teach, being able to know, being able to care, and being able to share. And for kindness, for courtesy, for chivalry, for tenderness, for compassion, I am grateful for all these things!

For every kiss, hug, hand held, squeeze, massage

For sunshine, sunset, sunrise, cloud, rain, snowflake, thunderbolt, hail.

For taste, touch, sight, smell, hearing

Every moment of our life is a gift, whether it brought joy or sadness, hope or despair, fear or courage, laughter or tears. Perhaps, it is unique in the entire Universe. Let us take the time to give thanks for it all.

January 1 Happy New Year

What if we didn't keep track of things? What if we just lived each moment without identifying and naming it? What if? We might just focus on the now. We wouldn't keep track of the past. We wouldn't worry about tomorrow. We wouldn't even have a name for a second, minute, day, week or year. We would see the sun rise and set, but we wouldn't keep track of when and why. What if you and I are these amazing particles of brightness who shine forever?

I wonder what life would be like if we hadn't kept track? I know for me, some of the happiest moments have been where I lost track of time, and I was completely in the moment. However, we do keep track of almost everything, and attach a lot of importance to it.

Last night on New Year's Eve we gathered together and counted down the seconds. We screamed, hugged, kissed and cried. For Lou Ann and me it is our wonderful evening; it is our wedding anniversary. We were married thirty-eight years ago in Scottsdale, Arizona. Then we immediately drove seven hours to Pasadena for the Rose Bowl and Parade. My youngest son Jim accompanied us there.

These three and a half decades have gone by in a blink of time. It is amazing how fast life seems to go. And yet, the two of us have done so much, it feels like several lifetimes rolled into one. I am so blessed to be with Lou Ann and see her daily, how she lives her life with such love, such grace, such honor and integrity. She lives full of joy, optimism and courage. Her gigantic heart touches almost everyone she encounters.

So, as long as we humans are going to keep track, I will join in and say happy anniversary to my lovely bride and wish her only happiness and prosperity all the days of her life.

And my wish for you in this coming year is to experience a greater fulfillment of the purpose for your life. May you get so involved with doing what you love or love what you are doing, that time stops for you!

Remember, we don't have to wait for December 31st to celebrate a new beginning. Each and every moment, we are reborn again to discover our divinity and to live our magnificence! From my brand new heart to yours, Thomas

Treasure every moment of this day and the next and the next and.....be happily conscious of living life with love, laughter and integrity!

January 2   The Year for the people

For many, 2017 was a difficult year in a lot of ways. There was so much natural destruction from fires, storms, floods, and in the United States, a stunning election that continues to cause concern for millions. I am not going to go into the specifics of the personalities involved. However, it appears that our country and our planet are in trouble. There are powers that have seized control, who do not value the beauty or sacredness of Mother Earth. And now it is our time to say stop!

It is time for all of us who love the planet and each other, to take a stand. To say enough is enough! Love is the most powerful energy and we get to stand up for love! We get to do whatever it takes to create heaven on Earth. We get to stand hand in hand and form a circle of love around our planet. In the United States, the upcoming elections give us an opportunity to take a stand for love.

Do whatever you can to be an agent who creates the kind of government we desire on all levels, local, state and federal. Let us campaign by not making the others wrong. Let us make our voices heard, exclaiming that goodness, mercy, caring and compassion are the hallmark of our campaign.

I would like to share with you an astrological reading regarding this full moon we are having tonight. It was just sent to Lou Ann thirty minutes ago with love, from a good friend named Cilandria who lives in Oregon. Here it is: *Full moon Cancer opposite the sun in Capricorn sets the tone for the year. Gratitude is the theme, enthusiasm, courage into the mystery. There is a strong need for emotional love and firm foundations. Now is the* time to create them. There may be tough truths, be clear, be the best you can be. What one identifies with, is who they become. Love everyone, everything, every situation. Look for the light and acknowledge it and you will shine! It's full throttle ahead. Be the light; align with your divine heart's purpose. Forgive, be compassionate, use your gifts, pursue your dreams, and travel LIGHTLY. Ask, does this let me shine in whatever I say, think or do. We are taking off with a blast! Namaste, Cilandria."

The stars are aligned with those who are standing in gratitude, aligned with those who are willing to love everything. It is our time! It is time that all of the wonderful, magical, angelic beings of light let their light shine even brighter. Then the darkness will realize that it is the light, as well! We will all dwell in this Garden of Eden, when we come from love! From my full throttle heart to yours, Thomas

Be the love and light for all the people in your life! They will shine too!

January 3 Universal Principles

Throughout our book we get to share with you Universal Principles. These principles were first shared with us by Arnold Patent in the early eighties. These wonderful axioms have been the foundation for how Lou Ann and I have travelled through life these past four decades. They are timeless and rich with fundamental truths that all of us can use to live a full life! There are nineteen principles on his list of the way Spirit shows up in manifestation all through Universe. I will italicize them so you will know the exact principle!

Universal Principle # 1 is Energy: *"the basic component of Universe, energy, occurs in either materialized or non-materialized form. All that we see and feel is an expression of energy.*

All energy is the love of the divine flowing through us. When we resist the flow of love, we experience discomfort. When we align with the love, we feel joyful and at peace."

We are energy and we get to choose whether we will materialize or not and how and what and where we might do so. When we incarnate on planet Earth as Homo sapiens we encounter this plane of manifestation in a unique way. All other forms of manifestation get to do so as well in their own unique way of expressing energy.

In the human experience it becomes apparent that as we allow our divine energy to flow through us, life feels easy. We feel joy and peace and love. When we attempt to take control of our lives and sometimes resist the flow of love it becomes painful. And often the pain gets so uncomfortable that we are moved to search for the reason of our discontent and it leads us to discover our true nature.

If you feel stuck in some way and are looking for answers to become unstuck; use the Universal Principles that I will be sharing here and see if they don't help you find your way back to your natural way of flowing with Universe. For more information about the principles please go to arnoldpatent.com and learn from the master!

Remember that you are love manifesting in your own singular unique way. No other form of love has ever been like you and never will there be another you. You are precious and valuable and capable and divine! From my heart to yours, Thomas

Let the energy of love flow through you in your own special way – know that you are Divine!

January 4   Remember the Love!

As I was sitting, eyes closed, being quiet, determining what I would share with you today, what came to me was the memorable song from the musical Rent—525,600 minutes. Lou Ann was sitting alongside of me and saw what I was writing. She pointed out to me that Alan Cohen, in his wonderful book, A Daily Dose of Sanity, shared the same concept. His title for today is 86,400 Big Ones. He is referring to the amount of seconds in a day. And he uses a quote *"Each day comes bearing its own gifts. Untie the ribbons."*

525,600 is the amount of minutes contained in a year. Of course it is all arbitrary. But the point is that in our lifetimes, we have a limited amount of time to do what we choose. I am asking all of us, how will we choose these moments of our lives? With what will we fill it? Most of us will probably use a third or 175,200 minutes sleeping. Some will use 175,200 working. That leaves another 175,200 to do what we choose. And, of course, we get to choose our work life, as well.

Our lives can be so much richer, when we can break it down into moments instead of years. When we choose to stay present to whatever we are doing or creating, life gets filled up with love. So many have discovered that when they give their whole heart to something, whether work or play or passion, they are overflowing with love.

Now, as we look back on this last year of 525,600 minutes, let us remember the love. Remember those who were with us and have now gone on their after Earth journey. Remember the kindness that someone did for us. Remember the laughter and the tears that lit up our soul. Remember the good things we accomplished and how we were supported by friends and family.

Choose each moment to be a sacred one. It doesn't have to be formal or religious. I believe that every moment is sacred. It can be watching a cartoon, feeding the cat or dog, going to the store, gassing up the car, washing the windows, making breakfast, hugging our loved ones or telling them how much we love them. Either everything is sacred or nothing is. There is only Oneness and we are part of it!

Enjoy your next moment and fill it up with every ounce of love you can muster. Then the next moment of love and the next until you use up your 525,600! From my minute by minute heart to yours, Thomas

Feel the love in your heart right now in this moment, embrace it fully and share it!

January 5   Healing Time on Earth

It is always healing time on Earth. There are no days off. It is a 24/7 365.25 days of operation. It can sure be overwhelming when we see what needs to be done. We humans have messed up the planet, so we get to clean it up and heal it. There are many organizations with which you can choose to get involved. Here is a list of some:

Friends of the Earth, · the Cousteau Society, · the Wilderness Society, · National Space Institute, · Save the Children, · World Wildlife Fund, · Friends for All Children, · the Alaska Coalition, · Nuclear Safeguards, · New Earth Exposition, · the American Indian Heritage, · Simpatico, · Environmental Defense Fund, · Fund for Animals, · Sierra Club, · Environmental Action, · Alaska Wilderness Preservation, − National Wildlife Federation, − Wildlife Conservation Society. Check them out and see if you can get involved.

There is also a lot of personal healing to be done. In truth, the personal healing can accelerate the global healing. When we feel good about ourselves and life, we generally make better decisions. These decisions can help us do our part in helping Mother Earth.

If you are feeling less-than, find someone and share your heart. It is so cathartic to let others in on our pain and suffering. When someone truly listens to us, something inside begins to shift. We then know at least one person knows what is going on inside of us. When we find trust like this, personal healing can begin. Then if we need to seek a therapeutic answer to our problems, we are better prepared to do the work.

John Denver sang a wonderful song titled Healing Time on Earth. Go to this YouTube link to enjoy it! https://www.youtube.com/watch?v=0wrDc8lx3_l

Come on, we can all do this! At the very least, the next time you see a piece of trash on the ground, pick it up and recycle it, and have recycle bins in your home. If you see water that should not be running, turn it off. Car pool or make your next car be a hybrid or better yet, electric.

Change old light bulbs to LED style. Lower your thermostat and wear a sweater. Lower the thermostat in your fridge. Go organic. Become Vegan! There are dozens of ways we can all help. Just go online and look it up. Now is the time for healing planet Earth. From my environmental heart to yours, Thomas

Healing ourselves and the planet can happen together! Let's begin it!

January 6   Time for Revolution

Just finished watching a new film titled *Happening-A Clean Energy Revolution* by James Redford. It is a documentary that clearly shows how far we have come and how the world is turning to renewable energy. We still have a long way to go because the fossil fuel business is still entrenched. We are now beginning to win the battle though!

In Buffalo New York they built the largest solar panel manufacturing plant in the western hemisphere. It is putting 3000 people back to work. At the Apple Corporation in 2016, 96 percent of the electricity used at their global facilities came from renewable energy, reducing their carbon emissions by nearly 585,000 metric tons. They're 100 percent renewable in 24 countries — and all of Apple's data centers. To go fully green, Apple has said it plans to "generate and source from more than 4 gigawatts of new clean energy worldwide by 2020," according to a document released this month.

California has soaked up enough rays to generate 67.2 per cent of its energy from renewable sources last month, smashing previous records. When combining California's largest grid with hydro-power facilities, renewable energy rose even further to 80.7 per cent of total energy generation on 13 May. Thanks to ample sunshine, full water reservoirs and more solar facilities, the California Independent System Operator, the largest grid in the state, beat previous records. California also set a new record on 16 May for wind power, producing 4,985 megawatts on one day. LEGO is now 100% renewable.

In Nevada, which tried to kill solar energy in 2015, they have passed nine new solar energy bills to bring back solar full time.

So, it is time for a revolution. Those of us who live in Arizona need to stand up and (march if necessary) and make the people on the Arizona Corporation Commission do what is right for the people of Arizona. Contact your local congress person and demand that you want Arizona to go 100% solar or renewable. We want to replace all fossil fuel energy and nuclear energy. Go to environmentarizona.org and sign up to get your voice heard!

There are many of you, in fact most, who read this, that live all over the world. Please do whatever you can to create renewable energy; it is more for our children and grandchildren than us. Let us have our ensuing generations sit around their solar or wind apparatus in the future and say how proud they were of us. Please, please, please get involved and make our planet green again! From my green heart to yours, Thomas

It ain't easy being green (as Kermit the frog would say) – you can do it though!

January 7 Avatars

Many years ago I gave a talk at Spirit Church in Sedona about Avatars. There is a highway through the Village of Oak Creek to Sedona which is the main thoroughfare from the interstate. The road is taken by most travelers from the south to get to Sedona. We locals of course, use the same highway and it is mostly one lane. Often I would head to town and there would be a large recreational vehicle going less than the posted speed limit.

One day, it occurred to me that Universe was putting those huge things in my way to slow me down. And when I slowed down, I would shift and be more present to the fabulous beauty that surrounded me. So, at church that Sunday, we gave the large vehicles the title of Avatars. An avatar is deity in some form. Since that time, I have a warm feeling when I am behind an RV, because I know Oneness is smiling.

Small events like this often come and let us know that we are connected. And that we often get to choose another feeling or thought that supports us in consciousness. I believe that life is always on purpose. We often are not aware of what life has for us. However, it is a powerful thing to surrender to Life and let it lead us to our highest good. Getting out of our own way and letting Spirit guide us is always a good thing! Many times, we think we have to be in control and know the answers about living. In truth, while we are in our Earth spacesuits, we have limited our knowledge so that we can have a total human experience.

So look for God in everything. Since there is only Oneness then everything is Divine. Try not to take even simple things for granted and you will have a much richer life experience. The next time you have someone slow you down or make you wait, stop and take a breath and smile and say "Thank you Spirit". From my patient heart to yours, Thomas

Laugh at what slows us down and be grateful for it! It has our best interest at heart!

January 8   Mind, Body, Spirit

When I was growing up, I rooted for the Cincinnati Reds baseball team. It wasn't a choice; my whole family was Reds fans. When my family moved to Southern California, I became a Los Angeles Rams football fan, a UCLA fan of all sports and a Los Angeles Lakers follower as well. As a young boy, I would play outside for hours doing all kinds of physical games such as Kick the Can, Hide and go Seek and capture the flag. I was fast and had good hand, eye coordination. In high school I lettered in basketball and baseball. In the Air Force I played softball and football.

I am eighty and I still love sports! I have literally watched thousands of games and events; everything from Little League Baseball to the Olympics. My mother knew the batting average and how many home runs players hit as well as my dad. Baseball is a sport of statistics. Knowing those details was a thing that actually bonded my family in a way. When the UCLA basketball team lost after it had won eighty-eight games in a row; I couldn't eat for two days! My four children also follow sports. My grandson Seth is a professional basketball player in Hungary.

In perspective, I believe professional athletes are paid too much. Someone can dunk a basketball and can earn millions per year, while school teachers have to buy school supplies out of their own pockets. Professional sports players and owners are among the one per cent of the wealthiest people. I wish it weren't so. I wish teachers and public safety officers and others who do so much for humanity could be paid a much higher wage.

And yet, I still watch the games. I love the games themselves and they taught me so much about life. Teamwork is essential to succeed. Each person has their role to play and they depend on each other. We learn to trust each other. We work hard, keep our commitments and follow through. Often, we eventually love each other. The motto all for one and one for all is a mantra for teams. And together we experience the ecstasy of winning and the agony of defeat.

To this day, I still play tennis four to five times per week. The other days I walk a few miles to keep in shape. My physical body has been so important to me these seven decades. I love to sweat and to exert myself and feel myself moving through space. I am sharing with you tonight not to enroll you in watching sports but perhaps to get physical. Our mental health is incumbent on our physical health.

We have chosen to come to Earth to express our divinity. It is a gift to incarnate in a physical body and have a mind that thinks and a heart that feels. I encourage you to take care of your physical temple as well as nourish your soul. Edgar Cayce channeled: "Spirit is the life, the mind is the builder and the physical is the result. When we take care of all three we get to live long loving powerful lives. From my athletic heart to yours, Thomas

Take care of your mind, body and spirit – they each matter equally!

January 9   Mother God

Many people don't believe in the anthropomorphication of Spirit, including me. Yes, there was a time when we could believe in a wise elderly deity who would take care of us; so many of us were taught that God was a male. I have noticed in my lifetime, that if God did have a form and personality the qualities would be feminine and not masculine. The feminine is what I feel when I feel God. The feminine nature is comforting, loving, caring, nurturing, sustaining and stable. That is what I believe to be the qualities of Deity. For me, God, Spirit, Oneness, All That Is, is the all-encompassing energy of everything.

Right now on planet Earth we have too long been ruled over, led by, the masculine energy. Masculine in the form of men is often brutal, uncompromising, destructive, proud, arrogant and unsustainable. Look at our country and how it is run. Look at all the wars that have been started by men. Look at Wall Street, our government, largely ruled by men who often seek to win at all costs. Half of our government should be women and women of all colors, races, beliefs and sexualty. Women are still underpaid and underappreciated.

If you saw the Golden Globes, you saw a wonderful speech by Oprah Winfrey. You saw a powerful black woman, who came from obscurity and poverty. She is perhaps the most recognized and potentially powerful person on Earth. In the U.S., we need her or women like her to lead our country in every aspect. If we truly desire peace on Earth, then it is women and the feminine aspect in goodhearted men who need to take the lead all over the world. As Oprah said "times up", time is up for the planet.

A new dawn is arising, led by people in their hearts and not their pocketbooks. It is time for all of us, women and men, who love the planet and all that is in it, to take a stand. Stand up for goodness, compassion, forgiveness, honesty, integrity and love of all creatures great and small. From my feminine heart to yours, Thomas

Feel the nurturing, loving and caring part of you and let it express itself!

January 10   We Light up Our Life!

A little parody on the hit song You Light up my Life! Lou Ann and I attended an Illuminate Film Festival meeting tonight. It is the first this year for our team and it was very exciting. We always feel energized and motivated after these events. The Illuminate Film Festival usually occurs the last couple of days in May and three days in June, here in Sedona.

We were brainstorming about marketing campaigns that would best exemplify who we are and what we do. We were using the word illuminate as a verb. We are inviting folks to attend the festival in which they might be more illuminated. Then hopefully, they will be inspired to take action so that our planet might be more illuminated as well.

As I write this, it reminds me that we are all light beings. Light beings have a choice about life as to whether we let our light shine brightly or perhaps dim it a little. The song You Light up My Life was written as a thank you to deity; that Oneness lights up our life and shows us the way. My parody also implies that as an integral part of Oneness, we too illuminate our lives!

We also focused on how important it is to take action. It is easy to get fired up around like minded people who are making a difference in the world. Then when we return to our daily lives, the true illumination gets to shine through.

I am always encouraging you to live your passion, follow your heart and make peace with where you are. I will share that a lot; it is vital! It is so important right now, to not only follow those suggestions, but to do it for humanity and the world. We have reached a place on Earth where what we say, think and do are more important than ever. Because social media has captured the interest of billions of people it is more vital that we let our lights shine!

If you desire to create more illumination in your life then please come to the festival as an attendee or volunteer to support the festival. Go to illuminatefilmfestival.com and scroll down to the "get involved" tab and select volunteer. We would love to have you join our team and you don't have to live in Sedona to do it. Now is the time to shine our lights so bright that the world will be a dazzling ball of light! From my illuminated heart to yours, Thomas

Be inspired and take action to illuminate your life and others!

January 11   Better to have loved

Tennyson's quote *"Tis better to have loved and lost then to never have loved at all"* fits other life lessons as well as love.

My advice in life is to go for it, in whatever area of life that you desire to create results. It does not matter if we succeed, as much as it does to have made the effort. Let us open our hearts to the infinite possibilities of life! I think one of the saddest things is to look back at my life and wish I had risked more. Even though, I have tried so many different things and failed at many; I still regret those times when I held back.

I have been married three times. Once, a family member said: "you don't believe in marriage do you?" "I replied if I didn't, why would I keep trying?" Well maybe I didn't believe as much as Elizabeth Taylor or Mickey Rooney (they were married eight times each)! I was just fortunate to have met Lou Ann.

So for me, it is better to have given it everything I've got, then to have not; only we know, whether we are giving it our all or not. This is not about success on some material level. Tennyson's quote is for each of us when we are at the end of this life; to smile and look back and know how much life we lived.

Don't wait for your ship to come in or for your soulmate to show up. Right now, find your passion, do what you love and do it for as long and as hard as you can! You and the world will be better for it! From my risk taking heart to yours, Thomas

Shoot for the moon! Even if you miss you will land among the stars!

January 12   Longevity

Ask yourself not how long you might live, but how much life is in the rest of your years? There have been studies about longevity and the answers are very revealing. Here are some ways to live longer and better.

Have a positive attitude. Happiness and attitude are very important. Optimism is a trait that is linked with longer life spans. Even studies support this. A 2011 study found that the group of older people that scored as the happiest had a death rate of 3.6%, which is less than half of the death rate of the least happy people, who scored 7.3%. Optimistic, outgoing, and easygoing people live longer.

So roll with it. Lou Ann and I have had the email and website name of positive place for some twenty five years. When people ask me my email address, they often remark what an excellent name that is. At the same time, as I keep repeating it, my mind keeps experiencing a positive image.

Laugh. Researchers in a 2012 study identified common personality characteristics of 243 centenarians. A love of laughter was on the list, and laughter was listed as an important part of life to them. Even people who smile more may live several years longer than people who do not smile as much.

Exercise. Regular exercise, be it walking, swimming, water aerobics, or riding a bike is going to extend your life. Exercises like yoga also help keep you flexible, improve your balance, and help relieve stress and anxiety. Getting 150 minutes of moderate exercise each week can add four years to your life.

Help others. Volunteer, donate, and help others when you can; doing this will do just as much for you, as it does for the people you help. Helping others allows you to contribute to your community, meet others, and find a purpose or a cause in which you believe. Plus, volunteers live longer than people who don't give their time.

Cook your own meals. A 2012 study found that people who cook at home up to five times a week live longer than those who eat out more often. In fact the homemade meal eaters were 47% more likely to still be alive after a decade. Eat organic and eat as much plant based foods as possible.

Living a long life is fun when we are healthy, happy, and prosperous and engaged in making the world a better place. We also live longer when we are being loving and being loved. Let us all live long powerful lives. It will be fun to do, and the world needs us to do it! From my youthful heart to yours, Thomas

Laugh more, have a positive attitude, exercise, help others and cook your own meals more often – you've got this!

January 13   Are We Up For It?

Teilhard de Chardin had a wonderful quote that goes like this: *"Someday, after mastering the winds, the waves, the tides and gravity, we shall harness for God the energies of love, and then, for a second time in the history of the world, man will have discovered fire."* Also he said *"There is almost a sensual longing for communion with others who have a large vision. The immense fulfillment of the friendship between those engaged in furthering the evolution of consciousness has a quality impossible to describe."*

He is talking about us right now. And now is the time for us to take action. We are standing on the brink of a planet in trouble. There are seven and a half billion of us and the birthrate seems unstoppable. We have destroyed so many of our species in the last hundred years. In that same century, we have aged the Earth the same amount as the last forty thousand years. These numbers are astounding and at our current pace they will only accelerate.

Let us find those folks who have the big vision for humanity. It might be one of us who reads this. Let's get involved in life in a way that transcends our limitations. Each of us gets to look inside our heart and decide whether we are part of the problem or the solution for our fragile spacecraft. I have shared on several occasions what many of us could do to help stem the onslaught of climate change.

Check out the David Suzuki Foundation for the ten ways you can stop climate change. Create a way that we can save this amazing planet for our children and their children. To paraphrase an old Pogo quote: let's say *"we have met our hero and it is us!"* Let us harness the energies of love and discover the fire that lights our hearts and saves our home. From my ecological, hopeful heart to yours, Thomas

Have a big vision of peace and love on the planet and begin creating it!

January 14 Coming Out

Lou Ann and I went to see the wonderful movie "The Post" tonight. The audience applauded three times during the movie. There were previews of upcoming movies which included a movie about a gay boy coming out. That term has always bothered me. Yes, I realize that it means coming out of the closet. And why were people in the closet in the first place? When did we decide that some of us "came out"?

Since the 1970's there has been a much greater acceptance of homosexual lifestyles. To love another, regardless of their sexuality is the essence of a joyful life. I know I am ranting and I feel good about it. I want no one to feel 'less than' for how they look, who they love or what they feel.

No one should ever have to "come out"! There was never any closet to be in as far as I am concerned. Let us unconditionally love and support each other, just the way we are, in all our magnificence! From my open heart to yours, Thomas

We each are so unique and incredible – acknowledge that in you!

January 15   The Simple Life

Lou Ann and I were driving to Costco today which is about 55 miles away from our home in Sedona. It was a bright sunny winter day and the air was so clear. We live in a wonderful area of Northern Arizona and you can see a hundred miles in most directions.

We heard the song "Give me the Simple Life" on the radio as we moved through the rolling hills covered in Mesquite.

The song reminds me that often we get caught up in life's activities and that we could miss the best things. Which reminds me of another song which is 'The Best Things in Life are Free.'

Both of these songs share the story that we often strive to create a life full of things and we miss the deep purpose of Earthly living. Life is about experiences that teach us how to be kind and loving. Other experiences demonstrate qualities of overcoming obstacles and persevering against long odds of achieving and never giving up. We eventually learn it is about with whom we share these amazing experiences. And then at the end of our life we can say we gave it all we had and we learned to love and be loved most of all!

I encourage you to find the balance in life as well. Give your love and passion to what you desire and make sure you are at the top of the list. From my simple heart to yours, Thomas

Give and receive love and kindness whenever you can today!

January 16 I have a dream

Those of us who were fortunate enough to hear the magnificent words of Dr. King will never forget that day! In August of 1963 I was 22 years old and had just moved to Washington D.C., actually the Maryland suburbs. I went there to get employment with the National Security Agency. I was married and had two children ages 20 months and 8 months. There was a delay in my job for ninety days, so I went out and found some work in a shoe store at a local strip mall. In less than three months I would be outside walking at that mall only to hear the horrible words "the president has been shot".

But on this day on the 28th day of August I was thrilled to hear the famous "I have a dream" speech from the steps of the Lincoln Memorial. I know that I am an idealist in many ways and that I mostly look for the "good". Some might say I am naive. I remember sitting on the steps of the Lincoln Memorial at other times and feeling the energy. I could hear words of the Gettysburg address in my heart. That all of us are created equal!

Living in Washington D.C. at that time was an exciting place to be. It was like no other time in my life. Eventually, I realized that working in intelligence work was not for a married man with two beautiful children. So I stayed in the shoe business and became a vice-president of a fortune 100 company.

In 1970 a series of paranormal events led me to enroll at the National Spiritual Science University. I studied all the religions of the world along with Quantum Physics and all the ways a person could read energy. Four years later, I graduated and started a spiritual center in Landover Maryland. Life was never to be the same. My soul had a dream and I was living it. And now, more than forty years later I am still living it; each and every day as I connect with you.

As a nation, we all still have a dream that black and white, straight and gay, liberal and conservative will not be judged by the color of their skin or their sexual orientation or their political belief but by the "content of their character." I hope all of you have a dream. I hope your dream is bigger than you can imagine. I hope your dream scares the pants off of you! I hope your heart and soul will never give up that dream. This world was built by dreamers. Never stop dreaming! From my dreamer heart to yours, Thomas

What is your dream? Let the content of your character help you fulfill it!

January 17 Universal Principle #2: Infinite Intelligence, God

Within all energy is an intelligence that is infinite, eternal and purposeful. This Infinite Intelligence, which we sometimes refer to as God, or simply love, is the source of all creative expression and the essential Power in the Universe. The way we view our Infinite Intelligence, or God, is precisely the way we see and feel about our Self and the way we experience life. When we perceive God as an unconditionally loving and supportive energy at all times and under all circumstances, we experience our world as totally safe, and everyone in it as loving and supportive.

> Remember:
> You are not your body.
> You are not your mind.
> You are not your job.
> You are not your hobbies.
> You are not your thoughts.
> You are not your actions.
> You are ever so much more.

You have come here from the farthest point away and yet you have never left and have always been here. You are love seeking itself. You have always been and will always be. There is nothing you cannot do. You have no limitations. So today, pause and remember that you are the light that has always shone and will always do so. Ask yourself what would an eternal limitless being do today? Then surrender to Universe. Don't always try to figure it out. Relax and let go.

I have this agreement with Universe. I simply say that I am right now in this limited form of expression and have purposely hidden my power. I have no clue. And you know everything. So in my finite form with restricted information I set a course of direction which I believe will best support Oneness.

Then I ask Oneness if I am not going in the direction which supports the highest good; please create whatever circumstances and events that reveal to me how I might manifest the results which serve all. May your days be filled with all that your heart desires! From my heart to yours, Thomas

What will your eternal limitless being do today?

January 18   What One Woman Can Do!

Today, a woman died that most people never heard of or knew. She was 91 years old. Dr. Mathilde Krim became a pioneer in 1981 when the AIDS crises erupted. She took the lead in getting people to stop judging the behavior and instead using their energy to find a cure.

Dr. Krim found a way to get science and medicine and social welfare to work together. She saved millions of lives. Indeed, thousands of people now alive with the virus today are leading full, productive, long lives, because she cared. It was an event in 1945 that would ultimately save people's lives decades later. As an eighteen year old, Ms. Krim saw a newsreel at the movies that depicted the horrors of a Nazi concentration camp. The memory of that experience defined her philosophy of life and made her a fierce opponent of prejudice and discrimination. She was awarded the Presidential Medal of Freedom in 2000.

There are so many people on our planet doing wonderful things like this and often we never hear of them. They are truly angels of mercy and love and compassion. May we all find ways to help our fellow human beings, by doing whatever it takes, to find our path of angelic purpose? From my purposeful heart to your, Thomas

We each can make a difference in another's life by our own kind and purposeful choices! Go for it!

January 19   Unconditional Love

Back in the days of Spirit Church, we used a saying often, to support each other. You say the person's name and share: *"I unconditionally love and support you, just the way you are, in all your magnificence".* We learned it from the Arnold Patent teachings. We would use it when someone would stand up in church and share about being in a challenging place in their life. The other day there was a program on NPR about two persons who had totally opposing points of view and still loved each other.

Today's politically charged climate is often driven by diametrically opposite ideologies. It might be time for some of us to just send a lot of love to the situation without judgment. We might close our eyes and take a deep breath and center our attention on our heart center. Then say: "we unconditionally love and support the situation, just the way it is, in all its magnificence. Join me in giving this a try and see how we might affect our society in a loving way. From my unconditional heart to yours, Thomas

We unconditionally love and support you in all your magnificence – it's being sent out to you now – receive it graciously!

January 20   You Are God, Get Over it!

This is the title of a channeled book by Story Waters that was published in 2005. There is a new expanded version and you can get it on Kindle for five dollars.

For many of us who were raised in "God Fearing" religions; there can be a resistance to saying oneself is God. We were taught that God was an omnipotent being who was located in another place beyond this Earth. We were taught that this God had rules that must be obeyed or we would suffer the consequences. It is no wonder that there might be some residual fear in us. Waters' book opened up a wider perspective of perceiving God. Many of us who followed Eastern philosophies have believed that the word God means Oneness or All That Is.

I have personally believed and taught for many years about the energy of love and that we are it! The human events in our world often separate us. Now, perhaps more than ever it is important to see the Oneness of everything. The old beliefs asked us to believe in a God outside ourselves. We have come to know the God within. We have learned to trust and follow that light within us all. Here is an excerpt from Waters' book:

"What you will discover once you have whipped the blindfold off and you look out into the new multidimensional reality that is your new realization of freedom, then the fun really begins. This is where and when you will create the dream in your heart. This is where you will create your most exciting self. This is where you discover that there is nothing you cannot be, for you are everything. This is when you will discover not only how amazing you are, but how amazing this whole reality system is and how incredible it is that you are here." – Story Waters

Now is the time to step into the power of who we really are. It is time to stop pretending. It is time to stop our limitations. It is time to let go and reclaim our divinity. You are all the limitless power of Oneness, and I invite you to live in the love that is our being, and to share that joy with the world. From my God heart to yours, Thomas

Really let yourself get this – God is within each of us – As you consciously breathe know that your breath is part of God!

January 21   Animal Loving World

There are millions of pets, warming the hearts of their owners all over the globe. On Facebook, many posts are filled with wonderful stories about people caring for animals. We had a dog named Angel who was with us for twelve years. Her health eventually failed her and we had to put her to sleep.   The picture of her loving, trusting eyes at that moment will forever be embedded on my mind. It was a tough choice and one that I felt had to be made.

Lou Ann and I made a choice to choose a plant based life four years ago. We had mostly eaten healthfully and wanted to take it a step further. However, the overriding element of this decision was to no longer harm any animal!

Maybe if all animals were pets, there would be more folks choosing a whole food, plant based diet. We are both advocates for creating a healthy climate as well. Eating animals accounts for more climate pollution than all the autos driven all over the world. What can we do as a conscious loving people? It might be time for many of us to step forward and consider the consequences of continuing to kill animals for our own needs. We do not need to eat them to get enough protein for good health.

I realize that this is a touchy subject for a lot of people. All of us get to choose about how we live our lives. At the risk of those who read this, getting upset with me, I encourage you all to consider making a change. I am asking for those sentient beings on our Earth who have no voice. People who eat meat are not bad people. We have been doing this for centuries. It no longer serves us to continue this way of living, let us live and let live. Let us create an animal loving world. From my heart to yours, Thomas

Make a healthy choice for you and the animals of our planet!

January 22   Choices

We met a lovely husband and wife couple today at the Sedona Veg Fest. We sat down and had a wonderful Vegan meal together. Our new friend James is an amazing artist and sculptor. He mentioned that he served in the Korean War. When lunch ended, I had a feeling of sadness.

James was born the same year as my oldest brother Bud. Bud was a very talented athlete who was offered a major league baseball contract while serving in the Army. He never got to fulfill that possibility of stardom. Bud died in 1985 of pancreatic cancer. Jim is a lively, happy, loving man who is contributing to the planet.

Here is an excerpt from James book: Art & Survival in the Twenty-first Century: *Today, we are faced with unparalleled challenges in the human experience. Can we, as artists, cut through persistent illusions; to actually see what lies before us? Can we summon the courage to hunt down the* unvarnished truth? Can our art open us to an honest dialogue about the times in which we live? Our very survival may depend upon the answers to these questions...

My sadness came to me both, because I miss my brother, and also the knowledge that he had made choices that perhaps didn't serve him as well as James had. One is not better than the other. It is just when we make less than healthy diet choices that cut our lives short; all of us are diminished in some way. A part of the Oneness is not able to shine as bright for all of us to experience. I encourage all of you to live the healthiest life possible for as long as you are able. If you desire to live a longer, happier, healthier life go to DoctorKlaper.com, your best life may just depend on it! From my healthy heart to yours, Thomas

Take a simple step today that will allow you to live your healthiest life!

January 23   Emmanuel

Every once in a while a book or a person or an energy connects with my life and I experience a significant change in how I see everything. The entity Emmanuel, channeled by Pat Rodegast is that kind of experience for me. I have been reading their material contained in three books for more than twenty years and those messages continue to surprise, enhance, entertain and shift my consciousness. The communications are so loving and consistent and inclusive about many aspects of our Earthly journeys.

Nothing in my four decades of personal search for the discovery of who I truly am has been as influential or profound. Pat Rodegast is no longer with us on the Earth plain. There is a memorial about her on YouTube, here is the link: https://www.youtube.com/watch?v=e7ncpRju0PU

Here is a sample of his/her pure wisdom. *"What does the voice of fear whisper to you? " Fear speaks to you in logic and reason. It assumes the language of love itself. Fear tells you "I want to make you safe." Love says "You are safe." Fear says "give me symbols, give me frozen images, and give me something I can rely on." Loving truth says "Only give me this moment." Fear would walk with you on a narrow path promising to take you where you want to go. Love says "Open your arms and fly with me." Every moment of your life you are given the opportunity to choose love or fear; to tread the Earth or to soar the heavens."*

There are three books filled with so much joy and childlike playfulness and profound eternal truth that will lighten your heart, enlighten your mind and fill your soul! Don't miss these; you will read and keep reading them all of your life! From my light heart to yours, Thomas

Let your playful self-come out! It will enlighten your heart, mind and soul!

January 24   Bring your soap!

In the 1980's in Japan, a phenomenon called Forest Bathing became very popular. The practice is proven by scientists to benefit physical as well as mental health. It helps lower heart rate, blood pressure, reduce stress hormone production, boost immunity and mood and improve overall feelings of well-being.

I remember growing up in Hollywood and traipsing through Griffith Park for hours. I was alone and surrounded by thousands of butterflies, dragonflies and birds of a variety of colors and songs. It was magical to be in so much green. The air felt like it was alive and of course it was. I have always been attracted to being out in nature. For me, there is a deeper connection to All That Is when I am in nature. I feel the Oneness of all creatures.

Now, forest bathing is starting to take off in the U.S. The Associations of Nature & Forest Therapy plans to train and certify about 250 new guides next year. "We're aiming to have 1,000 trained guides within three years," a wilderness guide Amos Clifford says. There's a growing body of evidence that the practice can help boost immunity and mood and help reduce stress. Of course, in winter in the northern hemisphere there is not the same kind of leafy experience available. Maybe we should all take a trip down under?

I am encouraging all of us to find some activity where we can interrupt our normal life activities. Let's make a connection with Mother Earth today and find that curious child within that wants to play! From my Forest heart to yours, Thomas

If you can today, get out in nature and feel bathed in its magic!

January 25   Synchronicity and Surrender

This afternoon I was talking with two of our vacation-rental guests at our home. I was sharing with them the titles on pages that I share with you each day. I sang a couple of lines of John Denver's Heart to Heart song. One guest shared that she grew up enjoying rock bands and never got into John Denver's music. She experienced a successful life living in Orange County California, but something was missing. Then she had the urge to move to Boulder Colorado. After moving there she heard a Denver song about coming home and her life totally shifted in a powerful way. She knew she was home!

It is the events in our life that are orchestrated by our True Self, that change our lives forever. If I hadn't been led by a number of synchronous events to move to Arizona back in 1977; I may have never met Lou Ann. I would have missed out on thirty eight years of unspeakable joy! ! Remember the John Denver song Sweet Surrender. Go to this link and drink it into your soul! https://www.youtube.com/watch?v=FakaHy5mlDl

So today's lesson, loved ones, is to surrender to Universe and follow your heart. You will create amazing adventures that will fulfill you in so many ways. From my serendipitous heart to yours, Thomas

Let the gentle nudge of the Universe and your inner most True Self guide you. EnJOY the ride!

January 26 Color of Change

Today I went for a walk in our neighborhood. I stopped and spoke with a man doing landscaping on his own property. We spoke about 15 minutes about the beauty of life. Then another neighbor was washing his car and I yelled out "it looks great" and he smiled and waved. I had a flash that I was living in Pleasantville.

Do you remember the iconic movie of the same name? It was a wonderful story of two teenagers living in 1998 current time who accidentally get transported into their television. It turns out they are taken to the town of Pleasantville. This is a town where everything is seemingly perfect. The entire place is in black and white. In truth, the folks in this town are living kind of a limited emotional existence. Our protagonists help the town discover real emotions and they slowly turn from black and white to the whole spectrum of colors.

This of course is a metaphor for all of our lives in some ways. Are we living in full color? Are we discovering the depth of our heart's desire or just some black and white copy? I know that I am so blessed living here in Sedona; where not only is the topography in brilliant color but so are the people. I encourage all of you to find your true colors and live your rainbow of life! From my colorful heart to yours, Thomas

Feel your inner gratitude for being alive, wherever you are now! Breathe it in then breathe it out feeling peaceful.

January 27   Intuition

Here are 10 things that people in touch with their intuition do, that helps create success in their lives.

    They listen to their inner voice.
    They take time for solitude.
    They create.
    They practice mindfulness.
    They observe everything.
    They listen to their body.
    They connect deeply with others.
    They pay attention to their dreams.
    They enjoy plenty of down time

They mindfully let go of negative emotions

This list sounds like someone who is living a peaceful, successful life. It would be a wonderful, to do list, for all of us. There is nothing in there about making a lot of money or about achieving a lot of things. There is nothing about hurrying to get things done; nothing in there about acquiring. Rather the list is about really connecting with ourselves our minds, our hearts, our fellow humans.

It would be wonderful if each of us took at least ten minutes a day to just stop and be. Be in a quiet place and be still and connect with our inner selves. I believe we would create the kind of life we would cherish. From my intuitive heart to yours, Thomas

Choose one or two of these intuitive tools and practice them today!

January 28   Gladys Naomi Fickert

Gladys is my mom and was born on this day in 1911, one of three girls who survived childbirth. Her mother Edna Jones had given still birth to two sets of twins. Her father, Paul Fickert was a police officer and a construction worker in Pittsburgh Pennsylvania.

Gladys was born in Cincinnati Ohio. She was a thin wisp of a girl and set the 50 dash record in junior high school. She married Oliver Christopher Bruck, who was born April 16, 1907 in Chicago Illinois. They were married on May 8, 1929.

The first of their children was a boy named Oliver Christopher Paul Bruck who was born April 17, 1931 and they called him junior. Their second child, another boy was named Robert Jerome Bruck, born June 13, 1936. Their third child – they wanted a girl - ended up being me, born on November 12, 1940. At the time my dad owned the Silver Dollar café in Cincinnati Ohio, the city where I was born.

Gladys and Oliver moved to Hollywood California in 1942. Oliver's family were horse racing people and deeply involved in horse race betting which was not legal in most places outside of the horse track itself. So Ollie as he was known was a bookie, a charmer and a drunk.

Gladys had to raise four kids, Oliver being one of them; and work full time and still run the home as many women had to do in the tough times between 1931 and the nineteen fifties.

Ollie died February 22, 1964 from alcoholism. Gladys remarried a man name Warner Zumwalt who was called Chuck. They met at Sears Roebuck while he sold sewing machines. Chuck died January 16, 1986. Gladys continued on.

Gladys left the planet on April 6, 2000 here in Sedona Arizona to the messages of the prophet Emmanuel and the stirring music of Robin Miller (a local musical artist) to a CD called Transcendence.

Gladys Naomi Fickert will never appear in any history books. In my heart she will always be "famous" for never quitting a tough life. Without her I wouldn't have written these words and you wouldn't have known the silent bravery of a life lived as well as it could be! From my thankful heart to yours, Thomas

Bless your family that brought you into this world, knowing they did the best they could!

January 29   Memories

Yesterday, we rearranged our bedroom. Put up new curtains and moved three dressers around.   On top of each was a collection of figurines, pictures and mementos. As I was collecting the items so that I could move the furniture; I began to experience the memories these items evoked. I felt tears well up in my eyes. They were tears of happiness, gratitude and thankfulness.

Our thirty-eight year relationship is one of mutual love, engagement, passion, joy and magic. Lou Ann brings lots of magic to our life! On one dresser there is a heart shaped photo of Lou Ann and I at Disneyland next to a statue of Quan Yin. On another dresser, pictures of our five children, thirteen grandchildren and five great grandchildren. They are surrounded by bunnies and dolphins and cherubs and angels. These are some of Lou Ann's gifts to our home.

These items are symbols of the path we have traveled over the years. I realize that we are so fortunate to have made this journey together. Both of us cook and clean and work and volunteer and exercise and eat well. We encourage each other to live our dreams and follow our heart's desire.

In our modern society we often depict life as too complicated, busy and challenging. I believe it helps to find the little treasures, share the simple moments and to look for the good in everything.

I encourage everyone to stop and find items that bless your life experience, whether alone or with others. It is so important to take time each day and remember who we are and to celebrate it! From my happy heart to yours, Thomas

Bring a touchstone with you to remind you of some of your magical moments!

January 30   Love One Another

There was a segment on MSNBC about a woman named Morgan McKay who owns the Oblio's Pizza restaurant in Denver Colorado. She decided to help the folks who have been put out of work by the government shutdown. She gives them free pizza and wine to eat. Then local folks heard about what she was doing and they began coming to her eatery to spend money and support her business.

It doesn't take much to create the kind of world we desire. Just see a need and fill it. We have created a planet where there is so much to be done to love and support each other. Perhaps one of the blessings of the current situation here in the U.S. is the opportunity for many of us to give to each other. We may have never taken the time to connect with each other in such a vital way!

Let us look for more ways to love one another. We don't have to wait for a calamity to occur to have this happen. The simplest act of kindness will create the loving world we all desire to have. From my uplifted heart to yours, Thomas

Find a way to be kind today to uplift yourself and others!

January 31   Angels We Have Heard on High

Angels are what I love writing about, because I am writing about all of us! We are all divine. We are all love. We are Oneness. Sometimes we forget about our divinity and can't find our wings. Somewhere deep inside we find the connection. It is fun to incarnate on places like planet Earth and take on this human form. .

We agreed a trillion years ago to come here and support each other in creating what we desire. We knew then, it was all a dance. Somehow we turned the dance into conflict and limitation. That is not real. What is real is the love that we feel and share.

We are the angels we knew would come. It is time for all of us to spread our wings and fly together in a beautiful heart formation. Then our sisters and brothers who still can't find their wings will remember who they are. Once we all remember, there will be peace on Earth. I invite all of us to shine even brighter than before. From my angelic heart to yours, Thomas

Breathe in the truth about your angelic nature, breathe out and shine!

February 1   Simple

Life can be arduous, painful, upsetting, difficult, challenging, complex.......peaceful. Joyful, loving, transformational, magic, ecstatic, prosperous, amazing.....simple! In other words, life is what we make it! For the most part, we get to choose our life experience. The challenge is to make our choices consciously. Through our choices, we often create circumstances where it seems we have no choice. However, there is always a choice; even if it is to only choose how we feel about our situation. I created the acronym below to help us focus on keeping life simple. Together, we folks on Earth have been making it more complex.

See

It

Making

People's

Live's

Easier

Let us take each day and see how we can make it simpler. For me, it has been to focus on not accumulating things. Becoming Vegan has simplified our life as well. We save a lot of time and money at Costco for instance by not buying meat or dairy. Shopping for organic food has also made it easier. It is a bit more expensive but we don't wander through most of a grocery store but stay in the healthy section. We exercise a lot, so hopefully we will remain healthy longer and not have to spend as much money on health care. It helps us live in excellence to the best of our ability.

Finally, Lou Ann and I see life as an adventure full of joy, love, prosperity and wonder. We enjoy focusing on these aspects of living and thereby finding simplicity in how we live. From my simple heart to yours, Thomas

Choose how you want to feel right now. It is that simple!

February 2   Groundhog Day

Every year on this day, Lou Ann and I keep watching the same movie over and over again! What if we only had one day? What would we do with it? If we knew we were going to keep getting that day again and again? Remember the movie starring Bill Murray?

He starts out as an egotistical weatherman. He has disdain for most people and things. Then of course, he keeps repeating the same day. He goes through perhaps thousands of repetitions. He spends his time getting what he wants, not really thinking of others. He gets so despondent about his situation that he tries to kill himself, many different ways.

Finally he begins to fall in love with his television producer. Then once he opens his heart to love, he totally transforms. Then he does all these amazing things to help support the people of Punxsutawney Pennsylvania.

The movie is a metaphor for life here on Earth. I believe that when we are only thinking of our self; life doesn't work very well. It is when we open up to our highest possible way of living that it begins to flow. When we get stuck in thinking our current life experience is so repetitive, we get to switch. One way is in service to others.

When we forget about our own problems and limitations and just give, we create magic. For our protagonist in the movie; each day was like a lifetime, kind of like reincarnation. We get to do it over and over again. When we do it from the heart, it is a joyful experience for all involved. May we all find that spark of love and service so that each day and lifetime is filled with everything our heart and soul desires. From my forever heart to yours, Thomas

Let the spark of love and service shine in you today! Repeat daily!

February 3   Winning

Some hundred and twenty million Americans watched the Super Bowl today. At the game today there will be a winner and a loser. The winners will be long remembered and the losing team is often forgotten. When fans interact with each other about any sport they will ask "who won the game?" It is clear to me that if you have dedicated your life to your art or craft; you are a winner. It doesn't matter if they ever print your name on some trophy.

To win at life is to get into the game. It is not to sit in the bleachers and watch from afar. Sometimes folks, don't try very hard because they don't want to lose. Once again, in sports, those athletes who participate lose more often then they win. I love tennis and enjoy watching Roger Federer play. He has won twenty grand slam titles in some fifteen years. This is the greatest achievement in men's tennis. Federer has lost about two thirds of the times he played in those events. Many of us who have been successful only one third of the time; would feel like we failed.

My thought tonight is winning is doing or doing is winning. When we attempt to create some results in life; just the attempt is a success. We don't have to be famous or wealthy or garner awards or rewards. We only have to take action. Find something you love and give it all you've got! From my winning heart to yours, Thomas

What we attempt to do is in itself a success. Let your life be in alignment with your true nature of love!

February 4   Healthy Choices

Every day we make choices that are mostly unconscious. We get up and have some breakfast, get dressed, perhaps go to work. Have lunch and maybe work some more. Come home and maybe eat again. Maybe watch some TV or read a book, etc.

I have been watching a movie about a man who has MS (Multiple Sclerosis). He contracted it when he was 19. It is now twenty years later and he is still healthy. He eats raw fruits and vegetables, lean meats and exercises. He never eats dairy or gluten. The irony is, he may have not been this healthy, if he had not contracted the disease. He is a wonderful representative for all of us on how to overcome unfortunate circumstances. He discovered that lack of vitamin D is a precursor. And of course, what we have eaten that didn't serve us, along with a lack of exercise. Modern medicine largely gives MS patients drugs that have no long term effect on the disease.

Now is the time for us to become conscious about our daily unconscious choices. Let us consider everything we eat. Let us find a way to move our body through space by walking, jogging, dancing or any other movement. We are responsible for our health; not our doctors, therapists, the AMA, the FDA or any other organization. We have the power to live long, healthy, happy, prosperous lives by making the best choices for ourselves. Now is the time! From my hopeful heart to yours, Thomas

Support your doctor and the quality of your life by being as healthy as you can, physically, mentally and spiritually!

February 5   Universal Principle #3, Oneness

Since the essence of everything is pure loving energy, in the truest sense, we are one. Oneness, love, is indivisible. Whenever we attempt to withhold love from anyone, we withhold love from everyone, including our Self. The truth of this principle becomes clear as we allow our hearts to open and feel our interconnectedness.

There is only Oneness, not twoness. Oneness is everyone and everything. When we do anything in Oneness it affects everything and everyone forever. While this can be a heavy burden it is also an energy freeing possibility. When anyone or anything is hurting we are all hurting. When one part of Oneness is experiencing joy, we are all feeling it. This is a powerful concept. We can then make choices that give energy and love to anyone anywhere.

It comes with it a responsibility to be aware of every word, thought or action we take. If we get out in front of ourselves we can be a wonderful healing force. Now is the time for all of us to look at our lives and see how we are living. Are we making choices that are not only helping ourselves; are they helping others? It is so important to include the welfare of everyone and everything in our powerful life choices! May we all sense the feeling of being one with all that is! From my oneness heart to yours, Thomas

We are all interconnected. As you allow your heart to open you can sense it! Breathe in and out with your hand or hands on your heart!

February 6   Listening to our Inner Voice

Yesterday, Lou Ann went to the post office and pulled up to the front door and got out of our car. A 96 year old man drove his car down the sidewalk that she was about to enter. The elderly gentleman hit the gas pedal instead of the brake and tore off our front bumper. Fortunately, Lou Ann saw him coming and got out of the way!

Later, we went to Enterprise car rental to pick up a loaner while our car was being repaired. We decided to purchase insurance for the rental, even though we have rented hundreds of cars without incident.

Today Lou Ann was checking out a location to teach her children's Yoga classes for the upcoming Sedona Yoga festival. When she left the grounds she ran over a rock which got lodged under the car and damaged the undercarriage of the rental vehicle.

You never know! I am always thankful, when we make a decision that supports us. We listened to our inner voice and went against our previous way of doing something, and it worked! You know the old saying of trust your gut?

I believe our challenge is that we are so bombarded with so much, in this information age; that it can be difficult to hear that little voice. Never the less, I encourage you to listen to that part of you that knows! It will support you in the best way possible. From my listening heart to yours, Thomas

Life can have twists and turns, when you are able, trust your gut!

February 7   The Rainbow Bridge

Lou Ann invoked Dr. Dispenza's create your day exercise this morning. She asked the Quantum Field for a day with happy surprises. We had just learned that we were not going to receive a stipend of $431 that we were counting on.

About three o'clock a giant, gorgeous, bright rainbow appeared in front of our house covering the entire expanse of red rocks. We both ran and got our cameras. I shot a couple of dozen pictures. When I closed the camera connection on my phone I noticed that someone had booked our Airbnb room for six days beginning on the 10th of February at the same time the rainbow was blazing! The total amount of the booking is $431!

The rainbow is immersed in nearly every culture throughout the centuries. The Irish legend is that there will be a pot of gold at the end of the rainbow guarded by a leprechaun. At the moment I took this pic, the legend smiled on us with a small pot of gold. The exact amount we needed. Life is fun when the spirit energy is in evidence. Thanks to Lou Ann for summoning the Quantum Field and filling our day with joy!

I wish for all of you to find your pot of gold. I hope it is more than money. I ask that it is filled with all of your fulfilled dreams, and that they be full of love, joy, abundance and a long life of health!

Our good friend, Ellie Cooper just called me and let me know that Nadia Caillou just passed away about the time of the rainbow. No wonder it was so bright! I had the honor of performing her marriage back in the early nineties. Life is sweet and sometimes bittersweet. Farewell Nadia, may your journey always feel like the brightest rainbow ever!

From my sad and sweet heart to yours, Thomas

Live life fully in the present – feel a rainbow around you and within you – filling you with wonder and joy!

February 8   Ancestry

When I got my Ancestry chart I found out I am eighty per cent Western European. I looked at a lot of the names of the men and women who lived and gave birth to my lineage. The chart only went back to 1715. It would be fun to trace it much further. Maybe some of those ancestors were me!

I remember past lives from France and Greece and England. I recall being in the middle east and inside the great Pyramids. Some of my past incarnation recollections have been helpful in this lifetime. I had an experience back in 1972 when I was learning Astrology. The instructor put my chart up on the wall for the whole class to see. She asked me if I had ever been in a physical fight. I told her I had not. She said that some planetary configurations indicated that I had chosen being peaceful in this lifetime.

Six years later I experienced a four hour massage in which the therapist played loud classical music. At the foot of the massage table sat a psychic who recorded her impressions of the session. At regular intervals, there would be a break so that I could share what I was experiencing. There were about fifteen lifetimes recalled during that whole massage. Me and the psychic tuned into seven of my lifetimes at the same time. Meaning when I was in Russia, she saw me there as well.

I recalled the time when I was a Russian military officer in the early 1800's. I was sitting on a horse while thousands of men, dead or dying were being carried on wagons. It was snowing and bitter cold. I remember feeling my hot tears running down my cold cheeks. I looked out at all the carnage and made a vow that I would never take a human life again.

Coincidentally, when I joined the Air Force in 1959, I was put into the Intelligence division. I was issued a card which declared I was a non-combatant; meaning I didn't engage in fighting. I also had an evacuation card that stated I was to be evacuated before other types of personnel.

Perhaps some of you have had past life connections that support you in this current life? Are you are repeating the same kind of pattern where you create results you don't desire? If so, you might want to find out like I did.

You see, when I was young, I avoided being in fights. I thought of myself as a coward. I judged myself harshly. Discovering that vow of peace I made 200 years ago helped me find more inner peace in this lifetime.

There is a wonderful book written on the subject you may want to check out. It is Dr. Brian Weiss' "Many Lives Many Masters" From my inquiring heart to yours, Thomas

Explore the possibility of past lives and perhaps bring deeper understanding into your life.

February 9   Count your blessings

Remember the song Count Your Blessings? *"When I'm weary and I can't sleep, I count my blessings instead of sheep. Then I fall asleep counting my blessings".* Sometimes it is a challenge to stay positive when our life circumstances get the better of us.

It is helpful to take a break and find a quiet place and count your blessings. Then take some slow deep breaths. Begin with the obvious things that you have created. You're alive. You may be reasonably healthy. You might have folks that love you. You may be able to pay your house payment. You may have a wonderful pet. You might be working at a great job.

Scan your body and be thankful for every part of it; your fantastic fingers. Your terrific toes! Your dazzling eyes! Be aware of your excellent mind and bless it. Thank yourself for having incarnated and created all of this!

My life experience has been that when I really appreciate all that I have; that I receive even more blessings! What you focus on expands; your life is in your own hands! It might be fun to call up someone we haven't spoken with in a long time and let them know how much we appreciate them.

I am counting all of you as some of my greatest blessings. Thank you for reading this and for responding and letting me know how much you enjoy it! We are all so very blessed in so many ways! From my blessed heart to yours, Thomas

Consider ten things you are grateful for – oh not your ten toes!

February 10   Secret Ingredients

This is a film that shows families who have contracted chronic diseases, even though they seemed to be living a healthy lifestyle. One family of five had twenty one different maladies. Their children were ill. One of them was diagnosed as Autistic. They discovered that the food they ate was not that healthy. They found out that they were eating genetically modified food. They found out their food had pesticides. Then the mother made it her mission to discover the answer to their illnesses.

They began eating non GMO'S. They started to eat Organic. In six months their chronic diseases faded away. Their son who was labeled Autistic totally recovered and became an A student and an athlete. Eventually they all became totally healthy. I have shared with you folks that Lou Ann and I are Vegan. We believe that this is the healthiest way to eat. However, even if you do not choose a plant-based whole-food diet, PLEASE make healthier choices.

If any of you are having chronic health problems, PLEASE explore what you are eating! We have a health epidemic on our planet and we can do something about it. Whatever you eat, PLEASE, make it organic, non-GMO and gluten free if you are sensitive to that. The film also showed infertile women become pregnant by following the above advice. *(Secret Ingredients is the title by Director Amy Hart)*

As they say "this is not rocket science". This is just making the healthiest eating choices for you. Your family needs you. The Earth needs you! To paraphrase Mr. Spock: "Live healthy and prosper." From my concerned heart to yours, Thomas

Whenever you can, eat organic – it can make you healthier!

February 11   Life is Too Short

My how time flies when we are in the body. Of course, we made up time, some time ago. I got to thinking about yesterday's blog about eating healthy. It occurs to me that sometimes we make poor health choices because we are attempting to fill up some hole inside. I know I have often been guilty of eating unconsciously. Occasionally, I will eat a meal and feel satisfied. Then not too long after, I find myself looking for a snack. It's not about being physically hungry. It's about me being emotionally undernourished.

It might be helpful to check up on how we are creating what we desire. For most of us, we have created a life where we choose to make ends meet. We get to pay the rent, buy the car, feed the family, feed the cat or dog, etc. Many of us find employment to create enough income to take care of those obligations.

When I was a manager back in the 1960's, I had a hundred people working for me. I would often give them a pep talk and say "I want you to jump out of bed and almost race to work" I want you to be here more than anywhere else that you might work. I want you to be doing what you love to do. If this is not that place for you, I want you to quit. Please find that place that creates a spark in your life. Don't settle for just getting by."

Life is too short to spend most of our time supporting someone else's dream. Unless doing so, is our dream as well! It might be helpful to take stock right now and ask ourselves "am I living MY dream?" If not, I believe finding our own dream will fill our heart. Then, perhaps we won't be filling the hole in our soul by filling our bellies. Who knows, doing what you love may be the new diet? From my inquiring heart to yours, Thomas

Do something that fulfills you even in the smallest of ways, so to nurture your heart not your tummy!

February 12   Leaves

We are gathering leaves to be part of the composting that we do on our organic magical food forest. We have been preparing the ground for some winter seeding and now Austin is recreating our greenhouse and Ashley is doing a lot of the compost work.

Ashley posted on the local Facebook page that we need leaves and lots of folks responded. One of them has a business over in Sedona named the Awakening. They do things like Aura photography and intuitive psychic services. When we were chatting I found out they are also connected to the local homeless organizations that will need more food; which is exactly why we are doing the organic garden.

I love the synchronicity of all this. We go looking for leaves and make a connection to partner with other organizations that will help us achieve our goal of being a food provider for others.

I was playing tennis today and shared with another player that we were gathering leaves. He suggested we come to his house and he would pay Austin and Ashley to clear his leaves.

I encourage all of us to follow our heart and it will lead us to the fruition of our dreams. It is the way of the soul, one step at a time. We don't have to figure it out. We only need to follow spirit as it leads us to discover the magic of being in harmony with the Universe. From my thankful heart to yours, Thomas

Follow your heart one step at a time and discover the magic of being in harmony with the Universe!

February 13   Mother Nature is watching us!

Find a Way

To stop climate change where you live:

Here are simple changes you can make to your diet to reduce its climate impact.

Eat meat-free meals.

Buy organic and local whenever possible.

Don't waste food.

Grow your own.

Take public transit.

Ride a bike.

Car-share.

Switch to an electric or hybrid vehicle.

Fly less (if you do fly, make sure you offset your carbon footprint).

Change to energy-efficient light bulbs.

Unplug computers, TVs and other electronics when you're not using them.

Wash clothes in cold or warm (not hot) water.

Dryers are energy hogs, so hang dry when you can and use dryer balls when you can't.

Install a programmable thermostat.

Look for the Energy Star label when buying new appliances.

Winterize your home to prevent heat from escaping.

Get a home or workplace energy audit to identify where you can make the most energy-saving gains.

Stop buying new things. Go to thrift shops and reuse.

Recycle everything you can.

Install solar power or wind power.

This commercial was brought to you by Mother Nature. Let us all find a way to stop climate change and create the world we want for our children and their children's children. From my sustainable heart to yours, Thomas

Pick one or two of these ideas as a treat to Mother Nature!

February 14   Funny Valentine

Lou Ann and I went on a Valentine's Day date today. We went to one of our favorite restaurants named Picazzos. We ate amazing organic Vegan pizza and pasta. Then we went to the movies to see Peter Rabbit. Lou Ann gets so tickled at this kind of movie that her laugh sets off the rest of the theater audience. She is such a joy! Her inner child, and her outer playful childlike being, is infectious. And in truth I laughed part of my gluteus maximus off as well!

I want to wish all of you a happy Valentine's Day. I wish for you to find love in each and every day. Mostly I wish for you to love yourself just the way you are. You do not need to do anything to be more lovable. We have made choices along the way that both our self and others judged. They were just choices and we always do the best we can do.....always!

So give yourselves some chocolates, some flowers and most of all, some loving kudos for being who you are. We are all valentines and gifts to each other. From my valentine heart to yours, Thomas

Let your playful inner child laugh right now! Feel the joyful gift you gave yourself!

February 15   Being Healthy

Many times I have covered what we eat. Tonight I would like us to discuss being mentally healthy. There are so many of us in pain both physically and emotionally. The world is not an easy place to navigate today. If we want to be healthy, we get to be loving. Love has been a curative for as long as there have been hearts that feel. Did you know that the heart sends more information to the brain than vice versa? Many of us try to think our way through life more than we feel our way through. The mind doesn't know enough about happiness. Happiness is a feeling. The heart feels. When we feel happy we are more able to be healthy.

Another way to create a more powerful, healthy life is to do something different. We are creatures of habit. We get stuck in these habits because it is comfortable. When we are too comfortable, we stop growing and becoming. Let's find ways to take a risk. It doesn't have to be a physical risk. It is when we move out of our comfort zone, that our life really begins. Let us take some quiet time and ask our heart what does it want to do? Then, whatever comes up for you, follow your heart's desire. Then take action.

Go for your dream and never let go. You may not achieve it, but the journey will change your life forever. I believe that when we do this we will be healthier as well. It is when we follow our hearts and live our dreams we become examples for others to do the same. From my healthy heart to yours, Thomas

The gate to happiness is self-compassion – open the gate!

February 16   Suspend your beliefs

Today I was in a training exercise with my tennis teacher Claudette. She is a wonderful tennis coach and an incredible human being. We are so fortunate to have her here in Sedona. During our training today, we both made statements that were limiting about our tennis play. I shared with her that it would be helpful if she suspended her belief and not soon after, she got to remind me as well.

Our beliefs create our reality here on Earth, and probably elsewhere too. What we believe is what we perceive. What we believe is what we create; there is no other law. We are unlimited beings of eternal spirit. Terry Cole-Whittaker tells us:

"The biggest lie is that we are born, continue for a while, and then die, when there is no possibility of death, given we are life, existence, and eternity. Another lie is; you cannot trust yourself, but all you can trust is your inner guidance and God within.

The mind is the greatest terrorist weapon ever invented and not qualified to guide or control any one. Learning to control, direct the mind, and meditate is most important or one suffers continuously from self-abuse, confusion, and unworthiness."

We all have beliefs that do not serve our highest good. Even a simple thing like hitting a tennis ball requires that we suspend any belief we might have that will not support us in doing it well. We make statements like; things are going to be challenging or difficult. And we are usually right.

We get what we believe. I think it is important to say, that if we just think a thought or say a word casually, it may not be a belief. However, when we attach our feelings to our thoughts they become powerful creators.

Let us take time to sit and write some of our beliefs. Then, let us suspend those that don't serve us. It is easy to see what we believe. We can take a look at what we have created in our lives and know this is the evidence of our beliefs. I wish you all, the success of discovering what you believe and creating the best possible results in your life. From my "expanded beliefs" heart to yours, Thomas

Be the observer of your thoughts today and know you are far more than them. Sense the bigger picture of who you are – a powerful creator of your magnificent life!

February 17   Meditation, A Way of Living

There is a lot of information about the practice of meditation. Meditation is the art of silencing the mind. When the mind is silent, concentration is increased and we experience inner peace in the midst of worldly turmoil. This elusive inner peace is what attracts so many people to meditation and is a quality everyone can benefit from. Meditation is usually done in a quiet place, sitting in a comfortable position, often with a straight back and crossed legs. Then we pay attention to our breathing and relax and allow our mind to be silent.

I learned to meditate in 1972 in a room above the Greyhound bus terminal in downtown Washington D.C. It was summertime and the windows were open, so we heard the bus engines and smelled the diesel exhaust fumes. Our teacher intentionally created this atmosphere so that we could learn that meditation was more than quiet or posture.

Meditation is finding the connection within us that is a part of the Oneness. So, it doesn't matter how we do it. In fact, our lives can be a meditation. When we learn how to focus and become completely present in what we see or do; we are meditating,

I am fortunate to go out in nature and walk frequently. I intentionally do not bring music with me so I can be in the moment with the sky, the trees and the red rocks. I encourage all of you wonderful beings of light to find your meditation practice, if you are not now doing it.

You will become more relaxed. You will find that little things don't bother you as much. You will become healthier. You will become more productive. Make it a way of living and you will be happy you did. From my relaxed heart to yours, Thomas

Find a meditative tool that works for you and watch your life transform!

February 18   What Are We Afraid Of?

We come into life and subject ourselves to limitations that require self-discovery from which to break free. Each lifetime is a chapter in the continuum of Earth travel. We are all writing our own book and as the author, we decide who the characters are in the novel. When we incarnate, we choose our parents and the environment we wish to explore. We set up lessons that give us perspective about our journey. Many of us don't quite learn all we need, so we come back again to find out more. As we mature, some of us gather enough wisdom to begin making choices that transcend our limited nature. We discover that the only thing that is real is the True Self.

We are not our jobs. We are not our personality. We are not our egos. We are not our excuses. We are not our stories. We are Oneness, in a Divine dance of celebration and exploration. The only thing real is the True Self. And the one who is not concerned about self (little 's'), becomes free. It is when we take total responsibility for our creations, we get to be free. We then become free from death, from failure, from our past, from choices, from everything that keeps us from the truth. We can then step into a place of pure inspiration. We are then free to create without limitation of the mind and ego. We create from the heart, the center of everything.

I encourage all of us to breakthrough our fear. Fear of losing, fear of suffering, fear of not being enough. Our journey here is about waking up, that is it. All the rest is entertainment, waking up to our magnificence, to our beauty, to our limitless Self. Then the journey is all we desired, before we were born.   From my awakened heart to yours, Thomas

Be your true nature, free of fear or ego, by being conscious of your True Self! Breathe it in and be it!

February 19   Movies

We had a wonderful Illuminate Film Festival get together tonight at the Briar Patch up in Oak Creek Canyon. A dozen of us gathered to eat delicious food, sit around warm fires and continue to bond together. We had a sharing experience where each of us told of movies that made a difference in our lives. There was a wide range of films from romantic to thriller to Freddie Krueger. Some of the titles were *Chariots of Fire, In the Wild, Powder, Love Actually, and Signs.*

Mine was *its A Wonderful Life*. I have seen it sixty times. Every year we watch it on Christmas Day. Every year I weep openly when it gets to the end and George Bailey discovers how much he is valued by his friends and neighbors. I cry tears of joy for George and I cry some tears of regret for myself. I see George as the man I had wished I could have been.

We all would be fortunate to find out that we have made a significant positive difference in the lives of others. When his brother Harry, raises a glass of champagne to toast George "He says "To George Bailey, the richest man in town". We are all rich who give so much to others. When we are loved by others, it is true wealth.

The Angel Clarence tells George: *You've been given a great gift, George: A chance to see what the world would be like without you*. We are all connected to everyone and everything. What we do and say matters. It can affect us all. We may not be famous or wealthy or educated. However, when we live from our heart we create miracles and change the world for the better. From my grateful heart to yours, Thomas

Just know that you touch others' lives being YOU!

February 20   The Pure Aloha Oath

Recently I went to the neighboring island of Oahu to play in a tennis tournament and I stayed with a wonderful friend Rytwin Lee who took me to Uncle Clay's Shaved Ice House of Pure Aloha and discovered an amazing oath about the business posted on the wall and here it is:

THE PURE ALOHA OATH

I solemnly promise to live every heartbeat of my life, from this day forward, with Pure Aloha.

Every single word that comes out of my mouth and every single action, be it large or small must first come from my compassionate heart and be supported by my thoughtful mind.

With an open heart and an open mind, I will unconditionally love every person who crosses my path of life, as a fellow member of our one world ohana.

If I truly try my best to do all these things, I will become the person I was born to be, filled with inner peace and complete happiness.

Living every heartbeat with Pure aloha I can bring love into the hearts of others and make our world a better place.

If you want to take the pledge, go to houseofpurealoha.com

I would love for as many people as possible on our Earth to live this oath.

From my pure aloha heart to yours, Thomas

When you love unconditionally all who cross your path can unconsciously receive that love into their hearts. Be pure aloha!

February 21   From The Present

The movie, E.T The Extraterrestrial, was playing on the TV tonight. I loved that movie so much. It came out the year Lou Ann and I got married. It might have helped us to turn on our heart lights even brighter.

I thought of another E.T. as well, Eckhart Tolle, and he seems extraterrestrial as well. One of his best books is *The Power of Now*. It's no wonder that it has sold over 2 million copies worldwide and has been translated into over 30 foreign languages. Much more than simple principles and platitudes, the book takes readers on an inspiring spiritual journey to find their true and deepest self and reach the ultimate in personal growth and spirituality: the discovery of truth and light.

Tolle introduces readers to enlightenment and its natural enemy, the mind. He awakens us to our role as a creator of pain and shows us how to have a pain-free identity by living fully in the present. The journey is thrilling, and along the way, the author shows how to connect to the indestructible essence of our Being, "the eternal, ever-present One Life beyond the myriad forms of life that are subject to birth and death".

So, it is time to phone home, meaning, make a connection with that place inside of ourselves that is eternal and only knows how to love. We could do it through contemplation and meditation or taking a walk in nature or looking in the mirror and smiling at the beautiful soul smiling back. After all, we are all extraterrestrials. We came here from spirit to shine so bright, that everyone who sees that light will remember their way home too! From my aloha heart to yours, Thomas

Read or re-read The Power of the Now – it is in the now that our spirit shines!

February 22 Have you ever:

Been bored listening to someone but acted interested?

Pretended to like someone more than you did?

Pretended to like someone less than you did?

Had trouble admitting you didn't know something you're supposed to know?

Had trouble admitting you are wrong?

Had difficulty asking for what you wanted?

Acted happy when you felt sad?

Had difficulty admitting you were attracted to someone until you found out how they felt about you?

Had a problem saying no or marking your boundaries?

Had trouble telling your sexual partner that you're not satisfied?

Reacted defensively when you thought you were being criticized?

Had difficulty expressing your anger, jealousy, or hurt without getting really angry?

Had trouble expressing your love, caring or vulnerability?

Avoided telling someone something that you feared might be hurtful?

Welcome to planet Earth! You are not alone. Many of us have created these circumstances in our lives. We are not bad or wrong or phony, just human. And as such, we get to work through a myriad of circumstances that develop our character, open our hearts and feed our soul.

Sometimes we forget who we are. It is time to fall in love with life. It is messy and painful and challenging and deeply rewarding when we face our stuck places and set them free.

The above situations are gifts we give to ourselves and others so that we may work through them and love each other at a deeper level than ever before. Happy healing and loving! From my inquiring heart to yours, Thomas

Face the stuck places inside, be with them then set them free!

February 23   Collateral Beauty

In December of 2016, our Illuminate Film Festival team had the honor of holding the United States grand opening of the film Collateral Beauty. It was a wonderful movie filled with emotion and discovery. The critics didn't like it. They don't like movies of the heart. They prefer high tech, hero movies that kill thousands to entertain us. This is my judgment of course. The movie starred Will Smith, Kate Winslet, Helen Mirren, Edward Norton and other notable actors. The story was about a man who would attempt to overcome some personal tragedy. His personal philosophy of life was what we often share here.

What is your why? Why did you get up this morning? What did you eat? What were your plans for the day? And on a bigger template, why are you here on planet Earth? What are you doing in this lifetime? In the movie, Smith gets letters from love, death and time. Each of us gets to utilize these elements in each of our lifetimes. Will we find love and give it? We have a certain amount of time that only our soul knows. How will we spend it? We will end this life at death. How will we be celebrated? How will we celebrate ourselves?

The term collateral beauty could be used to describe the meaning behind something. For example, when something bad happens to a person, they might want to check for the collateral beauty or the hidden messages behind the event, which could be a beautiful thing; even though at the time of the event, it is often too painful to do so. Collateral beauty is all around us and in us. We are an integral part of the beauty of the Earth. We are each other's collateral beauty. May we all be able to see that beauty and acknowledge it? From my collateral heart to yours, Thomas

The beauty of your life presence is so astounding! Be it!

February 24   Serendipity

Lou Ann and I watched the movie *Serendipity* again today. Please see it for yourself and let me know what you experienced.

In ancient Greece they didn't have obituaries. They only asked did the person "live with passion"! In a scene in the movie, one of the protagonists writes an obituary about the other and says *"Trager secretly clung to the belief that life is not merely a series of meaningless accidents or coincidences. Uh-uh. But rather, it's a tapestry of events that culminate in an exquisite, sublime plan."*

We are Divine and we get to live the plan. The wonderful thing is, we don't have to know what it is. We don't have to spend time figuring it out. It has already been arranged by our Soul. It wants us to have a life full of passion, beauty and prosperity. It doesn't matter if you find your soulmate, because you are it. The people who come into our lives are all the pieces of this divine tapestry.

We are here for each other to live our magnificence; if you are not experiencing it yet, no worries. Just close your eyes and surrender to your unknown life plan. Then say to Universe: "I am ready to live fully and freely from my heart and I let you lead the way". From my serendipitous heart to yours, Thomas

Will you begin sewing the tapestry of your life full of passion, beauty and prosperity right now?

February 25   Love Flowing

When I left the Sedona International Film Festival function last night, the car parked next to me had a license plate that said lvtolove (Live to love). When I got in the car and turned on the radio the song that was playing was Goodbye Girl by David Gates the lead singer of Bread. Richard Dreyfuss the male lead in Goodbye Girl is going to be at the film festival this week here in Sedona.

When I got home last night I noticed I had written my blog but somehow not posted it. I opened my computer to Facebook and on the left of the page was a post from Marsha Mason, Dreyfuss' co-star in the movie Goodbye Girl. Don't you love it? While at the function last night I was remarking to another person that when I am in the flow of following my inner guidance I have so many more magical events. When I get in a fear space and focus on money to pay the bills, I have less. Just sayin……. If this happens for you, I encourage you to follow your heart and you will never go wrong. From my flowing heart to yours, Thomas

Be in the flow of love in your life – trust and let go!

February 26 Universal principle #4: There Is Nothing Outside Of Us

"In order to have our human experiences, we have created the apparent reality that we are living outside the Oneness; that there are things and people that can affect us without our consent. The truth is, there is nothing outside of us; all that we see is our Self. This becomes our new reality when we open the belief in separation and accept the truth that we are one."

When we accept responsibility for our creations we no longer get to blame anyone else or ourselves. These are choices we make either consciously or subconsciously and we get to feel the power of our creation.

This can be a tough one for many people. We create everything in our experience. There is no other experience. If this is true it gives us the opportunity to consciously create every new outcome. What would you like to create? If there were no limitations, what would your life look like? This is not fantasy, this is physics.

As unlimited, eternal light beings there is an amazing wonderful world of possibilities for all of us. Look at your life right now and see all that you have created. If there are things in your life that don't feel like you, it is time to create it a different way.

Here is a new way of changing your life. I learned this from Arnold Patent as well. Look at what you created and then determine how you feel about it. Next, choose how you would like to feel right now in this moment. You don't need to do anything. Just focus on the feeling and stay with it until you feel it deeply. Stay with the feeling as long as you desire. Remember you are perfect just the way you are. From my heart to yours, Thomas

How would your life look right now if you knew you are an eternal light being? Choose how you want to feel right now knowing who you are!

February 27   it's Party Time!

We went to the Sedona International Film Festival as a guest. Lou Ann and I, and other team members of our Illuminate Film Festival have been able to see some wonderful films. At night there are parties where all the filmmakers and festival employees and guests like myself, get to mingle, network and support the industry. What I like most about it, is the passion the filmmakers have for their work. It appears that most are doing what they love to do. This festival is different from our Illuminate Film Festival. It runs ten days and has 168 films of all varieties and interests.

Here is the mission statement of The Illuminate Film Festival: Our mission is to elevate human consciousness and inspire lasting transformation through cinema.

ILLUMINATE is the world's premier film festival for conscious cinema. Dedicated to spreading enlightened ideas and pushing humanity forward, ILLUMINATE is a landmark destination event and centerpiece for conscious content. Founded on the premise that the language of film is universal and a dynamic force in carrying messages to the masses, the Festival showcases the best of conscious media to uplift, inspire and transform.

In a way, our volunteering for this is fulfilling the dream we had twenty years ago, to create our conscious television show. Cinema can certainly have an impact on the Earth. When it is done for the purpose of inspiring and transforming it takes on a larger meaning for me.

After I finish this blog, I will head out to the party and meet more exciting and committed folks who make me feel inspired. From my celebratory heart to yours, Thomas

Find what inspires you and share it!

February 28 Success

The wonderful life trainer Jim Rohn once said *"Success is something you attract by the person you become."* To expand that concept to all of life, I believe that whatever you attract in life is because of what you believe and often about what you have chosen.

I have been reviewing a film for the festival that is about a man who goes through a horrible life altering accident. His name is Hal Elrod and his film is The Miracle Morning, directed by Nick Conedera He then discovers success principles and develops a system to share them with others.   He then becomes wealthy and famous.

Later he is afflicted with a rare form of cancer. He battles this disease for months and is finally in remission. This ordeal shows him that he was obsessed with success and all the trappings it brings. He became a success-aholic. He spent way too much time doing that and not enough time being an excellent mate, father and friend.

What he discovered along the way is. Life is not fair, it just is. Things happen to us that we least expect. When they do, we get to choose how we are going to feel and how we will face them. It is often that our hardships define our character. Then, through the process of dealing with them, we discover something deep inside we didn't know we had. Our spirit, our life force can often rally and perform and create beyond our wildest dreams.

When it is all said and done we often discover that the love, the sharing, the caring, our families and friends are our success. Let us support each other to help discover the gifts, the energy, the joy, the passion, the courage to be successful in life! From my encouraging heart to yours, Thomas

Our success is sharing, caring and loving family and friends – begin now knowing this!

February 29   Last Words

This belief about life has been shared many times on this blog. However, perhaps it will carry more weight coming from a multi-billionaire.

The last words of Steve Jobs –
I have come to the pinnacle of success in business.
In the eyes of others, my life has been the symbol of success.
However, apart from work, I have little joy. Finally, my wealth is simply a fact to which I am accustomed.

At this time, lying on the hospital bed and remembering all my life, I realize that all the accolades and riches of which I was once so proud, have become insignificant with my imminent death.
In the dark, when I look at green lights, of the equipment for artificial respiration and feel the buzz of their mechanical sounds, I can feel the breath of my approaching death looming over me.
Only now do I understand that once you accumulate enough money for the rest of your life, you have to pursue objectives that are not related to wealth.
It should be something more important:
For example, stories of love, art, dreams of my childhood.

No, stop pursuing wealth, it can only make a person into a twisted being, just like me.
God has made us one way, we can feel the love in the heart of each of us, and not illusions built by fame or money, like I made in my life, and I cannot take them with me.
I can only take with me the memories that were strengthened by love.
This is the true wealth that will follow you; will accompany you, He will give strength and light to go ahead.

Love can travel thousands of miles and so life has no limits. Move to where you want to go. Strive to reach the goals you want to achieve. Everything is in your heart and in your hands.
What is the world's most expensive bed, the hospital bed?
You, if you have money, you can hire someone to drive your car, but you cannot hire someone to take your illness that is killing you.
Material things lost can be found. But one thing you can never find when

you lose: life.
Whatever stage of life we are in right now, at the end we will have to face the day when the curtain falls.
Please treasure your family love, love for your spouse, and love for your friends...
Treat everyone well and stay friendly with your neighbors. Nuff said!
From my heart to yours, Thomas

Feel the love in your heart, embrace it in the now! Know that life is precious and so are you!

March 1   Belief

Our beliefs are our reality. In 1989 Wayne Dyer wrote a book titled *"You'll See It When You Believe it"* It is profoundly true! Simply one of the most important books you'll ever read. If you're struggling to survive or to thrive, Mr. Dyer will show you the way. One observer said "Just read it I dare ya!" It was a landmark book in my life!

There is an important movie titled "*What the Bleep Do We Know?* There is a scene in that movie where they explain that the Native Americans who inhabited this continent were partially defeated by the fact that they had never seen an ocean ship. When the Spanish came to the shore they had a distinct advantage before landing. The only warning the natives might have had was from a wise leader who could see the ships because they were part of his belief.

Right now there are probably so many things we cannot see and they are only not visible because of our limited beliefs. One of the ways to personal freedom is to radically shift our limited beliefs. When we take time to let go of those thoughts and understandings that hold us back, miracles can occur. The moment you shift your belief, you realize that what you're chasing has been right in front of you.

What are your limiting beliefs? One of mine is I won't achieve what I planned to do before I incarnated. Take some time and just write down a list of any of your beliefs. When you are finished, look at the list and check off those that are limited. Then draw a line through them and declare that they no longer have power over your life! From my believing heart to yours, Thomas

Our beliefs are only a small part of who we are, we can choose differently in this moment to be our Divine self!

March 2   Star dust

Tonight we went to a party at the Sedona International Film Festival. I love being around filmmakers. They are like grandmothers. I meet them and ask them what their film is about. Their whole countenance lights up! Not unlike grandmothers when you ask them about their grandchildren. They get so passionate about sharing their movie. It is their child of sorts. They give it all of their time, money and energy. It is central to their purpose in life, a lot of times. We should all be so lucky.

Find what you love to do and give it everything you got. Your days will feel more fulfilling. In fact, you may not even know what time it is, at times. You will feel there is a special reason for you doing what you love. And only you can do it in your unique way.

There is a book by Barbara Sher called *Wishcraft, How to Get What You Really Want*. She says: *"If you've been waiting for a job that rewards you with more than a paycheck…or for the perfect moment to take that "long-lost" dream off hold…it's time to stop waiting and start creating a life you can truly love!"*

My wish for all of you is that your whole life feels like the heart of a grandmother. From my wishful heart to yours, Thomas

Love this moment you are in, so you can create more of them!

March 3   Nothing in Our World Like Love

Wondering what I might share with you folks tonight and this song began to resonate in my brain: Nothing in Our World like Love

Nothing in our world like love

Nothing in our world like love

Some say love makes the world go round

Not enough love, makes us frown

What in the world is love?

Some say love is easy

Some say love is hard

Some say love lasts forever

Some say love never comes their way

All I know is, love is who we are

Souls all traveling to the farthest star

Nothing in our world like love

Love is where you are

Love is near and far

Love is happening every day

Love is happening in every way

Nothing in our world like love

I don't know where the songs come from. I may be doing something unrelated to writing and I will hear the tune and the words. Love is always a good theme for us to focus on! From my tuneful heart to yours, Thomas

Know that you are LOVE!

March 4   Let It Shine!

The Sedona International Film Festival is complete, so now I can get to bed at a decent hour. It was a wonderful experience for me. I love being around the energy of folks making a difference on our planet. These talented artists and creators are giving all of their energy into what they believe. They are like shining lights in the darkness.

They are not any different than you and I though. They remind me of that exciting quote from Marianne Williamson: *"Our deepest fear is not that we are inadequate. Our deepest fear is that we are powerful beyond measure. It is our light, not our darkness that most frightens us. We ask ourselves, who am I to be brilliant, gorgeous, talented, and fabulous? Actually, who are you not to be? You are a child of God. You're playing small does not serve the world. There is nothing enlightened about shrinking so that other people won't feel insecure around you. We are all meant to shine, as children do. We were born to make manifest the glory of God that is within us. It's not just in some of us; it's in everyone. And as we let our own light shine, we unconsciously give other people permission to do the same. As we are liberated from our own fear, our presence automatically liberates others."*

Sometimes we get caught up in a pattern of not letting our light shine. We are all unlimited at the spiritual level. We only believe that we are not. We have forgotten who we are. And it is never too late. No matter what our choices have been in life. No matter what we have created that doesn't seem to support us. In the very next minute we can change by bringing up the feelings we are experiencing that are less than helpful. Once we access them, say the word "change". Do this anytime you feel stuck in any way. You can reprogram the mind and let go of the blockage. This one small step can help us begin to break through our self-imposed limitations and our lights will be able to shine again! From my shining heart to yours, Thomas

Bring up the feelings that are less than helpful, notice them then say the word 'change'. Be the light being you truly are one stuck place at a time!

March 5   PTSD

The movie 'Almost Sunrise' is being sponsored by the local mental health coalition and Mary D Fisher Theater and Illuminate. 'Almost Sunrise' tells the inspiring story of two young men, Tom Voss and Anthony Anderson, who, in an attempt to put their haunting Iraq combat experiences behind them, embark on an extraordinary journey – a 2,700 mile trek on foot across America. I saw the trailer and it is thrilling.

We have been looking at a lot of films about military service personnel who have PTSD. We have sent these men and women off to kill other humans to support our country's policies. And to support the military industrial companies that get rich off of these young folks.

Enough! We need these young Americans to be here in our country, living long, productive, happy and prosperous lives. Too many leaders of our country have sent these brave young people to their deaths. And then thousands return home with horrible memories of doing something against the nature of our souls. Let us do all what we can to take care of these wounded heroes. Let us also take a stand in any way we can for peace. Let us find a way and work together for peace on Earth! From my peaceful heart to yours, Thomas

When we find peace inside of us, others can feel it inside themselves too if they choose! Let the ripple effect happen!

March 6   Satsang

Have you been to a Satsang? It is a traditional activity in the East Indian spiritual context, meaning "being with good/righteous companions." Satsang is a sitting together with an enlightened person who usually gives a short talk and then answers questions.

My first experience was with a lady named Gangaji, thirty years ago here in Sedona. At Satsang, we gather together and sit quietly without speaking. Many at the gatherings meditate and allow themselves to find the silence within. Then the Guru or teacher comes in and we continue in silence. Usually the teacher will begin speaking extemporaneously and share whatever is in their heart. After they stop, people often get up and ask questions. They are sometimes stuck in their perceptions about life and the teacher will listen and lead them to a place of understanding.

It is hard for me to put into words the feelings that I have during this whole experience. In short, I feel at home. I resonate with the words shared by the teacher but even more with their presence. My inadequate words are; I am filled with joy and love and possibilities.

I was reviewing a possible film for our festival tonight and it was about Mooji, a Satsang leader. Mooji's teachings are simple and he encourages his followers to avoid the mind's influence. Then, abide in the Self which is the witness of all phenomenal existence. It is before any "thing," including thoughts and all that is perceived with the five senses. He teaches that to be in your spiritual heart, the part of you that knows. The world does not need the ego's help. Truth and freedom occur at the end of striving.

If he were here tonight he might say: there is nothing to do, there is nowhere to go, and you are already there. Once we give up the notion that we need to do or accomplish, we begin to connect with the essence of who we are. It is then we can live in peace and let life flow from us and through us. Simply put, we are what we have been searching for and have found our way home. From my Satsang heart to yours, Thomas

Be in the true essence of your spiritual heart throughout your day today!

March 7 Held back, kind of broken voice

A delightful teacher named Kathi Bellucci has been giving me voice lessons. She is teaching me to make my whole body an instrument for sound. We have been training for a few months and the progress has been slow. No fault of the instructor. I don't do my homework. She is infinitely patient with me though.

She has been teaching me posture and how to support the sound with my ribcage and diaphragm. She also has been showing me how to direct the sound in my head so I can sustain the higher notes. Today in the lesson, she was sharing how I could do some of these things so that I could avoid my "held back kind of broken voice!" I howled with laughter. It was a perfect description of her imperfect student.

I told her today how much I love her and her spirit and her joyfulness and her longstanding patience in dealing with a recalcitrant student. It is such a joy to be learning from her. I am so blessed and so is Lou Ann, who is her student as well (and a good one)!

I got to thinking about my "broken voice." It mostly breaks when I am not holding the body structure and I am in fear of a high note; so I hold back. Sounds like a lesson for life. I got my palm read at the yoga festival by an amazing lady. She noticed my right hand is deformed. She shared that I have a fear about reaching fame and success. I am holding on too tight to my fear. She claimed my hand would relax and heal when I release my fear of fame and success.

I am asking all of you good folks today; where are you holding back? What do you fear that might be keeping you from achieving your dreams? If you are not creating what you desire it may be time for a "checkup." You may want to connect with a "trusted, sensitive being" and find an answer. I wish for you all to find your path, fulfill your dreams and to fill up your heart with all the joy and love and abundance you desire! From my heart full of love to yours, Thomas

Breathe in more fully today and exhale out with a hum, laugh or song as often as you can!

March 8   Saturn Return

In the early seventies I became a professional astrologer. I did it for several years and had some wonderful experiences. There is an aspect of Astrology that is important to discuss. When we are born, the planets in our solar system are in a position which is called our natal horoscope.

There are ten planets including Earth (third rock from the sun). The planet Saturn is the sixth planet from the sun. It takes Saturn 28-30 years to complete its orbit around the sun and through the Zodiac. It is masculine energy and rules both Capricorn and Aquarius, and the Tenth and Eleventh Houses.

The orbit of 28-30 years is significant. When we arrive at the age of twenty eight to thirty in our life, we often get tested in a variety of ways. Saturn doesn't make things easy. That's the role of the taskmaster of the zodiac. Saturn commands us to get to work and to work hard. Discipline and responsibility are important to this planet, yet if we're eager to conquer the world, that's okay, too. At the ages of 28 to 30 people often change jobs, relationships, get divorced, get married or move to another place. Our spirit is encouraging us to check in with our life purpose. Our astrology chart is a road map of our life. It gives us directions on how to succeed at what our soul wants to accomplish. We often get off track and Saturn is there to remind us of our mission. This is the Saturn return.

If you are near 28, 56, 84 you will be awakened to how you are doing. It is then that we can glance at our natal road map and stay on our personal interstate highway or perhaps take a detour or two. As in other decisions in life they are all perfect and on purpose, that's the way we designed it! Safe travels, from my exploring heart to yours, Thomas

Wherever you are in your journey, know it's the perfect place for now!

March 9   Universal principle #5: Perfection

"God is perfect and expresses this perfection as unconditional love and support. Whatever unfolds is God happening. When we see and feel other than unconditional love, we are seeing and feeling the disguises we have created with our beliefs. We create disguises to explore the experiences that make up our human journey. When we are ready to see and feel with greater clarity, we embrace whatever is before us in unconditional love, trusting that Universe, in its constant expression of unconditional love, is sending us the perfect support to expand our joyfulness. With practice, our clarity grows, along with our gratitude for the unconditional love, support and joyfulness that is always present."

We are eternal spiritual beings choosing to be here on planet Earth. We come here because we choose to. There is no Karma to repay. There is no greater purpose to achieve. There is only us choosing each second and playing a game of let's pretend.

We pretend we are limited. We pretend that we die. We pretend we are finite. We intentionally do this so that the game we play on Earth will have meaning. If we knew the truth about our limitlessness the game would be over. It wouldn't work. So we all agree that this one life is all there is and we have a limited amount of time to work with.

It is like going to watch a movie. When we go to the movies, a part of our consciousness suspends belief for a while so the illusion on the screen will work. It is more entertaining to lose yourself in the story and be sad or happy or inspired, etc. Life is like this. However, we almost totally buy into the illusion that all of this is real and we keep up the pretense for as long as it takes for us to play the game.

We each are the directors, writers, producers of our own unique movie. We are also the casting directors who invite all the actors who may have prominent roles or extras. Remember there are no small parts in your movie. And each scene has been carefully crafted in alignment with our soul's desire. Today you have all you need to create your perfect movie. So give it everything you've got. Leave nothing on the cutting room floor. Today is the grand opening, the world premiere of your blockbuster movie. Let the world see your greatness! From my heart to yours, Thomas

Know what an opportunity today is and truly live it!

March 10 Appreciations

The other night Lou Ann and I went to a meeting with the Inspiration of Sedona group. It was part of a series of movies about Peace. We often think about peace in a global context. Peace on Earth is what so many people desire. I am reminded of the Sy Miller and Jill Jackson song. The opening lines are "Let there be peace on Earth and let it begin with me!" In truth this is the only way to achieve it. It has to come from deep within each of us to make it happen.

When we appreciate someone or some things in our life we create a peaceful feeling within and with each other. Early in Lou Ann's and my relationship she taught me the priceless value of appreciation. She would thank me for doing the simplest things. When she did so, I got a feeling of being loved and cared for. When that occurred I felt peaceful inside. Then I would want to do more loving things both for her and others in my life.

I learned a valuable distinction when I took the Radical Honesty course. Dr. Blanton taught us a deeper way to share appreciation. When someone does something nice for us we often say "I appreciate that!" When we tweak it and say to the person, "I appreciate you", it becomes so much more personal and connects us heart to heart.

Let us find ways to appreciate more things in our lives. Let us find ways to appreciate each other until we create a deeper peace within us all! As the above mentioned song says:

Let peace begin with me.
Let this be the moment now.
With ev'ry breath I take
let this be my solemn vow:
To take each moment
and live each moment
in peace eternally.

Let there be peace on earth
and let it begin with me!"

From my appreciative and peaceful heart to yours, Thomas

Let the people in your life know you appreciate them!

March 11   Animal Rights

Each year, humans kill ninety-six billion animals, yes billion. Seventy five million farm animals killed daily.

Most of you probably know about PETA. It stands for People for the Ethical Treatment of Animals. With the help of a global army of kind people, PETA has revolutionized the way the world thinks about animal rights. Now, people aren't just asking if the tanks at Sea World are too small—they know that it's wrong to confine and display intelligent, sensitive orcas at all, and they're speaking out about it. They aren't just avoiding fur coats—they're seeking out vegan leather shoes and vegan wool sweaters made of other materials. They're not just decrying cruelty to dogs and cats but also demanding an end to the horrific cruelty that animals raised for food endure every day on farms and in slaughterhouses.

Sometime during the Neolithic age, we became farmers and we domesticated animals. So for the last several thousand years, the human race has dominated animals. Now we are destroying the rest of the planet with our selfish decisions. It is time for us to change this scenario. It is time to take a stand for all animals of our planet. We are the only voice that animals have. We are the only ones who can do the loving and nurturing things, to help all these wonderful creatures. Please join all the animal lovers of the world and do whatever you can to support and care for God's precious beings! From my hopeful heart to yours, Thomas

Give the animals in your life an extra hug today! Or give yourself a hug! Find a way to protect animals even in the smallest way!

March 12   Edge of Paradise

Each day I enjoy sharing my thoughts and feelings with all of you. I hope you are nurtured by it in some way. We just watched a film about a group of young adults, who gathered together on the island of Kauai, in the early seventies.

At first, there were just thirteen of them and they lived on the beach in tents, away from the other folks on the island. These free spirited folks were eventually arrested for the way they lived. Then, Elizabeth Taylor's brother bought several acres and allowed them to live on his property.

Soon, others followed and they built living structures from wood and plastic to shelter themselves. Some fell in love, had children, and raised a family, some were veterans of the Vietnam War, others were against that war, most just wanted to live free. They wore very little clothing and some smoked pot. They were escaping the harshness of the world at the time.

They called their enclave Camp Taylor and it lasted eight years. The local Hawaiians were envious of the freedom of these young Americans. Soon the authorities got the place shutdown and destroyed. The movie looks back at this idyllic time, in these folk's lives, through photos and current interviews of the people. Almost to a person, they said it was the best time of their life and many said it made their life better because of it.

Lou Ann and I lived on the Big Island of Hawaii from 2009 to 2013. We felt a kindred connection to these young people. There is the energy of the islands, the sun, the weather and the beauty that is so attractive. Both of us were always treated with honor by the island people. Lou Ann entered a local Hula group and learned the sacredness of the dance and culture. I played a lot of tennis and walked many miles along beaches and mountain trails and felt so at home.

It is called paradise by many. I believe that each of us can create our own paradise, by being in our heart and feeling the connection, to the Earth and its inhabitants. It is said that home is where your heart is. I could paraphrase that and say paradise is where your heart is. May all of you find your paradise and live in peace and beauty all the days of your lives. From my island heart to yours, Thomas

We each are living in Paradise right where we are!

March 13   Ask, Listen, Act

Lou Ann and I watched a short film, five minutes long, called Intuition, it was brilliant. It was about our intuition. That part of us that communicates with us, often in a silent whisper or a knowing. We call it our gut. It is our connection with why we are here. Life on Earth today can be overwhelming. Consider what the human race has created and continues to do so; seven and a half billion souls making choices that affect everyone else. The challenge is, most of us make choices in an unconscious way. We are products of our environment, heritage, upbringing, education and genetic and reincarnation imprint.

Life comes at us at such a frenetic pace, that we choose quickly, and often it doesn't serve us. It is time to slow down. It is time to stop, listen and then act. Let us take a few moments each day and ask "Universe, how can I serve you today?" Then listen for the answer. It may come as an inner voice, an idea, a hunch or a feeling. Whatever form it arrives, it is then we get to act. When we do not, it can have repercussions that keep us from what we desire. When we trust that inner part of ourselves that is connected to Oneness, magic can happen.

I know for me, some of my greatest accomplishments occurred, when I surrendered to that still small voice. Once I got out of the way, my life was never the same! I encourage us all to go within as often as possible and ask, listen and act. The world will be a better place when we do. From my intuitive heart to yours, Thomas

How can you serve the Universe today?

March 14 Equality

We hold these truths to be self-evident, that all men are created equal, that they are endowed by their Creator with certain unalienable Rights, which among these are Life, Liberty and the pursuit of Happiness. I would add "all people" and all sentient beings to this declaration!

We saw a movie about Erin O'Flaherty who is an American beauty pageant titleholder who held the title of Miss Missouri in the Miss America 2017 pageant. She is the first openly lesbian contestant to compete in Miss America. The movie depicted the challenge that she went through while competing for this beauty opportunity. There were many who criticized her participation as you can imagine. The Declaration of Independence says all are equal and are entitled to life, liberty and the pursuit of happiness.

Let us be the people who make a change on our planet. Let us create so much love and caring that all feel nurtured. Let us create a society where no one ever has to "come out". There is only one human race and it does not need to be categorized as a letter such as LGBTQIA. We are better than that. In our heart of hearts we know we are one. And that Oneness is made up of separate and equal parts. From my egalitarian heart to yours, Thomas

Nurture that place in you that feels less than, so you can have compassion for others that may be judged as less than or not equal!

March 15   Daily Wisdom

Lou Ann reads from two books every morning and she has been reading them daily for years. One is Mark Nepo's The Book of Awakening, a daily spiritual sharing for each calendar day of the year. Nepo's book tells us there is a Buddhist precept that asks us to be mindful of how rare it is to find ourselves in human form on earth.

So what will you do today, knowing that you are one of the rarest forms of life to ever walk the earth? How will you carry yourself? What will you do with your hands? What will you ask and of whom? Tomorrow we could die. But today we are precious and rare and awake. It ushers us into grateful living. It makes hesitation useless. Grateful and awake, ask what you need to know now. Say what you feel now. Love what you love now. Here are things we can do.

Sit outside, if possible, or near a window, and note the other life forms around you.

Breathe slowly and think of the ant and the blade of grass and the blue jay and what these life forms can do that you can't.

Think of the pebble and the piece of bark and the stone bench, and center your breathing on the interior things that you can do that they can't.

Rise slowly, feeling beautifully human, and enter your day with the conscious intent of doing one thing that only humans can do.

When the time arises, do this one thing with great reverence and gratitude.

Life is precious in every lifetime whatever form we take. As a human being on Earth, we get to have a mind and soul and feelings to experience the magic of life. Don't take any of it for granted. Have each day be a sacred connection to All That Is. From my learning heart to yours, Thomas

We are rare and truly blessed – take time today to feel it and know it!

March 16   Love in Action

Just saw another wonderful movie about an American documentary filmmaker and a Cambodian lady who are personally saving Elephants, titled Love and Bananas! It is a beautiful story about these amazing giants. They are being slaughtered like all wild animals across the Earth. This film was so well done and so full of heart. The Cambodian woman has rescued forty five Elephants and has them sheltered in a reserve. It is just a small amount of the hundreds of thousands that have been killed.

It reminds me of the story I first heard many years ago by Eve Hogan of Hawaii. She said there was this girl walking the beach and the tide was bringing in thousands of Starfish. As the waves broke they would get stranded on the shore and die. She would pick them up and toss them back into the ocean. A man passing by noticed the girl and asked her what she was doing. She replied "saving Starfish"! He said "there are millions of them, you can hardly make a difference" The girl bent down picked up another Starfish and flung it into the water. "Made a difference to that one"!

Sometimes, with all that is going on in the world that is harmful, we feel overwhelmed. However, each of us can make a difference every day by doing the smallest things. Just the other day I saw someone hold open a door to a retail store for someone who was quite a ways away. In a couple of moments, the person who had the door held open for them did exactly the same thing.

This is not rocket science. This is love science! Let us all get involved in whatever way we can, to help each other and especially those that have no voice! It is time for love in action! From my activist heart to yours, Thomas

How can we make a difference to the 'starfish' in our lives?

March 17 The Shadow of Your Smile

Lou Ann and I just watched another excellent film about how we all perceive life. Each of us has developed a story about what has happened to us. This story is a combination of our life experiences and our understanding and reaction to them. It often replaces what is really going on. We believe in it so much, that it keeps us stuck and prevents us from fulfilling our magnificence.

In the movie several attendees went through four weekend workshops. They got in touch with their shadow side, that part of our unconscious that records everything. They also found out how wonderful they are from the other participants. They went through deep processes so that they could live their lives in the present, not in their story. It is something that would be of value to almost everyone.

Synchronistically, our good Astrologer friend in Hawaii sent us how the current configuration of the skies may affect us. Here is what she shared:

New Moon, Sun, etc. in Pieces, Depths of emotion, intuition, spiritual existence (to many it is the unknown). Let go of the past that hinders your connection to your true Divine Love. Bridge Heaven & Earth, use your imagination, meditate in your own way, and come to unconditional Love & Forgiveness. Lift the Veil & Transcend. Release aggression, resolve conflicts. BREATHE. MOVE forward without hurting others. Renew your relationship with the invisible; reconnect with your divine truth- UNION. Rest, spiritually replenish. Allow silence & let creative energy flow. Deep wounds may surface and it may be an opportunity to practice *unconditional Love & acceptance. Open to Love & all Truths. We all have shadows, we are all holy. We are preparing to bring our creations and dreams into reality.*

It was almost identical to the message of the movie. Thank you Universe! I would encourage anyone who has not looked at how they hold their life story, to examine it. It will set you free! From my inquiring heart to yours, Thomas

Resolve conflict within you with self-compassion! Know you are loved!

March 18   Healthier Us

This post was on Facebook, it is important for all of us to read. These are not my words but I think they have value. What is preventative medicine? A sustainable diet found innately in all humans to avoid sickness and disease

What is this diet?
Fruits should be eaten in more quantity than any other food group or element. Eat raw vegetables or boiled. Eat store bought foods with 5 or less ingredients and know what it is you are eating and how to pronounce it.

Do not eat foods that will not spoil. Avoid all processed foods to include white salt, white sugar, and white flour, and chemicals whenever possible. Abstain from eating meat and to find the least amount of protein in our diets is required, not what most as health experts want you to think.

A good diet leads to a healthier you, healthier animals, and a happier planet!!! While saving 30% off your food budget and eating more foods that are good for All Humans. We need to remember that not all foods are good for us. Instead of eating one plate of meat we could eat two plates of Vegetables; allowing us to eradicate starvation and poverty.

There are major challenges for the human race. Poverty, climate change and hunger and they are all tied together. We humans are deforesting our planet and instead creating grazing land for cattle. Cattle produce more methane than fossil fuels. The carbon dioxide from the fossil fuels and the cattle are destroying the ozone layer. We are having more floods and droughts.

The majority of our planet goes hungry every day. We cannot sustain eating beef and our bodies are not made to digest meat. We need to eat a sustainable healthy diet for our personal good and the welfare of the Earth and all of its inhabitants! From my Vegan heart to yours, Thomas

Try having a meatless meal with lots of veggies once or twice this week!

March 19   Making a Difference

Lou Ann and I have been working on sourcing, finding, screening and reviewing movies for the past four months. Our team is near the end of the process. Six of us spent the day going over about eighty films we thought worthy of being in the Illuminate Film Festival. It was exciting to be a part of this event. We look at films in several possible ways. Do they inspire? Do they transform? Are they well made? Will they make a difference? Are they marketable from a distributor's point of view? We include categories such as healthy food, life purpose, personal healing, climate change, overcoming poverty, saving animals, the environment, spiritual wisdom and many more.

We have a lot a fun being together and we also take our task seriously. We know that cinema is a powerful medium to make a profound effect on our planet. We fall in love with some films because we see the passion filmmakers have about their subject. We watch people save elephants, giraffes, wolves, whales, dolphins, gorillas and apes.

All of these wonderful creatures have no voice except for the brave committed filmmakers who tell their stories. We worked ten hours and finally came up with the final twenty two, plus a couple of alternates, that will be in the festival this coming June. Now we get to invite the amazing folks who made these films to be a part of our fifth year.

It will be exciting letting them know that their hard work has been noticed and rewarded. If you have a chance, go to illuminatefilmfestival.com and purchase a pass or become a member. It will help make our world a better place "for you and for me and the whole wide human race". Just sayin…. From my illuminated heart to yours, Thomas

*Many inspiring films from Illuminate Film Festival can be seen on line –
go to Illuminatefilmfestival.com to learn more!*

March 20   I Set Myself Free

*Today's just like any day but it's not any day. Today's the day I finally
found the courage to give myself a lift. Everything's much clearer since I
gave myself this gift. I set myself free; I set myself free, free to be the
best me I can be. I set myself free, I set myself free, since I stepped out of
my way, there's no stopping me. I'm diving into life from an exhilarating
height and refusing to be held back by a little thing called
fright. Growing stronger branching out like the strongest tree, I set
myself free.*

*Watch me grow, watch me grow; truth is all I ever want to know. As I go
forward one thing is clear, the only thing that matters is right here. And
all the stumbling blocks that held me back came tumbling down, I'm
lighter than I've ever been and two feet off the ground. I'm filling up with
love and I let it overflow, watch me grow.*

*Just breathing in and breathing out, got me on the track, I found myself
again and it's good to have me back. And I will conquer any obstacle
somehow, and the most important time is happening now. And giving up
the fight was an incredible release and for the first time in my life I feel a
total inner peace. Growing stronger, getting better, making changes,
loving more, I will open any door, getting closer every minute to the
person that is me, I set myself free, Oh I am free, yes I am free!*

These are the lyrics to a fantastic song, written by Dale Gonyea; Lou Ann
and I learned some thirty years ago. I am writing them from memory so I
am sure they are not exact, but close enough. It was performed and
recorded by Michael Byers a fabulous singer/actor/dancer. This song is
in Amazon Music under That Kid Can Fly. These lyrics should be copied
and put up on all of our bulletin boards, mirrors, refrigerators or any
place that you can see them daily. I hope you will adopt them as your life
mantra or personal declaration of total independence. From my
"free" heart to yours, Thomas

*Listen to the lyrics to the song I Set Myself Free about 3 times and feel the
magic that happens inside you!*

March 21   Let the Light Shine Through

Lou Ann and I went to see A Wrinkle in Time today; huge movie with a stellar cast and a wonderful story about all of us. There was a line in the movie that said "wounds are where the light shines through". All of us have wounds and we patch them up both physically and emotionally. Many of us try to hide them or forget them when they carry too much trauma. This movie line was perhaps a paraphrase of the remarkable Persian poet Rumi. He said "The wound is the place where the light enters you."

This is what some of the greatest thinkers in existence knew, and what every person who wants to be at peace should: your suffering is not punishment. It is a tool, like anything else, to deepen your awareness and expand your consciousness. In other words: to make you more present and more capable of feeling the joy and light and gift of that present moment. That probably sounds deliriously, annoyingly optimistic, especially when you're in the thick of it, but remember that anger is recognition, and the inability to accept.

The paragraph above was written by Brianna Wiest. Here are some other quotes: "I think that we are like stars. Something happens to burst us open; but when we burst open and think we are dying; we're actually turning into a supernova. And then when we look at ourselves again, we see that we're suddenly more beautiful than we ever were before!" C. Joy Bell C.

"The most beautiful people we have known are those who have known defeat, known suffering, known struggle, known loss, and have found their way out of the depths. These persons have an appreciation, sensitivity, and an understanding of life that fills them with compassion, gentleness, and a deep loving concern. Beautiful people do not just happen." Elisabeth Kubler-Ross

"Out of suffering have emerged the strongest souls; the most massive characters are seared with scars." Kahlil Gibran

"Pain and suffering are always inevitable for a large intelligence and a deep heart." Fyodor Dostoevsky

Perhaps we can be thankful for the pain and suffering we have experienced in our life. They have honed and designed us into the magnificent beings that we are. When we finally surrender and allow the light to shine through all our life experiences we do indeed get to be a shining star! From my shining heart to yours, Thomas

Let the light shine through your life experiences – this is a gift to yourself and the world!

March 22   Your Destiny

Back in 1995 Lou Ann and I attended a business seminar that had as its theme "Teamwork Makes the Dream work" Tonight we decided to have some Vegan chocolate chip cookies. Lou Ann was the chief baker and I was her sous baker. I chopped the pecans and cleaned the bowls and utensils. We laughed a lot as we were preparing the delicious dessert. We love to cook together! We often laugh a lot about life.   Both of us are the card suit of Clubs in the Destiny Card deck. Lou Ann is the nine of clubs and I am the eight of clubs. Ahhhh!

Here is an explanation of the deck. This system is the deck of the common 52 playing cards. Each birth date of a person is assigned one of the 52 cards called Your Birth Card. Once you know your birth card, you will know who you are and be able to know in advance what will happen in areas of love, family, work, finance, health, legal matters, travel and your spiritual life.

People who are clubs love to read and to learn new things and thrive on conversation and communications in all forms. The Clubs person is here searching for the perfect truth. Clubs people are creative and experience life through talking and learning. We both love words and their meaning. We both play with words all the time. It is one of the things we laugh about most.

If you want to find out about your Destiny Card, just go to cardsoflife.com and put in the month, day and year of your birth. Once you find out about your card and those folks you know; the cards can help improve your relationship with them. As they say "it's in the cards!" From my happy heart to yours, Thomas

Have fun discovering your destiny cards! Let it be another way of learning more about yourself!

March 23   How Sweet It Is

Lou Ann and I went to Prescott Valley Arizona, fifty five miles from Sedona, to see our grandson Seth play a professional basketball game. He played in a basketball league in Hungary for a few months. He said it was good to be home, meaning the United States. He played college basketball for the University of Maryland and the University of Virginia Tech. He is six foot one and weighs 193 pounds. He is left handed and has a good three point shot.

His dad and I used to play playground ball back in the early eighties in Phoenix Arizona. The courts were outside with metal chain rims. Seth's dad Joe, who was about twenty at the time, and I would play on the same team on those Phoenix courts. I was in my early forties, more than twice as old as any of the other men and boys playing there. I started playing basketball when I was twelve and played in high school at Hollywood High. I was an excellent long distance shooter. Little did they know! Joe would get the rebound and pass it out to me and swish I would sink a long shot. This scenario kept repeating and finally one of the players exclaimed "somebody guard the old white guy" The three point line didn't exist in college basketball until 1987. It was sweet to do something so well!

Another sweet thing is Seth's smile when he plays. So many players are so intense and even angry when they play. Seth has this big grin on his face a lot of the time! He is the product of good parenting and having a good attitude toward life. May we all find something in life that we enjoy so much, that we go around with a big grin on our face! From a proud grandpa's heart to yours, Thomas

Feel the sweetness in your own life and let it bring a smile to your face!

March 24   March for Our Lives

About 750 people showed up and marched and listened to talks and music and then we walked a couple of miles down the main highway in Sedona.   Hundreds of well-wishers drove by and waved and beeped their horns.

This was different. This wasn't about the environment or the mess Trump has made of our country. This was about children's lives. There were powerful signs displayed as we marched together. One sign said "A uterus is more heavily regulated than an assault rifle", a teacher's sign said "arm me with books, not bullets". One more said "actually guns do Kill people!" My favorite was "One child's life is worth all the guns on Earth!" I couldn't have said it better!

The man who made this sign was a Native American who has narcolepsy. He had to stop and rest several times along the route to catch his breath. Many other elderly also had to pause and rest and they kept on going.

Now the real work begins. We cannot let this moment pass and not get some action taken about banning assault weapons. It is you and I and all the people who care about our children being slaughtered in their classrooms.

We must do whatever it takes to vote people out of office, which will not stand with us and will not pass common sense gun laws. If I had my way, all guns on Earth would be rounded up and melted to make statues of all whose lives have been senselessly lost. We could honor their lives as well as our fallen heroes.

I hope this day was meaningful for you as it most likely was for millions of people all over this planet. This day we have drawn a line in the sand and said "Enough is enough." "Never again." Please find a way to get involved like you never have before. From my hopeful heart to yours, Thomas

It's up to each of us to take a stand to protect our children!

March 25   Just Learning

When Lou Ann and I became vegan about five years ago, we looked for a substitute for butter. We chose the Smart Balance products only to discover one of the ingredients is palm oil. Oops! Here is the problem with that. Palm oil is literally everywhere – in our foods, cosmetics, cleaning products and fuels. It's a source of huge profits for multinational corporations, while at the same time destroying the livelihoods of small holders. Displacement of indigenous peoples, deforestation and loss of biodiversity are all consequences of our palm oil consumption. How could it come to this? And what can we do in everyday life to protect people and nature?

What can we do?

1. Enjoy a home-cooked meal: Use your imagination: why not try almond-coconut-pear biscuits? Or pizza with potato and rosemary? A meal cooked from fresh ingredients beats processed foods containing palm oil every time. Oils such as coconut, olive, rapeseed or flax seed are ideal for cooking and baking.
2. Read labels: As of December 2014, labeling regulations in the EU require food products to clearly indicate that they contain palm oil. However, in the case of non-food items such as cosmetics and cleaning products, a wide range of chemical names may still be used to hide the use of palm oil. A quick check of your favorite search engine will turn up palm oil-free alternatives, however.
3. Remember that the customer is king: Ask your retailers for palm oil-free products. Write product manufacturers and ask them why they aren't using domestic oils. Companies can be quite sensitive to issues that give their products a bad name, so inquiring with sales staff and contacting manufacturers can make a real difference. Public pressure and increased awareness of the problem have already prompted some producers to stop using palm oil.
4. Sign petitions and write your elected representatives: Online campaigns put pressure on policymakers responsible for biofuels and palm oil imports. Have you already signed all of Rainforest Rescue's petitions?
5. Speak out: Protest marches and creative action on the street raise public and media awareness of the issue, which in turn steps up the pressure on policymakers.
6. Leave your car at home: Whenever you can, walk, ride a bicycle or use public transport.
7. Be informed and inform others: Big Business and governments would like us to believe that bio fuels are good for the climate and that oil palm plantations are sustainable. Spread the word – share this information with your family and friends and encourage them to rethink their consumption habits. It's in our hands!

One other thing you can do is make your own butter as we have. Go to lovingitvegan.com for the recipe. From my learning heart to yours, Thomas

Begin today to make a small difference in your life through one of the above suggestions!

March 26 Universal principle #6: Beliefs

A belief is a thought hooked to a feeling. The feeling gives the thought a perception of power and creates an illusion that is experienced as real. Under the guidance of our Souls, we adopt beliefs to provide us with the precise experiences we are having, and that we planned before we entered this realm. The urge to explore life beyond our beliefs is a signal that our Soul Selves are ready to guide us in freeing the flow of Divine Love, disguised by our beliefs.

Tough one! Our beliefs are our perception of life and create our experiences. We cannot see something until we have the ability to believe that it exists.

I have had many amazing events in my life. Several were when I traveled to other countries. In 1978 I went on a mystery and healing tour with 43 other medical professionals. At the time I was one of the directors of the Edgar Cayce medical clinic in Phoenix.

We were visiting Greece and were traveling on a bus with a local guide. I was sitting in the rear of the bus with three other friends. The guide was describing the ancient temple of Apollo located in the town of Delphi. She was describing the temple and as she did so I jokingly said to my friends that what she was sharing was not quite accurate. I went on to describe how I thought the temple would be. When we arrived the temple was just as I had shared. We were blown away. How could I have known? I was just being playful about the information that I told them.

Later we were at a stadium. It was a large stone amphitheater. I left the group and went to the top of the stadium. I sat down to meditate; it felt so familiar to me. The buses horn startled me out of my reverie. The people were yelling to me that it was past time to leave and for me to hurry down. At first I thought I will go down the stone steps the way I had climbed up. Instead I got this idea to go up a few rows higher. I went up and there was a path that I knew I had been on before. I ran down the hill and I was at the bus before the others arrived even though I had been farther away.

My friends were surprised when they saw me waiting for them. How did all this happen? I believe I had been there before in a previous incarnation. Maybe I got to see it because I believed it? From my heart to yours, Thomas

Let the flow of Divine Love move through you!

March 27   We Are Oneness

In the rush of daily life, we sometimes forget about our divinity. We are all perfect just the way we are. We are eternal limitless particles of Oneness. In our Earth spacesuits we have imposed ourselves with limitations. We are born and live and die, only to do it over again as much as we choose. It is important to understand the big picture of who we are and at the same time, give our time and energy to what is occurring now.

Our Earth is being threatened by our choices. Species are being eliminated every day. Scientists say: "We know that the drivers behind species loss are mostly increasing – land conversion and degradation, pollution, climate change. And of course the human population is still growing and consumption is growing – and most of that consumption is not sustainable."

All species are part of Oneness, like us. They are us and we are them. So, even though we are immortal spiritual beings, we have a responsibility to all the parts of Oneness. We get to treat them like our family. We get to become involved in any way possible to prevent our rampant consumption. Each of us can do our part. Here is a list.

<u>1. Think twice before shopping.</u>

<u>2. Make sure your big purchases have big environmental benefits.</u>

<u>3. Ditch the plastic.</u>

4. Boycott products that endanger wildlife.

5. Take extinction off your plate: Eat less meat.

6. Be water wise.

7. Drive less, drive green.

8. Green your home.

9. Choose renewable energy.

10. Pay attention to labels.

11. Choose to have a smaller family.

12. Use your voice and your vote.

From my oneness heart to yours, Thomas

Choose ONE of the items on this list and work on it for a week! Let the Oneness begin!

March 28   Thank you, Richard Gere

"I don't regret anything. Everything happens for a reason-it's part of the healing process. Life is a healing process.

The reality is, we can change. We can change ourselves. We can change our minds. We can change our hearts... and therefore the Universe changes.

As custodians of the planet it is our responsibility to deal with all species with kindness, love, and compassion. That these animals suffer through human cruelty is beyond understanding. Please help to stop this madness.

What we all have in common is an appreciation of kindness and compassion; all the religions have this. We all lean towards love."

The above quotes are from Richard Gere. I love how he matured and found the beautiful center of his being. I have found that many folks like movie stars, rock stars and sports stars and people with enormous success, discover the true meaning of wealth. It is not about things and comforts. It is about connection, caring, compassion and making a difference with what we have been gifted.

Most of us who live in developed countries have so much abundance that we sometimes take it for granted. More than three billion people live on less than $2.50 per day. While we can't immediately solve this crises, we can do the best we can for anyone we know who is in need and help them out.

If all of us, who are aware of the less than fortunate, pooled our resources and took action, we would change the whole world. To repeat one of Gere' quotes: *"The reality is, we can change. We can change ourselves. We can change our minds. We can change our hearts... and therefore the Universe changes.* Let us change whatever it takes and be the change! From my changed heart to yours, Thomas

Let this day be one of connection, caring and compassion!

March 29   Hump Day

We name days of the week to reflect our feelings. Wednesday is Hump day because it is in the middle of the week. When we get to Wednesday, we only have two more days until the weekend. Monday has often been called Doomsday. There are more heart attacks on Monday morning than any other time. We are too stressed. Friday of course is TGIF. We can't wait for the weekend when we work Monday through Friday; mostly because we are not doing what we love to do for our vocation.

I am renaming my days. Monday is now Marvelous Monday. It is the day we get to renew our plan for success in life. Tuesday is now Terrific Tuesday. The day that we will remember what magnificent beings we are. Wednesday is now Wonderful Wednesday. The day we choose to remember how awesome life is. Thursday is now Thankful Thursday. The day we hold to how grateful we are. Friday is now Fun Friday. The day we can remember how much fun we are having. Saturday is now Sensational Saturday. The day we get to create more sensational events in our life. Sunday is now Special Sunday. The day we get to remember that every day of the week is special because we are experiencing it.

Let us treat each day as the sacred occasion that it is. It is sacred because we have created it and we get to choose whatever we want as part of that day. There are no bad days, unless we declare them to be. Every moment of life is the opportunity to rediscover our divine nature and the joy of being alive! From my sacred heart to yours, Thomas

Let's explore a new perspective of each day of the week – make your life amazing starting today!

March 30   Love Your Precious Self

Hold yourselves gently as you pass through this life. We all make choices we wish we had never made and will probably make more. We are infinite spirit, housed in finite space suits, sometimes walking in the dark. There is no one to judge us that counts except ourselves. And it would be helpful if we were lenient. Life is a challenge in a lot of ways. Most of us were raised by well-meaning parents without a lot of child care experience. They were learning while we were. In the midst of this two decade parental training experience, we created a story of our life and that story runs us.

It may be time to give up that story and rewrite a new one that serves us better. Everyone is always doing the best they can all the time without exception! Remember this poem that was so popular many years ago? It may have even more relevance today!

While reading these next few passages, visualize the night sky filled with millions of stars!

Desiderata

Go placidly amid the noise and haste, and remember what peace there may be in silence. As far as possible without surrender, be on good terms with all persons. Speak your truth quietly and clearly; and listen to others, even the dull and the ignorant; they too have their story.

Avoid loud and aggressive persons,
they are vexations to the spirit.
If you compare yourself with others,
you may become vain and bitter;
for always there will be greater and lesser persons than yourself.
Enjoy your achievements as well as your plans.

Keep interested in your own career, however humble;
it is a real possession in the changing fortunes of time.
Exercise caution in your business affairs;
for the world is full of trickery.
But let this not blind you to what virtue there is;
many persons strive for high ideals;
and everywhere life is full of heroism.

Be yourself.
Especially, do not feign affection.
Neither be cynical about love;
for in the face of all aridity and disenchantment
it is as perennial as the grass.

Take kindly the counsel of the years,
gracefully surrendering the things of youth.
Nurture strength of spirit to shield you in sudden misfortune.
But do not distress yourself with dark imaginings.
Many fears are born of fatigue and loneliness.
Beyond a wholesome discipline,
be gentle with yourself.

You are a child of the universe,
no less than the trees and the stars;
you have a right to be here.
And whether or not it is clear to you,
no doubt the universe is unfolding as it should.

Therefore be at peace with God,
whatever you conceive Him to be,
and whatever your labors and aspirations,
in the noisy confusion of life keep peace with your soul.

With all its sham, drudgery, and broken dreams,
it is still a beautiful world.

Be cheerful.
Strive to be happy.

A poem written by Max Ehrmann in 1927

Take time to look in the mirror and smile. Then wrap your arms around you and give yourself a hug. You earned it! From my precious heart to yours, Thomas

Know that you are a child of the Universe! You are sweet, imperfect and awakening to whom you already are!

March 31   The Present

"We are living in a culture entirely hypnotized by the illusion of time, in which the so-called present moment is felt as nothing but an infinitesimal hairline between an all-powerfully causative past and an absorbingly important future. We have no present. Our consciousness is almost completely preoccupied with memory and expectation. We do not realize that there never was, is, nor will be any other experience than present experience. We are therefore out of touch with reality. We confuse the world as talked about, described, and measured with the world which actually is. We are sick with a fascination for the useful tools of names and numbers, of symbols, signs, conceptions and ideas." Alan Watts

It seems to be true. There are times when I am playing tennis or in a meditative experience with Lou Ann that time doesn't exist. However, most of the time there is a part of my mind that is recalling what occurred or anticipating what will happen next. We are so conditioned by the artificial invention of time.

Perhaps the meaning of life is just to be alive. It is so plain and so obvious and so simple. And yet, everybody rushes around in a great panic; as if it were necessary to achieve something beyond them.

We are a function of what the whole universe is doing, in the same way that a wave is a function of what the whole ocean is doing. We are the infinite experiencing itself. It might be time to relax and just enjoy the now. From my present moment heart to yours, Thomas

For as often as you can today, breathe, relax and BE in the moment.

April 1   You Are Love

Here are some more wonderful quotes to warm our hearts.

"In a deep moment of love, thinking stops. The moment is so intriguing; the moment is so tremendously powerful, the moment is so intensely alive, that thinking stops. You are simply in awe, a great wonder surrounds you." – Bhagwan Shree Rasneesh

"The spiritual life, for me, is a dance between making it happen and letting it happen, between falling down and rising up again, between holding on and letting go, between unlearning that which would keep me from love and remembering the love that I am.

Life is a sweet balance of give and take, and the remembrance that it's all really one and the same.

Spirituality is my personal journey of releasing anything that would separate me from another or from love, joy, union, and peace. I do believe that we are all spiritual beings on a human journey." Jennifer Williamson.

We all need to be inspired from time to time. We can get stuck in patterns and habits that become comfortable and can keep us from moving forward in our lives. We can also inspire ourselves. Take a moment and find a quiet place. Then after a couple of deep breaths to center ourselves; ask the Universe what would you have me do today to make creation a more beautiful, loving experience! Then listen for the answer that comes from deep inside you. From my inspired heart to yours, Thomas

Pick one of these quotes today and live it! Have a happy day!

April 2   Universal principle #7: Feelings

Our Soul communicates to us through our feelings. The more willing we are to feel our feelings, the more able we are to connect with the love that resides in them. Love, fully, freely and joyfully felt is the true Power in the Universe—a totally peaceful Power. This Power does not belong to each of us; it emanates from the Divine and manifests through us when we surrender to it.

This can be a challenge for some of us, to fully feel our feelings. When we do we are rewarded with a deep sense of connection. When we share these fully felt feelings with others, miracles can occur! Remember the movie Pay it Forward? When we go out of our way to do something nice for someone else; and they in turn do the same for others. It is not a communicated agreement to pass this love on; it is simply a result of feeling so cared for we automatically do it.

The Universe is a very loving place and when we surrender and do kind loving things, and then often, wonderful things happen to the giver. Universe pays it forward! From my feeling heart to yours, Thomas

Feel the power and peace of love within and let it emanate outward to others!

April 3   Farming

We had a wonderful young man named Gary come over to our property and help us with our plans for permaculture.

The three core tenets of permaculture are:

- *Care for the earth*: Provision for all life systems to continue and multiply. This is the first principle, because without a healthy earth, humans cannot flourish.
- *Care for the people*: Provision for people to access those resources necessary for their existence.
- *Setting limits to population and consumption*: By governing our own needs, we can set resources aside to further the above principles. This includes returning waste back into the system to recycle into usefulness. The third ethic is sometimes referred to as Fair Share, which reflects that each of us should take no more than what we need before we reinvest the surplus.

Instead of having flat rows of many varieties of food; the vegetables, plants, trees and fruits all work in harmony with each other; to create a synergy of support for each other. So you might have fruit trees next to the broccoli and nut trees against the tomato plants.

We have one acre of natural desert landscaping with a hundred pine trees spread throughout. By growing more green plants, fruit and nut trees, vegetables and herbs, we can reduce our personal carbon footprint. At the top of our lot sits our house. We plan to terrace and build water channels to capture water during our rainy season. From June 15th to September 1st is called the monsoon season. We get eighty per cent of our rain in this ten week period. It is incumbent upon us to collect and store as much as we can. We get about eighteen inches of rain and each inch is about 28,000 gallons per acre. We will be working hard to capture as much as we can.

Ultimately, we want to create enough organic produce to give most of it away, to food banks and those with not enough to eat. If any of you want to join in the fun, please let us know!

Our farming is part of our overall plan that we call Enriching Life Forever or ELF! I am sure that Lou Ann will be enlisting the little people to help us grow our garden. I encourage everyone to plant as much as you can of organic food to supplement your personal health. From my healthy heart to yours, Thomas

What will your own oasis of green look like?

April 4   Longer Life

Here are ten factors I saw on a TED talk that help you live a longer life. Here they are in the reverse order of importance. In other words numbers nine and ten are the most important factors in having us create a longer life.

1. Clean air
2. Hypertension Rx
3. Lean vs. overweight
4. Exercise
5. Cardiac rehab
6. Flu vaccine
7. Quit boozing
8. Quit smoking

9. Close relationships
10. Social integration

Number nine includes those people in our lives that will sit with us when we are in despair. They will take you to the hospital. Call the doctor if you are not feeling well; loan you money if you need it. The groups of people who love and support us make a difference in our lives.

Number ten is about how much you interact with people as you move through your day. Also how many people a day do you talk to? Do you talk to the person who makes your coffee or the person who delivers stuff to your home or office? Do you talk to the woman who walks her dog by your house every day? Do you play bridge or belong to a book club? Those interactions are one of the strongest predictors of how long you will live.

So if you are like me and you eat well and exercise well and you don't smoke or drink; it is more important to surround yourself with various kinds of people. They give us a connection to life when we interact with them and give us greater meaning to being alive. Perhaps we could contact members of our family and friends and let them know how much they mean to us and do it more often. From my healthier heart to yours, Thomas

Take time today to be with one of your tribe!

April 5   The Sweetness of Life

Lou Ann and I are watching one of our favorite movies: Chocolat. It is a story of a vagabond woman and her daughter who travel from town to town dispensing cacao remedies. The cacao tree is native to the amazon valleys. It was domesticated by the Olmec and Mocayas (Mexico and Central America).

More than 4,000 years ago, it was consumed by pre-Columbian cultures along the Yucatan, including the Mayans, and as far back as Olmeca in spiritual ceremonies, but I digress. Chocolat tells the story of Vianne Rocher, a young single mother, who arrives in the French village of Lansquenet Sous Tannes at the beginning of Lent with her six-year-old daughter, Anouk.

Vianne has arrived to open a **chocolaterie**, which is on the square opposite the church. During the traditional season of fasting and self-denial; she gently changes the lives of the villagers who visit her with a combination of sympathy and a little magic.

Her chief adversary is the Comte de Reynaud who runs the town using strict rules and intimidation. Soon Vianne shares her sweet deserts and people become freer and find their loves and passions. It is a metaphor for how many of us limit ourselves by rules we learned from our parents and instructors. Yes, there are rules that serve us, like stopping at a red light. However, we also stop our lives using an emotional red light that stymies our growth and kills our dreams. The metaphorical Reynaud may live inside each of us. He has personal hurts in life that have caused him pain and he takes out his anger on others.

For me, life is meant to be sweet. We are here to enjoy all the joy, love and abundance our hearts will allow. We are not here to march to anyone else's music. We are the embodiment of the beauty of the Universe in all its glory. We are here to be a sweet partner of Mother Earth and all of its inhabitants.

And along the way, maybe have a few cups of hot chocolate, seasoned with some Mayan chili pepper. I would love for us to create a dialogue   For instance, how have you learned to fulfill your life journey with your love of life? From my sweet heart to yours, Thomas

If there is a self-imposed emotional red light in your life that stymies your growth, notice it and let it go!

April 6   Simply kind

Step over ants,

put worms back in the grass,

rescue baby caterpillars,

release spiders back into your garden,

open windows for bees to fly home,

they are all little souls that deserve a life too!

These thoughts are from Wilder Child

If you want to do something nice for a child; give them an environment where they can touch things as much as they want....Bucky Fuller

The quotes above are for the "little creatures" and children.

"The first step in crafting a life you want is to get rid of everything you don't." — Joshua Becker

Every day, more stuff comes into our lives: stuff in our houses, stuff on our calendars, and stuff on our minds. All that stuff gets in the way of where we really want to go and who we really want to be ... it's time to make a change. From nosidebar.com

The above quotes are for those of us who want to simplify our lives as an act of kindness to ourselves. Most of us have too much stuff in our homes, cars and workplace. Much of it has not been used for months and sometimes years. Not only does it occupy a place in our living spaces; it occupies a place in our minds.

When we live more simply, we have more time, money and energy to create the kind of life experience that gives us joy and peace. Let us love ourselves and our environment enough to live simply, reduce our consumption and accumulation of stuff. It is a kind thing to do. From my simple heart to yours, Thomas

Spend time out in nature playing and exploring, even if only for ten minutes!

April 7   Reclaim Your Life

Brian Gardner shared a list of ways to live a fulfilling life on his website nosidebar.com.

Eight ways to reclaim your life:

1. Travel — go places you've always wanted to visit.

2. Social media — unplug from your devices every now and then.

3. Have conversations — seize the day and talk deeply.

4. Declutter — remove the unnecessary junk in your life.

5. Try new things — have no fear and enter the unknown.

6. Reminisce — look back and remember things that matter.

7. Solitude — spend time all by yourself, with nobody else.

8. Rest — stop what you're doing, and do nothing.

It would be fun to create a dialogue about this and share our experiences around these eight suggestions. Lou Ann and I love to travel and we have conversations with almost everyone. We enjoy trying new things; it brings a lot of zest into our lives. It is healthy to look back at our life and remember the things we did well. I love going for long walks by myself and commune with nature. Most of us would do well to stop and just hang out without doing anything.

We bought a house that came complete with all the furniture, fixtures, dishes and household items, now it is time to declutter! It only takes an hour a day, so we get to spend more time with each other. How do you plan to reclaim your life, if any of it needs it? From my heart to yours, Thomas

Choose one of these 8 ways today to reclaim your life!

April 8   Fun Stuff

Life is such a wondrous adventure! We had a clogged up toilet and shower in the same bathroom. A fellow tennis player referred a plumber to me, who works on Saturday and doesn't charge extra. His name is

Jerry, and he came to our home about 2:15 and took about an hour to clear up the issue. We had never met before.

A couple of hours later Lou Ann and I drove eighteen miles to Cottonwood Arizona. I got in a checkout line and the plumber Jerry, who had been at our house, was standing in front of me! Love it!

Speaking of checkout lines; there is a theory that when customers are standing in line and being served by a person; it is helping keep more folks employed. So, we stood in line about fifteen minutes today rather than let the robots do it. I don't know if the theory is true or not, however it felt good to think that we were supporting the folks who need to work at stores.

Then we went to a Mexican restaurant and ordered a wonderful vegan burrito and our server said his name is Alphonso. He said we could call him Fonzi. Aaaaayyyyyy! We love the Fonz!

We came home and the two visitors at our house were having a snack, out on our deck. They said they had just had their eyes "read" by a local therapist. Then we learned they were big fans of Wayne Dyer, Deepak Chopra and many others that we both admired. It just keeps happening over and over. The more we follow our hearts, the more delicious and synchronistic life is! From my very amazed heart to yours, Thomas

Look for the synchronicities all around you! It's magic how they appear when you look for them! EnJOY!

April 9 Arrogance?

Last week we had some vacation-rental visitors who spent a couple of nights with us and they got sick and lay in bed for two days. They had a lot of booze in the fridge and ate a lot of food that was not healthy. I thought to myself that they might have been better off if they had chosen more wisely.

The next day, it was my task to clean up the mess. It was difficult and took quite a while. I wore gloves. The following day I got the same symptoms they had of retching and eliminating in an unpleasant way. As I lay in bed for most of two days I mused about here I was, a non-drinking plant eating person, having the same awful experience. It was a kind of mental karma of sorts.

We each get to make choices. Some of those decisions empower us and some do not support our conscious desires. I searched my mind to get in touch with my choices. I am not a "better" person because I choose not to eat animals or drink alcohol. For me it is simply a "better" choice for my own health.

It is easy to get trapped in how we picture ourselves and others. I want to always be loving and as non-judgmental as I can be about others choices, as well as my own. It is also my wish that as many folks as possible would choose a whole food plant based life. It is better for the planet but it doesn't make those who choose this lifestyle "better!"

So, the next time someone gets sick or anything else I may judge that is less than. I get to remind myself, that there are only choices and when they are made they are often from a limited understanding. We get to choose again! From my humbled heart to yours, Thomas

When we judge others we lock the energy around the experience. Choose again and forgive the judgment and the other person as well!

April 10   Ten wonderful Qualities

On Facebook there was a list of eight characteristics of a toxic person. The list may be valuable if we are in a relationship with someone who has a lot of those qualities. I attempt to mostly look at the positive and loving ways to live. Our website is positiveplace.com and it is also our email address, which we have used since 1995. Tanya and Lana Bloch kindly bought us the domain at the time. So, tonight I immediately looked for a list that would exemplify what are the best qualities in people. I found this one titled; the ten best qualities in any person. Here is the list:

The 10 Best Qualities in Any Person

By Cathryn Conroy

If you want to be a better person—or a better spouse, parent, friend or employee—it could be a simple matter of adopting the right traits. Based on numerous Internet discussions and lessons learned from life, here are the top 10 best qualities for any person.

!. Be honest

Honesty is a way of life. It means you don't steal, you don't cheat on your taxes and you keep your word.

2. Be happy

It's not about money, looks or status. Being genuinely grateful for what you have and looking forward to the dawn of each day can make you feel a kind of happiness that is contagious.

3. Be respectful of others
When you treat others as you would like to be treated, you are showing the ultimate kind of respect.

4. Be easygoing and fun
As the old saying goes, "Live, laugh, love." Slowdown from life's frantic pace and have fun—whether it's an unscheduled day playing hooky from your responsibilities or just a few minutes respite from the grind.

5. Be confident
Once you accept there is always someone out there who is better than you, you can realize your own abilities. Be confident in what you can—and cannot—do.

6. Be emotionally open
Be open and honest with those you love. Express your opinions and listen to theirs without criticizing.

7. Be disciplined
No one is watching over your shoulder when you slack off—except you. Self-discipline means you have a finely tuned sense of ethics, of what is best, and you act accordingly. You are strong enough to say 'no' to life's many temptations.

8. Take pride in yourself
While too much pride does not serve us, we all need to feel some pride

in who we are, where we live and what we do. That kind of pride helps define us in our world.

9. Be compassionate
Being empathetic to the needs of others and doing good deeds to ease others' suffering is one of the most basic acts of kindness and goodness we accomplish as human beings.

10. Have a sense of humor
You have to be able to laugh, especially at yourself. There is humor in almost every situation. You just have to find it. And laughing is almost always better than crying.

Instead of the Ten Commandments, these could be the Ten Adjustments. We are all learning the best ways we can be and we are constantly changing and becoming. It is not how we follow hard and fast rules so much as how we access the love in our hearts and live from that place. From my heart to yours, Thomas

Which of these qualities speaks to you today?? Be that!

April 11   Mr. Rogers Neighborhood

There is a video going around showing the time that Mr. Rogers testified before congress for six minutes on the value of public TV. It has had 109 million views on Facebook. He shares with senator Pastore his communication on each show with children. He said that he gave an expression of care to each child and let them know that each one was unique.

Here is what he said to children during each show: "You've made this day a special day by just being you. There's no person in the whole world like you and I like you just the way you are." Senator Pastore replied *"I'm supposed to be a pretty tough guy and I have had goose bumps for two days listening to you."*

The senate was considering a grant proposed by Lyndon Johnson for twenty million dollars for public television programming. Richard Nixon wanted to cut it in half. After the testimony public television got the full grant.

Lou Ann and I heard Mr. Rogers speak several years ago and were blown away by his wisdom and heart. He shared this: "When I say it's you I like, I'm talking about that part of you that knows that life is far more than anything you can ever see or hear or touch. This is that deep part of you that allows you to stand for those things without which humankind cannot survive. Love that conquers hate, peace that rises triumphant over war and justice that proves more powerful than greed."

May we continue to create "Neighborhoods" of peace, love, understanding and inclusion! From my neighborhood heart to yours, Thomas

That deep part of you is the you I like – feel the wisdom and truth of this!

April 12   True Success

Success is being friendly when another needs a friend;

It's in the cheery words you speak, and in the coins you lend;

Success is not alone in skill and deeds of daring great;

It's in the roses that you plant beside your garden gate.

Success is in the way you walk the paths of life each day;

It's in the little things you do and in the things you say;

Success is in the glad hello you give your fellow man;

It's in the laughter of your home and all the joys you plan.

Success is not in getting rich or rising high to fame;

It's not alone in winning goals which many hope to claim;

It's in the person you are each day, through happiness or care;

It's in the cheery words you speak and in the smile you wear.

Success is being big of heart and clean and broad of mind;

It's being faithful to your friends, and to the stranger, kind;

It's in the children whom you love, and all they learn from you.

Success depends on character and everything you do. By Edgar Guest

I was chatting with another tennis player today about successes and failures in life. He and I both lost our fortunes in the real estate crash of 2008. I shared with him the concept that when a person is at the end of their life; they don't exclaim "I wish I had spent more time at the office". Having a nice home and car and job are great to have.

However, they have little to do with happiness or true success. As the poem above declares, it is how you relate to others as perhaps the highest kind of success. How kind we are. How we show up for our family and friends. Our smile, the little things we do or say that makes the world a better place and our life a success. From my successful heart to yours, Thomas

Pay forward kindness today and it will most assuredly grow!

April 13   The Soul of Money

The above, is a title of a book by Lynne Twist. The subtitle reads "Reclaiming the Wealth of Our Inner Resources". Another book written by one of my greatest mentors is, Money and Beyond by Arnold Patent.

Many of us have a challenging relationship with money. Some of us chase after it like it is the most important thing in life. Some of us have negative training about our relationship with it. Money is just a symbol of an exchange of energy. We give our time and energy to create income and then we trade it for other things we perceive have value. It isn't good or bad. It, or the love of it, is not the root of all evil.

I grew up like so many young people, in the nineteen forties, without a lot of money. My father was an alcoholic and my mom worked underpaid clerical jobs, to support three young sons and her itinerant husband. He hardly held a job because of his drinking, so cash flow was low most of the time. I recall having to put cardboard in my shoes to cover the holes in the bottoms.

We lived in Hollywood, so there was a lot of affluence. It was tough for a little boy not to see the difference and wonder why? There was a local grocery store that had soft drinks sitting outside in cold water; I would take some without paying.

I have learned that things money can buy are of much less importance than the inner beauty and love that we all have inside. So, if like me, you have had an up and down relationship with money, don't let it derail you in any way. We and all of creation are beyond value. We are priceless and great treasures of love, compassion and prosperity.

Arnold Patent once said *"Abundance is the natural state of affairs in the Universe. And we are that abundance".* If, right now, you are patching holes in your soles, remember there is no hole in your soul that needs fixing. Let us love money and all of creation, for what it is and enjoy being wealthy in every way.

May we all live this kind of life and when we are at the end of our life we will say *"I am so happy that I spent more time being with those I love".* From my abundant heart to yours, Thomas

Know that you are abundant. Treasure the wisdom of your Divine Heart and embrace it fully!

April 14 In the Universe

There is no one like you. You are unique in the entire Universe. There will never be another you. Yes, one of the most amazing things about Universe is, no two things are alike in every way. And that is wonderful. We get to live our life in our own way. We get to choose whatever we desire to be, do or have. And we will do it in a way that has never been before and will never be repeated.

Wow! What a gift to be part of Oneness and to realize our uniqueness. And the irony perhaps is that we are interdependent on all the other parts. Every part of Oneness affects every other part.

So let us continue to express our individuality in all we do, and at the same time, support all the other parts. Right now there is a rash of divisiveness that is rampant on this little blue planet. We have lost our way. We are captured by our fear and we act out on our environment and each other. The challenge for us, is being loving, while we honor our own path and to not give away our power. This power is that each of us gets to determine our destiny in every lifetime.

Let us celebrate who we are and love others for who they are. May we open our hearts and minds and create a planet where all can love and play in peace and prosperity. Whether we be, humans, animals, oceans, trees or inanimate objects; we are all one and we are all love. May it always be this way! From my unique heart to yours, Thomas

As a gift of Oneness, recognize your uniqueness. Open to this with love and playfulness!

April 15   Beautiful and Prosperous Life

This morning Lou Ann and I were headed down to the Phoenix area. I said a little affirmation that our day would be filled with beauty and love and joy and prosperity.

We first drove down to an area north of Phoenix to pick up a utility trailer to help us with our garden project. When we arrived at the place the seller showed us his trailer and shared that one of the almost new tires had a slow leak in it. He said the local tire company where he purchased it would fix it up for us for free.

We drove about a half an hour further south into the Valley of the Sun and a car was passing by and waved frantically at us. I looked in the rearview mirror and discovered the right side of the trailer had sunken down. We pulled over and discovered that the "slow leak" had other intentions. Just at that moment a police officer pulled up behind us, with his lights flashing.

The police officer asked "Do you know why I pulled you over? I replied "the tire!" He said "no, you went through two stop signs when exiting the freeway!" He shared that a lot of people from out of the area do not see the signage. He said he was just giving us a warning. Then he offered to stay behind us for safety as we pulled into a large parking area.

We got out and went into our own car to get a lug wrench to loosen the nuts on the wheel so we could put the spare on. We discovered that our lug nuts were much larger than the ones on the trailer. Lou Ann was inspired to go into the closest grocery store and ask for help.

She inquired at one of the check-out lines as to whether anyone there had the tools we needed to pursue our task. A lady several feet away heard her inquiry and shared that she had a whole adjustable wrench set with a bar to turn the sockets. We discovered she was a Naturopathic physician here from Wisconsin. A few minutes later with her help, I was able to take off the old trailer tire and attach the spare.

Then we headed home and I reflected on my morning affirmation. It was true that we discovered a flawed product which was concerning. Then we had the tire fail at high speeds on the highway. Then we were admonished about running a stop sign by an officer of the law.

However, we would not have met the angels in the grocery store who rescued us. We would not have met a man who was honest about the possibility of the tire on the trailer. And then gave us a portion of the sale back to help us out.

For me, I feel abundant about the monetary gifts we were given. Even more about the gifts of love and caring we also received. The day did not unfold as my conscious mind had envisioned. The Universe had a better plan. I truly feel like it was a "beautiful and prosperous" day.

May we all discover the wonderful gifts of life that come in perhaps mysterious ways. Let us celebrate the magic of Oneness and how it opens up blessings for us each day! From my beautiful and prosperous heart to yours, Thomas

Perceive your day today as beautiful and prosperous!

April 16   The Universe is Always in Charge

Lou Ann and I went to an Easter soiree' at Ranjita's house up in Oak Creek Canyon. Ranjita is one of the most unique persons that I have ever encountered. The three of us met in an aerobics class back in 1988.

Ranjita went on to create a healing sanctuary called "Your Heart's Home". It is located right above a trout farm about four miles north of uptown Sedona. Over the years, Lou Ann and I and many others went there for her transformative body, mind and spirit healing therapies. However, Ranjita had a tumultuous relationship with someone in the neighborhood.

Ranjita purchased this multiple acre parcel on the side of a mountain and over the years created so many healing spaces and sanctuaries. Many times she invites her friends and loved ones to delicious parties as she did today. There were dozens of smiling, hugging, laughing folks of all ages and ethnicities celebrating life together.

Lou Ann and I were driving up the circuitous dusty road to Your Heart's Home and I had this thought that wouldn't it be wonderful for Ranjita and the people who owned the property below to find a way to heal their past experiences and create a wonderful spiritual partnership.

We arrived at her place and she took me aside and said "guess what, I have had a wonderful miracle!" There are new owners of the property below and they are catering this event today. We are also going to work together in creating a loving partnership in a business together. I smiled and shared with her my thoughts I had as we drove up to her place.

We all get to create our lives as the best we can. We make choices that are sometimes painful and other times joyful. We get to do this in a Universe that is always on purpose. It is always rooting us on! It is always waiting for us to remember our connection to Source. When we do, even unconsciously, the results are amazing! From my ever reborn heart to yours, Thomas

What wonderful miracle do you want to create?!

April 17   Imagination

Albert Einstein said: I never came upon any of my discoveries through rational thinking. This didn't make any sense until I looked it up...the part that's missing is what he said after it. "Logic will take you from A to B, imagination will take you everywhere."

Don't let the imaginary person in your head keep you from loving the one staring at you in the mirror. Our imagination is magical! Our imagination lets us free to be the person we were meant to be. When we let go of preconceived ideas and rules and ways to behave, we are able to create a life full of fun and wonder.

For those of us who have lived long enough to be classified as adults; it would be wonderful to let go and let our imagination run free. Take some time tomorrow and find a peaceful place, perhaps outdoors and let your imagination create a whole new path to take. It is time to let go and follow our hearts to Wonderland! From my imagining heart to yours, Thomas

Remember Alice in Wonderland – she sometimes believed as many as 6 impossible things before breakfast – this is a great practice!

April 18   Beggars Can Be Choosers

There are so many old phrases that jump into my mind unconsciously. I am of that age, that many sayings were passed down from generation to generation. There was no television, or Wikipedia or such. We heard what our elders said and often repeated it. I found myself thinking about a situation today and my mind said "beggars can't be choosers!" Then my next thought was, maybe they can.

Life is difficult for a lot of people. We see so many people asking for money or food on street corners. We have no idea what lead them to being in that position. And we don't need to judge them for creating that life situation. So many people today live paycheck to paycheck and have little reserves to keep them going. An unfortunate experience can devastate us.

In my belief, we always choose. Many times conscious and many more times unconsciously. In the big picture of life, we choose to incarnate and perhaps to choose parents and our environment. Then once we incarnate we keep on making choices that sometimes do not serve us. That doesn't make us wrong or deficient. It makes us human.

So those of us who appear to be less fortunate have made choices that seem to have not worked out. And the beauty of life is we get to keep on choosing. It would be great if those who have made choices that worked out pretty well could help those who didn't. We are so blessed and so abundant. May we share our bounty, our love and our caring to

help anyone who needs support! From my begging heart to yours,
Thomas

When your day feels unpleasant, choose again how you want to feel!

April 19   Never Let Go of Your Dream

You were born with a dream that lies deep in your soul.

You were born with a need to reach out to a goal.

Swear by all that you know, that you'll never let go of your dream.

When the road seems too long and your hopes turn to clay

That's the time to be strong, with a will there's a way

Though the way may be slow, you must never let go of your dream.

If you're living without trying, that's not living, just a slower way of dying.

Unconsciously. I *So hold on tight to what you want*

And you will wake to some great golden morn,

when the world seems to say, this is why you were born

here it is, here's your day.

And you'll reap all you sow, let your cup overflow

If you never let go of your dream

Never let go of your dream

The lyrics above are from a song we used to sing in Canyon Singers; written by Sheila Davis, music by Tommy Zang. Canyon Singers was a group who performed in Sedona for twenty five years. We were lovingly directed by Sandy Reid, who has since moved to Iowa.

I love living life more when I am connected to a dream. It is more powerful when the dream is my own. However, right now Lou Ann and I are on the staff of the Illuminate Film Festival and we are dreaming together.

I encourage all of you who have some dreams hidden inside to wake them up! Find a way to live a life full of passion and adventure. Please don't settle for less than a life lived, full out. In my experience, it is not worth it! From my always dreaming heart to yours, Thomas

Live your passionate and adventurous life fully now!

April 20   Deep Friendship

For the eighteenth time I was reading volume seven of the Harry Potter series this morning. Yes, I know I'm addicted; to perhaps, some of the most brilliant, entertaining writing ever. The book is titled Harry Potter and the Deathly Hallows. There is a scene in the book where Harry is following a bright silver doe through the woods. He eventually comes upon a small pond covered in ice, in which the Sword of Gryffindor is resting on the bottom. Harry jumps in and tries to extract the sword. However, he is wearing a cursed locket around his neck and it attempts to strangle him. At the last moment, his estranged friend Ron, jumps in and pulls him out, exclaiming "are you mental?" At this moment my throat always constricts and I get tears in my eyes.

Harry and Ron are the best of friends and have been together through a lot of chaos and danger. Ron has left Harry and their classmate Hermione, because he was wearing the same cursed locket and it made him act crazy. Upon his return and his saving of Harry I get very emotional about the love I feel between two friends, even in a book of fiction.

I wish that kind of friendship for everyone on planet Earth. If there are people in your life, for which you would jump in a frozen pool. Contact them right now. Tell them how much you care! They can be relatives of course. The connection though, is a deep bond of believing and loving each other, no matter what. If you don't have that kind of connection with someone, I urge you to create it. Your life will be rich beyond measure. From my friendly heart to yours, Thomas

Cherish your deep friendships today by calling one of them and let them know how much you care!

April 21   Who Decides?

Lou Ann and I love to people watch. We were having lunch in the Scottsdale Fashion Square mall today, thousands of folks passed by, while we ate our lunch. I see people and my mind immediately begins a conversation with myself about them. I might notice their age or their hair color or their nationality. I will observe how they walk, the look on their face, how they carry themselves. I make up stories about whether they are happy or sad or divorced or awake to life. I notice some as attractive and some not so. And here is where the challenge for me occurs.

Who decided what is attractive or beautiful or not attractive and not so beautiful? As the saying goes, clearly the judgment of anyone else is in the eyes and mind of the beholder. In society, why is slim more attractive than heavy? Perhaps in some parts of the globe it is just the opposite?

The point is, it is all a judgment, based on some kind of general agreement that has no bearing about the truth of it. Meaning, each of us gets to decide what we like and who we like, physically, emotionally, spiritually. In the grand scheme of things, it means little. We are all here as members of one human family and we appear in about seven billion different ways.

The truth is, we are all one. Each and every one of us is Divine and perfect. We don't need to measure up to anyone else's standards of how we look, who we love and what we choose. Yes, it is fun to sit and observe my fellow human race in all of its variety and uniqueness. May we see each other as a treasure of the Universe! From my sometimes unconditional heart to yours, Thomas

Forego any judgment today and see only the beauty of each soul.

April 22   Life

"What is life anyway? A series of events, some stuff that happened; some stuff that happened to me, all along the way, made me who I am today." These are lyrics from a Michael Byers song called "You Are My Friend". I am typing on Lou Ann's computer. Mine crashed and it doesn't work at all; along with all of my film festival information, my solar business and our Airbnb business.

Oops! I can't locate our computer fix it guy, Jake. It feels weird not being on my computer for hours today. I can do a lot of it on my phone, so I get to adjust to this creation of mine. All of the events in life that happen and how we handle them make us who we are. This is not tragic - not life threatening - just inconvenient. So I get to create in a whole new way perhaps. Maybe you folks have had days like this where you get to look at things a little differently.

I have become so comfortable doing my blog and our businesses in a certain way. Maybe something will shift for me and I will do it in a different and more productive way. Maybe I will do something completely new.

Maybe you are up against something that is not flowing as well as you had hoped. You might want to surrender to the situation and know that there's a spirit that guides us, a light that shines for us. It has always been that way and will always be.

We don't need to know everything about the path that we are on. It may be enough to know that it is on purpose and divine! From my surrendered heart to yours, Thomas

We are on purpose when we love ourselves and others! Shine bright!

April 23   Little Blue Spaceship

Lou Ann and I attended an Earth Day celebration in the little town aptly named Cornville Arizona. The event was at a place called Maggie's Farm. It is a couple of acres of sustainable living. Sustainable living is the practice of reducing your demand on natural resources by making sure that you replace what you use, to the best of your ability.

For instance, reusing and repairing things in our home and workplace, instead of going out and buying the fanciest new versions. Another would be to consider purchasing local, instead of places like Amazon, who have to use a lot of energy to get us the product.

There were talks on beekeeping, using gray water and permaculture; which is what we are doing to our little acre here in the Village of Oak Creek. Permaculture is defined as consciously designed landscapes which mimic the patterns and relationships found in nature, while yielding an abundance of food, fiber and energy for the provision of local needs. In our case, we are going to grow as much organic produce as we can and give it away to the less fortunate.

Life will always find a way to live. Our global thoughtlessness about our planet has destroyed ninety per cent of the forests. It's frightening but true; our planet is now in the midst of its sixth mass extinction of plants and animals — the sixth wave of extinctions in the past half-billion years. However, no matter how much carnage we humans do to our beloved Earth, it will find a way to live. The problem is: our children and their children's children will suffer so much because of us.

Even if you only find a way to have some tomato plants and herbs on your patio, it will help. Anytime we grow organic fruits, vegetables and trees, we help sustain the world. .

Please, do all you can to be sustainable about your life and perhaps we can save this gorgeous place for all those who will come. From my sustainable heart to yours, Thomas

Find a sustainable technique that will work for you and do it!

April 24   Love Yourself No Matter What

The greatest happiness of life is the conviction that we are loved; loved for ourselves, or rather, loved in spite of ourselves; and that we get to love others in the same way! We spend a lot of time seeking happiness in an amazing variety of ways; too much time looking outside of ourselves in our search for joy.

Life is way too short to be looking for something or someone to make us happy. We have always had the capacity to love ourselves; we just forgot who we are. There is nothing broken that needs mending. Remember the words to one of my favorite songs. *I love myself the way I am, there's nothing I need to change. I'll always be the perfect me, there's nothing to rearrange. I'm beautiful and capable of being the best me I can. And I love myself just the way I am.*

The point of the song for me is, there is only one you and that you, is the perfect you in every way. Our minds often get in the way and try to convince us that we are not okay. Our hearts know the truth. So, whenever you are not sure about how you are doing. Just remember that you are beautiful and capable at the most important thing in the world. And that is being you! And you are the only one who can do it. From my one in seven billion hearts to yours, Thomas

Be the love you wish to create in your life and it will be attracted to you!

April 25   Universal principle #8: Mutual Support

"Our Universe functions as a mutual support system in which each and every thing in existence relates to and affects every other thing. Every person and circumstance in our lives is there to support us by reflecting back to us the beliefs we hold in our consciousness. The prevalent belief that we are naturally competitive and adversarial is just a mirroring back to us of our acceptance of that belief. Releasing beliefs from our consciousness frees the love of God to flow through us and to those with whom we interact. Mutual support then reflects more of our natural state of Oneness, and becomes the foundation for rebuilding community based on love, from family to village, city, state, nation and world. The more we look for the love that is present in each event and circumstance in our lives, the more we appreciate how perfect the Universe's support for us truly is."

We have created it all. There are no accidents. Everything is in Divine order. Since we are these amazing creators of our existence; we get the opportunity to create our life experience exactly as we desire! The entire Universe is conspiring for you to have it all! We are supporting each other every step of the way. What is it that you desire? What dreams lie hidden somewhere in your consciousness? Now is the time to realize that they can come true for you.

Find some unconditional loving persons who want the best for you. Have a brainstorming session with no limitations. Share from your heart exactly how you want to feel every day. Then have your team of loved ones formulate a specific action plan to create your dream.

In 1997 we had a group of friends help us create a television show called The Positive Place Television Talk Show. It was a program that features the best that people can be. The show focused on all the wonderful folks who are making the world a better place every day.

It never made it to the air but it is still a good idea and the formulation of that show changed another television show that has affected millions in a positive way. You will be amazed how many people are out there who will support you in consciousness. The world needs you and your dream. Remember the words of Goethe:

"Whatever you can do or dream you can, begin it. Boldness has genius, power, and magic in it."

As soon as you trust yourself, you will know how to live. Knowing is not enough; we must apply. Willing is not enough; we must do. Correction does much, but encouragement does more. None are more hopelessly enslaved than those who falsely believe they are free.

Every day we should hear at least one little song, read one good poem, see one exquisite picture, and, if possible, speak a few sensible words. Nothing is worth more than this day. Magic is believing in yourself, if you can do that, you can make anything happen. I love those who yearn for the impossible. All the knowledge I possess everyone else can acquire, but my heart is all my own." From my mutual supportive heart to yours, Thomas

Look for the love and support in your life this very minute! You are so blessed!

April 26   Hope

We are a world adrift in chaos. Wars, starvation, racism, lying, cheating, verbal and physical abuse are rampant. A report came out about the life expectancy in the United States. For the first time since the early 1960s, life expectancy in the United States has declined for the second year in a row, according to a CDC report. American men can now expect to live 76.1 years, a decrease of two-tenths of a year from 2015. American women's life expectancy remained at 81.1 years. The change was driven largely by a rising death rate among younger Americans. The death rate of people between the ages of 25 and 34 increased by 10 percent between 2015 and 2016, while the death rate continued to decrease for people over the age of 65.

The tragic part of that report is the dramatic increase in deaths of folks between 25 and 34. The major change is caused by drug overdose and suicide. Our younger adults are giving up. They are living in a world largely created by their parents and it has become unlivable for them. So they resort to taking drugs to deaden their despair or even worse; they end their lives because of the intense pain of living on Earth today. They are without hope.

What can we do? Here is a list of things I found on Life Hack that might help each of us.

Conduct a hope audit of your life. How are you doing? In health, work, relationships?

Take good care of your health.

Have a stress reduction strategy.

Meditation, breathing exercises, physical exercise and favorite forms of recreation all reduce stress.

Being in nature does as well.

Create hopeful relationships.

Learn to forgive.

Develop a daily journal writing habit if it helps you to let go of negative experiences and emotions.

Help others see the best in themselves, notice their desire to make meaningful contributions and help them find their path to becoming hope makers for themselves and others.

Look for ways to make hopefulness tangible. Don't let it be just something for the future. Hope is all of the little things we do each day to make our lives better. Everything you do contributes to hopeful living or takes away from it. That may seem heavy. But hope is that important. It needs to be treasured. From my hopeful heart, Thomas

Go inside your heart and let go of any doubt about the love that you are and breathe in and out 'Hope' - let it fill you with more light and love!

April 27   Blessed

Soon I will have my new computer and I will be able to share directly on my own Facebook page. Thanks for finding us on Lou Ann's page. I have shared with you the story about how I came to start this some ten months ago. The essence of that story is that Kwan Yin came to me through a local sensitive. She kind of reprimanded me in a way. She exclaimed that "there are millions of people on planet Earth who are suffering. They have lost hope and have given up." She went on to say that I have the experience and knowledge and heart to support them with my words. I hope these words have been some help to you folks who get to read them.

I knew I was going to be a minister when I was in high school. I became one at the age of twenty seven. Later I enrolled in a metaphysical university in Washington D.C.; then started a spiritual center in Maryland in 1975. So I have more than forty years of experience of listening, learning and sharing spiritual principles. I have been blessed to study with some of the most wonderful teachers and masters over the decades. Their words and experience are melded into my own personal philosophy of how to live the most loving, caring, giving life possible.

The most profound guidance I have to share is "Follow your heart!" Your spiritual heart is the essence of all truth. It will never let you down.

When we come to a place where we desire to know what the best possible outcome is for all; it is advisable to find a quiet place and take some deep breaths. State your query and then be still and listen. If you do not get a clear indication of what direction you should take – do this. Surrender to your higher self and then make any decision that you choose to do. Once you set off in a particular direction, you will be given all the contacts and experiences that will lead you to your greatest good. From my blessed heart to yours, Thomas

Place your hands on your heart, breathe and feel a sense of hope there! Let it charge you throughout your day!

April 28   Self Esteem

Lou Ann and I went to see the movie "I Feel Pretty". Amy Schumer does a great job playing someone who has little self-esteem until she bumps her head. Then she sees herself as she has always wanted. This is one of the most important lessons in life. In truth, everything is exactly as we perceive it to be.

We create everything. What we deeply believe will be created. This is so powerful. There is no one outside of us creating any event in our life. If we believe there is karma, there is. If we believe this is the only life, it is. If we believe that anything is possible; we create an internal narrative that supports that idea. Belief invites us to "be on the lookout" so we can gather evidence to support our theory. Once confirmed we begin to weave the belief into the pattern, fabric and garment of our lives.

Our beliefs can be expansive or very limiting. There is evidence of our beliefs. Look at your life. What is in it? What do you own? Who do you love? Who are your friends and family? Whatever you currently have in your life, you have one hundred per cent intention to have it. This is where the power is.

Right now, if you have created something that doesn't enhance your life. You get to change it. We no longer have to look outside of ourselves to create life the way we want. And, we don't get to blame anyone or anything for what we have. When we realize how powerful we truly are, our life changes dramatically. We then can love ourselves just the way we are. There is no higher self-esteem than that. From my powerful heart to yours, Thomas

Expand your perception of self-love within so you can love others more easily!

April 29   When You Care Enough

My new computer is just a thing, but I love it! It serves me well right now. Tonight, Lou Ann and I watched a Hallmark Hall Of Fame movie. These movies have a lot of emotion and feeling to them; more than a regular weekly program. The story tonight was about a woman dying of cancer. She has a daughter who is angry with her, so there is a lot of healing to take place. The Hall of Fame movies also have fabulous commercials. They use the Hallmark saying of "When you care enough to send the very best" and expand upon it. The commercials are real life stories of people making a difference in their communities. One of the themes was "When you care enough to be someone's hero! They showed a group of people who gather together to help each other with the most basic things like food and shelter.

When we serve in a bread line we are someone's hero - when we bring a blanket to keep them warm - when we give them shoes to cover their feet. When we paint their house, mow their lawn, take them to the doctor, help them buy groceries, we can be their hero. When we march for veterans or teachers or people limited in their civil rights, we are heroes.

We don't have to be rich or educated or smart. We only have to care enough, to take the time to do what will help our fellow humans and other sentient beings. From my caring heart to yours, Thomas

Create a small way to make a difference in someone's life today!

April 30   Magical Music

Lou Ann and I went to a benefit concert to support the local elementary school which may be shut down. There was a group of performers singing and playing guitars. Three of the performers have meant a lot to us. When we moved to Sedona in the late eighties, Patrick Ki played his guitar at the Hideaway restaurant. He would strum out tunes as he walked the aisles. When he came to our table, we requested a John Denver song and I would sing the words as he played.

Robin Miller another composer, guitarist and key board player wrote a piece of music called Transcendence. It is a wonderful piece of music that allows the listener to connect with a deeper part of them.

In April of 2000 my mom Gladys, was nearing the end of her life. Lou Ann and I sat beside her and read the wonderful spiritual messages of Emmanuel while we played Robin's Transcendence music. We felt the light in the room magnify and it felt like angels were present as she left her body. I let Robin know how much that meant to us and what a gift it was to Gladys as well.

Eric Miller, Robin's son has become an amazing Flamenco guitarist. He and Lou Ann's daughter dated back in the late eighties; and he has become a good friend. The fourth performer was vocalist and percussionist Susanna Martin. As we sat there and listened to this wonderful group of musicians, perform at such a high level, I felt so blessed. I had this gorgeous thought of how beautiful life is and how fortunate we are to live it full out! From my deeply appreciative heart to yours, Thomas

Listen to some music that makes life feel magical to you!

May 1 Journey to God

We spend many years attending seminars and retreats, reading books and sharing in discussion groups about our concept of God. All of these may be helpful but God is not to be 'figured out' or deduced through reason. God is to be experienced through our connection with all of the beauty of life. This is done through our feelings. Our feelings reside in our spiritual heart. Connecting with God is an inner journey. Everyone and everything is God. It is the only energy in the Universe. When we feel our alignment with this energy it occurs deep in our heart.

We have created a conscious mind which can interfere with feeling our connection to God. Often our lives do not work very well and when we reach a crisis point, we come back to God. Of course, in reality, we never leave, but we think we do and that is when the pain and suffering occur.

It is the coming home to our God connection which is the essential purpose for living. In this journey, home is the richness and passion of life. It is the grandest of all journeys and filled with risk and reward, but it is the only journey we ever truly make. There are many principles which can aid in our journey, but the ultimate one is to know you are divine and eternal.

There is a wonderful book written by Martia Nelson titled Coming Home: The Return to True Self.

It guides us into our true self where we find a wealth of unconditional love, happiness, prosperity, and connectedness with all life. Each page evokes self-love and a feeling of being seen and understood at the deepest level. Coming Home offers deep insight into the nature of the field of pure Divinity within us all. It will help all those who seek fulfillment from the level of being rather than Doing. Deepak Chopra said: "Coming Home is the clearest, most powerful explanation of the universe and how it works that I have ever read. It's brilliant. This book will be on my bedside table for quite some time."

Check it out, your life will never be the same after you read it and follow the guidance. From my true-self heart to yours, Thomas

Home is found in your heart – nurture and connect with it often!

May 2   There is such a thing as a free lunch

The Illuminate Film Festival is coming up at the end of this month in Sedona. One of our featured documentaries is The Free Lunch Society. It is a film about the concept of a basic income for everyone. Fact: The world produces enough foods and goods to feed a happy world. Fact: The world is more than prosperous enough to end all inequality. Fact: The Walmart-family owns just as much as 160 million Americans. Fact: Lotto winners keep on working even if they don't have to. Fact: A tax on money-and finance-transactions will fix this inequality. Fact: It would boost the economy to give more people a decent income.

The system of today, where the richest get richer by the day and the middle class can't even survive on the income of two badly paid jobs, we need a new system. What would you do if your basic living needs were paid by our government? Some have said that it would lead to laziness. People wouldn't work; they would lie around all day doing nothing. However, once people's needs are met they can relax. The pressure will be off. They will have more time to spend doing things they love. There will be more time to spend with their families. That would have a huge benefit to society. To have one or two parents available for their children and each other. People may become more creative. They will have more time to work on their hobbies and dreams.

Finland is studying basic income and Kenya already is enacting a program. Hawaii is even looking at enacting it for its citizens. To learn more, go to iTunes.com to find this movie; from my relaxed and creative heart to yours, Thomas

Life gets better and better as we open to the possibilities!

May 3   Familiarity Breeds Contentment

The expression "familiarity breeds contempt" is all too familiar. Yet, as the case with many common sayings, we might benefit from taking a look at whether or not it truly makes sense. When we don't examine these beliefs they tend to become self-fulfilling prophecies. Ordinarily, the expression "familiarity breeds contempt" refers to what often happens in long-standing relationships and marriages. Regrettably, over time too may relationships begin to see their happiness wither! Yet, the question remains: is it actually familiarity that causes this disappointment?

Yesterday Lou Ann shared something with me that she had said the day before. When I first heard it I thought of that old saying I mentioned above. And yet I had a different reaction to her sharing. I laughed and we both laughed together. It is part of my enchantment of Lou Ann. We have been communicating things to each other for more than thirty eight years. There has to be a lot of repeated words and sayings. We both grew up in families that shared a lot of old sayings. So we are very familiar with our exchanges.

I believe that when we don't feel good about our self, we act out on each other. So that kind of familiarity would breed contempt. However, just the opposite is true.

If a soft kiss, an appreciative hug or the simple feeling of being cared for becomes familiar, then familiarity in fact evokes and sustains love. In loving relationships that embrace emotional support and respect, familiarity produces a wonderful life. What we become accustomed to should become the focus of our attention.

We have said many times that what we focus on expands. Let us open our hearts to each other and create the kind of familiarity that breeds contentment and love. From my familiar heart to yours, Thomas

Open your heart to contentment and love more fully than ever!

May 4   May the Fourth Be With You

Today is the fourth day of May, so I thought I would have some fun with the old Jedi quote of "May the Force be with you."

Actually it always is. We can never be without it, because we are the Force. There is only Oneness. Everything is a part of it. There is not a Two-ness. The word Oneness is all inclusive, by definition there is nothing outside of it. It is thrilling to think about that. We are all a part of creation. Each and every part of creation is unique and therefore equal. There is no good or bad in Oneness. There is only the creative energy of all that is.

When we realize on a personal level that we are an integral part of the whole, we should celebrate. We are never less than. We are all equal and necessary to the whole. Without us, it would not be whole. There would be a sacred vital part missing. We get stuck sometimes and play the game of life in a small way. Remember the words of Marianne Williamson:

We ask ourselves, 'Who am I to be brilliant, gorgeous, talented, fabulous?' Actually, who are you not to be? You are a child of God. Your playing small does not serve the world. There is nothing enlightened about shrinking so that other people won't feel insecure around you".

We are the Jedi Knights, not in a battle with the Empire, but with our perceived limitations. We forget that we are the Oneness and that we have limitless energy, incredible talent, unlimited gifts and eternal vision. We get to stop playing the game of "let's pretend" and to take back our power through self-realization. Today, let us declare that we are the Force; a Force of love, compassion, healing, understanding and inclusion. From my Jedi heart of love to yours, Thomas

Be the creative, brilliant and fabulous energy that you are!

May 5   It's All Good

Yesterday we drove over to Prescott Arizona which is about fifty five miles from our house. About half way there, a huge sleet storm blew across the highway. There was a three inch accumulation for a few miles. It was thirty seven degrees this morning. Saturday it will be ninety for the high. You never know, do you? Life is such an amazing variety of experiences. So full and so rich! Most of us live in such abundance. I have some tennis player friends that sometimes complain about traffic or weather or some insignificant thing. I encourage them to see it in a different way.

We stop and take time to look around at one of the most beautiful places on Earth. We acknowledge how healthy we are. We share how many friends and loved ones are in our circle of life. Remember the wonderful song from Lion King? Here is the link from YouTube with Elton John singing this inspirational song:

https://www.youtube.com/watch?v=IwH9YvhPN7c

Life is even more fun when we find our place on the unwinding path. Our place is in our hearts, our dreams, our surroundings and our journey. I wish you all the best possible life, filled with everything your heart desires. From my deeply grateful heart to yours, Thomas

Treasure your circle of life and let it expand!

May 6   No Goal but this

Lou Ann and I went to a Deva Premal chanting concert tonight. Her partner Miten sang a song with the title of our blog tonight. At our core, there is nothing to do, but be. We don't need to accomplish anything. We are connected to our essence and just being is enough. I realize that when we are in this temporary thing we call life on Earth; we feel the need to do and have. It is not necessary. We entered life without anything and we will leave in the same way. In between birth and death we get to choose whatever we desire. However, we are Oneness being Oneness all the time; when we realize our divine nature, than we really do not need any goal except to be.

Deva Premal and Miten use a process of "natural selection" to choose the mantras on their albums. Premal has said she gravitates toward Sanskrit mantras, rather than mantras from other languages. She says that, for her, removing her ego from her understanding of the mantra allows the creative process to express the true meaning of the mantra.

The purpose of her work was explained: "Our objective is to be open to the Goddess of music – to be true to ourselves, as musicians, as 'teachers;' as partners, and ultimately, as individuals – fellow travelers. We accomplish this by not 'trying' to accomplish anything. We take very little credit for what is happening around our so-called success (we have sold over a million albums now!) – We see ourselves as messengers of a 5,000 year old tradition...so, our part in the process is simply to show up and chant".

Deva and Miten warmed our hearts and inspired us to remember who we truly are. We chanted along with them and danced and laughed and were filled with joy. I wish for all of you to experience them sometime. From my en-chant-ed heart to yours, Thomas

Find one thing that enchants you today and do that!

May 7   Like a Good Neighbor!

We bought some furniture the other day on a local Facebook site. We drove through a sleet storm and didn't get home until dark. We called our neighbor down the block for help and he and his wife both came and helped me carry in a very heavy sofa. They told us of a sale two doors down from them, of people who had sold their home and were selling everything.

When we got there yesterday we found an eight piece sectional, hardly ever used for $200. Our same neighbor Terry, met us at the house and helped me load the sectional and a king size bed that was never used as well! I told him that either Lou Ann or I did something really wonderful in a past life or he and his wife are piling up points for the next life! Then our friends, two miles away, let us use their truck to transport it all.

This is what I describe as spiritual living. It is not about showing up at a place of worship. It is not about attending classes to learn valuable life principles. It isn't even about praying or meditating. It is about loving acts of kindness. I personally don't believe in an actual place like Heaven. If there were, these kind folks would probably get a front row seat!

Many folks are wondering how we will ever turn things around on planet Earth and create the society we desire. This is it! Be a good neighbor! When enough acts of kindness outweigh our not so thoughtful acts, we will create Heaven on Earth. Exactly where it should be! From my deeply thankful heart to yours, Thomas

Be a good neighbor today at work or home or wherever the opportunity arises!

May 8   There is no path

With each trip around the sun, more and more people come to the realization that there's somehow more to life than meets the eye. It is an awakening process that leaves many of us wondering what the true nature of reality is all about. Part of this ongoing transition is that people are no longer satisfied with living a purely materialistic lifestyle based on superficial possessions. Instead, they actively seek to enrich their life by adopting a more spiritual worldview.

As a result of feeling connected to a source greater than them, many embark on a spiritual journey in order to find themselves and to seek God. They begin realizing that they are so much more than just this body. Instead of being defined by their human body, they come to the conclusion that they are spiritual beings inhabiting physical bodies.

We have never left. We don't need to be found. We are not lost. We have always been. We are always on purpose. There is nowhere to go. We are already there.

The human task is to simply remember. We are divine and don't need improving. When we do awake to the awareness of our magnificence, then life can become a joy ride of infinite possibilities. Surrender and let go, you won't regret it. From my heart to yours, Thomas

Connect to Source each time you can today. Notice how Divine you truly are!

May 9   I Remember You

At the illuminate Film Festival we all got to see a very haunting and romantic film titled " I Remember You" It is also the title of a song written in 1941 with the lyrics by Johnny Mercer. Here is a link on YouTube that features a gorgeous romantic rendition by Tony Bennett: https://www.youtube.com/watch?v=epWCk2mvq0g

The lyrics are so romantic when we think about "telling the angels, the thrill of it all". The song was written for Judy Garland by Mercer. Even though it is a personal love song, we could expand it to include all of the things we remembered about our life that gave us a thrill.

Things like looking at the Milky Way, and my first ride at Disneyland; and the birth of all my children. All the games we played together. All of the road trips we took. Every moment I spend with Lou Ann. My list would go on and on.

Life here on Earth has been a thrill. It has of course, had its ups and downs. However, it has been astounding and beyond words really. I wish for you to recall all of the best moments of your life and perhaps you too, could record them somehow. We could start the I Love My Life Association. From my thrilled heart to yours, Thomas

Focus on the thrill of it all – the sweet simple events that make our lives richer and meaningful!

May 10   Universal principle #9: The Mirror Principle

"Everything we see and feel is a reflection of the state of our own consciousness. Every person we attract into our lives is showing us a perception we hold about ourselves. Every feeling expressed by another, mirrors a feeling deep within us. This reflection is a gift, for it allows us to be aware of the beliefs we hold, and the ways we have blocked the free flow of Divine Love through us."

In the series of experiences that make up our life there can be time for reflection about the whole purpose of it. We are so busy in doing, that we have little time for being, which is after all what we are: human beings not human doings. Many of us stick to the script; we see life as a one-time event of some four score years and then hope there is an afterlife.

Then what? Perhaps if we played our hand right, we get a heavenly home, if not, a horrible fate. Then there is the possibility that we are here many, many times before exiting stage left. If we are eternal souls who have a consciousness that endures in some form, then why not keep coming back?

The gospel means "good news." Good is a judgment. The good news is, we are here and experiencing life. However, the planet is a mess. The human inhabitants use up its natural resources and even kill each other a lot.

The Earth is a reflection of who we all are. Right now we are not doing such a good job of caring for our planet. It is up to each of us while we are here to do all we can to nurture and love our amazing planetary home. Recycle, become sustainable, and treat everything as sacred, because it is. So before our own journey to our spiritual home, let's make this one the best ever! From my heart to yours, Thomas

Be the reflection you wish to be – caring, kind and loving!

May 11   Never Give Up!

The immortal football coach of the Green bay Packers Vince Lombardi, once said to his players "Fatigue will make cowards of us all" He was encouraging his team to give even more effort in practice, even though they were exhausted. So that during a game, when they were once again drained of almost all of their energy; they would find a way to dig deeper and win.

When we spend most of our energy, it can be a challenge to keep on going. One thing Lombardi didn't mention, but was perhaps implied - football is a violent physical sport which takes an enormous amount of energy to play. However, as I said a while ago, it is also very mental. I think he was also inferring that when we get so tired we want to quit, it is our mind that wants to throw in the towel.

And so it is in many of our lives, that we, who do not overexert ourselves physically, get exhausted as well. We may put in a lot of mental and emotional energy to create our desires; only to come up short of our goals and dreams. This can be just as exhausting as some extreme physical task. We give so much to our passion and it sometimes crashes and burns!

The key to Lombardi's success is that his Sunday football games were won on Monday through Friday on their practice field. Let those of us who still have dreams and goals to achieve, continue to persevere. Let us know that if we do not give up on our passion and keep on practicing, we will win our own personal Super Bowl.

I wish for you all to find the energy, courage and strength to push on through to your dreams. From my never quitting heart to yours, Thomas

May 12   The Rainbow Connection

Forty years ago Kermit the frog sang the wonderful song The Rainbow Connection in the Muppets Movie. It was brilliantly written by Paul Williams. He was born in the magical year of 1940. The Academy Award winning song that year was, When You Wish upon a Star!

I have never learned the lyrics to the Rainbow Connection before now. I have heard it on television and radio. Today my gifted voice teacher Kathi Bellucci surprised me with this magical song to learn today. Now Lou Ann and I are learning to sing it and will share it on our Enriching Life Forever Vlog. Here is a wonderful rendition of this magical song on YouTube: https://www.youtube.com/watch?v=GNM6R6QV9vo
When I sing these words I am transported to a place where my heart is full. I am filled with wonder! The innocence of the lyrics reminds us of the place in us that "never grows up!" I urge us all to rediscover our rainbow connection and live from that place; the lovers, the dreamers and us; from my rainbow heart to yours, Thomas.

Listen to your rainbow heart – its laughter is contagious!

May 13   Loving Life

We went to a local restaurant here in Sedona the other day with one of our dearest friends, Ellie Cooper. We have known Ellie since 1995 when Lou Ann and I were sharing Spirit Church. We also collaborated on the development of the Positive Place Television Talk Show.

Later on, I had obtained a job as a medical courier after the TV show didn't fully materialize. After four and a half years, Ellie took over that position when we moved back to Northern Virginia. When we all come into the restaurant named Picazzos, we are greeted by the server and one of the food bussers named Bertha, who comes and gives us hugs and kisses.

Tonight we went into another local restaurant and several of the waiters (who were not our servers) came by to say hello and greet us as if we were family. It is like a Hallmark movie! We are so blessed to be loved and nurtured by such wonderful people. When we go out to restaurants, we always want to know about our servers. We ask them about their work experience and their personal lives. We also ask them about whether they will continue to do food service or do they have other plans and dreams? It is a wonderful exchange of energy and it makes our life richer for it.

When we humans take the time to know others at a deeper level, we appreciate it and the world becomes a more loving and beautiful place. In some ways, it is like paying it forward. The more that all of us take time to be present with each other, the more we will all feel loved, and peace on Earth will be easier to achieve. From my well-nourished and grateful heart to yours, Thomas

Find time today to ask someone about their lives and really listen with your heart!

May 14   What the World Needs Now

Mother's Day is the third biggest retail holiday of the year. And rightly so! Mothers are celebrated highly because we know in our hearts how much they love. I was the youngest of three sons with an alcoholic father. My mother worked constantly to keep the family fed and together. She had to, as far as she was concerned. I will always be grateful for the amount of time and energy and love my mom Gladys, showed me in my sixty years that we shared in this lifetime,

Most mothers have gigantic hearts that do not have the word 'quit' inside them. They are all in! I watch how Lou Ann is with her daughter Uma. She is always there to support her, no matter what. There isn't anything she wouldn't do. She has indomitable energy to serve her daughter, and of course, her grandchildren as well. Mothering is the epitome of the feminine energy. And sometimes it is done by men.

There are a lot of problems in the world, mainly caused by men. Women, whether or not they are mothers are what keeps the world from totally unraveling. The nurturing aspect of motherhood or the feminine is the link that makes the planet strong. Even Mother Nature is threatened by the masculine desire to conquer and obtain. Of course, Mother Nature will never lose. No matter what we humans do to her. She will survive.

It is time for the world to not only honor and love mothers on Mother's Day, but to do even more. We have a paltry percentage of women in our primary governmental offices in the United States. We would not have the crime, corruption or current prison system if women were in charge.

Men need to open their hearts and learn the lesson of the divine feminine. The Divine Feminine is experiencing a re-emergence—a rebirth into the collective consciousness. For centuries she has been downplayed, demeaned, removed from her place of honor and reverence by the dominant patriarchal culture.

We are now in a time when the Divine Feminine is the subject of intense interest and many conversations and she is beginning to receive the veneration and devotion she deserves. The Divine Feminine represents the supreme level of feminine expression and manifestation in the universe. She comprises the best of the feminine in all its measure.

And the divine feminine is in all of us, women and men alike. People are coming together in refreshing ways to nurture the planet, create sustainable communities and work for social change. Veganism has hit the mainstream; yoga and meditation studios abound on every corner.

In lieu of sticking it out in corporate jobs, more professionals of all ages are walking away from empty paychecks to live their dreams and nurture their truest soul callings. This awakening of human consciousness is creating movement towards greater creativity, compassion, and wellness, communion with nature and a sincere respect for religious, ethnic and gender diversity.

On Mother's Day let us celebrate the wonderful, nurturing, giving, loving, caring women who have chosen to be mothers. Let us also celebrate those women who have chosen not to be mothers and still exemplify these traits of the divine feminine. What the world needs now, is love sweet love, not for some but for everyone! And mothers always do that! From my nurtured heart to yours, Thomas

Honor the feminine in yourself. Breathe in and out slowly and know we are all made of masculine and feminine energies. EnJOY!

May 15   Treasure Hunt

Last fall, Lou Ann and I traveled back to Virginia by car, where we had lived for seven years. We picked up about twenty boxes of assorted books, mementos, writings, art work and clothing, that we had left behind. We were also looking for two necklaces that each of us had, from some thirty five years ago. They were gifted to us by a wonderful woman named Helen Dimit. They are 24 carat gold and they have a metal piece which has a six pointed star. In ancient days the two equilateral triangles were symbols of the seven original planets in the Zodiac. It is now referred to as the Star of David. In the center of our medallion is the Christian cross.

We had thought we had lost these beautiful gifts. When I was unpacking today, I discovered them in a colorful cloth bag. I got goosebumps when I saw them because the bag had lots of dragonflies embroidered on it. Many of them blue, the symbol of my oldest brother Bud, before he left the planet on May 8, 1985.

This is often the way my life works. I had intention of cleaning up a mess and making our living space better. Then, as often occurs, we receive a gift from Universe! I have shared with you folks before that a powerful way to create, is to just do something. You don't have to have a goal or reason. Take action and Oneness shows up in all of its magnificence! I encourage everyone to surrender and let The Great Spirit give you its gifts. From my magically overwhelmed heart to yours, Thomas

Today take one tiny active step to reflect your own magnificence!

May 16   Keeping the Dream Alive

Back in 1995, I had the opportunity of going to Los Angeles to the Income Builders International training seminar. It was a seminar that taught people who had a dream, a book, a business or a passion to create a plan to market it.

We were living in Sedona and we met Gloria Reeder in February in a brainstorming circle to help folks create their desires. When it came my turn, I said *"You know the talk shows on TV, including the better ones like Oprah and Donahue, mostly focus on what is wrong with society. I shared what if we had a television program that focused on what is wonderful about our world?"*

We began to create the show and it took us a couple of years and we eventually ran out of funds. I had a chance to do it again in 2000 but that didn't work either.

It is still a good idea. I know that the media people believe that negative things create more attention. It is often tragedy in some form or other that gets the headlines. However, the world has changed a lot in the last twenty years. Good things are happening, as well as the challenging events. It would be exciting to see a program about local heroes all over the globe, who are making a difference in a positive way.

I got news tonight that I will be in the filmmaker lab after the upcoming Illuminate Film Festival. The lab is an immersive, hands-on workshop in conscious cinema, ideal for filmmakers with a project in development.

This three-part lab involves experiential exercises allowing you to tap into your creativity, set intentions and goals, and provide you with practical solutions to sharpen story and find your audience.

I will be presenting the still excellent idea to celebrate the beauty and magnificence of our planet. I would encourage any of you who still have a dream to not give up on it. Mine may never come to pass as I picture it. However it makes a difference in consciousness when we make the effort.

The energy we send out even in attempting is never wasted. There is a song that goes *"You were born with a dream that lies deep in your soul. You were born with a need to reach out to a goal. Swear by all that you know, that you'll never let go of your dream"* From my never ending dreaming, heart to yours, Thomas

What did you want to be when you were small? Maybe some part of that can be reawakened?!

May 17   Universal principle #10: Non-judgment

"At our request, we have been carefully taught to evaluate and judge much of what we experience. However, 'right' and 'wrong', 'good' and 'bad' are just beliefs, disguises for the unconditional love that is always present. The truth is that everything that occurs is just another event or circumstance that we have created in our imagination. Judging something keeps whatever we judge the way we judge it. Also, judging anyone or anything tells us that we are judging ourselves in the same way. Judging creates discomfort that can only be relieved by opening our hearts, first to the judgment and then to the person or thing we have judged. Freeing this openhearted energy leads to the joyful feeling of unconditional love for ourselves as the wholeness and completeness of who we really are."

Often judgment is the thing that creates what we do not want to experience. We are meaning making machines. We make up stories for most of the events of our lives. These stories are our judgment of what has occurred, is happening or might take place in the future. This judging keeps us locked into the stories and often prevents us from the life that we desire to have. Of course, we often judge ourselves the harshest. We sometimes are not aware of this and cannot figure out why life is not flowing.

Remember the line from the song The Wings that Fly us Home? "Is a hero's blood more righteous than a hobo's sip of wine?"

Not to me! In our society we have it that those who succeed are more valuable than those who do not. It's analogous to saying that our left eye is more valuable than our right one. They are both valuable and when working in tandem they give us greater vision.

We have created life on Earth that makes it more difficult for some people than others. "To the victor go the spoils", has been an edict and way of life for centuries. In the United States we have a fixation on material and societal success. Hardly anyone can name who came in second in any major sporting event. A team could win all of its games until the final one and consider itself a failure in our judgment of success.

This begs the question; what is spiritual? Most of us would not consider a hobo's sip of wine as equal to a hero's blood. We have been caught in our mind's trap to judge everything. However, our judgments do not always serve us. The hobo and the hero both left the womb with the same potential to create their life experience. They both made choices. Those choices led them to exactly where they are now. Choices are just choices. It is we, who say the choices are good or bad. We could disagree about whether they serve us or not. It is just our opinion. From the perspective of oneness they are the same, just choices. We get to have a huge breakthrough when we can suspend our judgments and just notice. When we notice and refrain from judgment we maintain the energy of oneness. From my heart to yours, Thomas

Give up judgments as much as you can today! When you notice, switch to being grateful even if it's just grateful for your pinkie finger!

May 18   May I Be Happy

Another wonderful movie we presented at the Illuminate Film Festival is "May I Be Happy". It is a movie about mindfulness.

Mindfulness means maintaining a moment-by-moment awareness of our thoughts, feelings, bodily sensations, and surrounding environment, through a gentle, nurturing lens.

Mindfulness also involves acceptance, meaning that we pay attention to our thoughts and feelings without judging them—without believing, for instance, that there's a "right" or "wrong" way to think or feel in a given moment. When we practice mindfulness, our thoughts tune into what we're sensing in the present moment rather than rehashing the past or imagining the future.

Mindfulness helps you to cultivate happiness from the inside out. It also allows you to be better in touch with who you truly are. Even more so, the habit of self-reflection will help you find more meaning in your life's experiences.

This can be accomplished by picking up the habit of meditation, or by simply trying to pay the greatest attention to the present moment. And you can also find time to reflect on your life and your actions. It will help you to identify patterns that let you know what is really important to you.

"May I Be Happy" reveals the significance of mindfulness practice in transforming the lives of young people in the classroom. Covering varying approaches to mindfulness by a range of San Francisco Bay Area programs, this feature documentary reminds us of children's natural capacity for well-being, resilience and happiness.

I invite you to see this movie and be thrilled to see that there are wonderful things being taught in our schools that will change the world forever! Go to mayibehappy.org. You will be thrilled! From my hopeful heart to yours, Thomas

Be 'mindful' of your breath and your heart today – let it guide you to more love and happiness!

May 19   Tough News

You know that I mostly focus on the positive side of life. For me, there is too much attention given to all the things we do wrong. Today would be an exception, another mass shooting in a school. Parents sent their children to school today and ten priceless treasures didn't return. It is unfathomable for a parent to experience this.

Today's episode was done at a high school, where Lou Ann's niece teaches and 2 grand-nieces attend. There were anxious moments before we heard that they were okay. I know that pro-gun folks say, that guns don't kill people, people do. However, there is always a person at the other end of the gun who pulls the trigger. A person who is in so much pain; and they have so much anger that they would commit a horrible act of violence; often to people they know. And there is also many innocent youngsters gunned down because they got on a yellow school bus and trusted.

My view is, for humanity to day by day, learn how to love. Learn how to love the unlovely. The perpetrators of these heinous crimes were lonely people, that didn't feel loved in some way. Even if they were mentally ill and incapable of experiencing love; we as a society, let them down.

A famous psychiatrist once said that people we call insane are like us or we are like them in some ways. He said that if we had experienced the exact same life as they had, we would probably have made the same choices. We literally do not know the heart and soul of another, totally.

Here we are again. There will be lots of discussion following this incident and not much will ever be done, to prevent it from happening again and again. Until most of us model for others how to live from a place of love, it won't end. Until we find a way to care so much for those who do not love themselves, it will continue.

Let us find a way to love so much, that eventually no parent will ever have to experience what happened at Santa Fe High school. From my very sad heart to yours, Thomas

Send a caring smile to others today, so they can pay it forward to another!

May 20   Mental Illness

Having had the privilege to undergo a lot of mental and emotional counseling in my life, it occurred to me that most of us would be well served by having feedback about our choices in life. We are all the result of our environment, our parenting, peer pressure and our uninformed choices. The world is a challenging place to be in at times. However, there are those among us who genuinely have mental illness that need attention.

Lou Ann and I went to a movie tonight put on by the local mental health association titled Beyond Silence. There were three people featured in the film. One was diagnosed with Bipolar 1, one with Bipolar 2 and one was schizophrenic. One of them committed murder by following the voices in his head, the other two wanted to kill themselves. They were about as sick as one can be. However they found their way back to wholeness. One found his way by getting a Golden Retriever. The lady in the film used Yoga as a vehicle to wellness. The third took up bicycling to find his freedom.

Yes, they all went through traditional therapies. However their hearts were opened to the possibilities of life through service to others. It is often, that those who become the finest teachers, leaders or therapists are the ones who have experienced the deepest amount of pain and worked their way through it.

I encourage anyone who feels like they are unable to cope with life, to seek counseling. Don't go through life in a lot of pain and try to get through it yourself. We are here for each other. It may be as simple as getting a loving dog or other animal that loves us unconditionally, that allows us to open our heart to the possibilities of our magnificence.

If you see others in emotional distress or behavior that does not serve them; please get involved and help them find support. Underneath the silence of our broken hearts is a place of love for all of us. From my heart to yours, Thomas

Remember we are all in this together. Be compassionate today instead of judging – what we put out comes back to us!

May 21   What Would You Do?

There was a story on Facebook today that had an interesting conclusion. A man was asked to answer the following question in a job interview. What if you were in your car and you pulled up to a bus stop and there were three people waiting there. One was to be your soulmate. The person you would love and with whom you would spend the rest of your life. The second was your best friend who previously had saved your life. The third was an elderly lady who was ill and needed medical attention. Who would you pick up?

Here was his answer. He gave his car keys to his best friend to take the elderly lady to the hospital. He remained behind to meet and get to know the person he would love forever. He clearly answered outside of the box. We don't always have to make one choice. We can use our innate ability to find a solution that supports everyone. This Facebook article was shared by NTD.TV Inspired Life. Here is who they are:

At NTD we believe the integrity of our world hinges on the accurate and truthful spreading of information. We dedicate ourselves to provide a source of truth, no matter the odds, and shed light on major issues that the world deserves to know. We cover the stories that others don't. Our unbiased news provides critical information and insights. Our focused, exclusive analyses cut through the complicated political landscape and provide a clear perspective. We are responsible to society by steering clear of the sensational and producing our news with the utmost integrity.

We try to bring humanity into everything we do and to better understand who we are today by looking at history, culture and our civilization. We are inspired by timeless stories that promote universal values and humanity. We believe that if the stories and ideas we take in embody positivity, we can create change for a better future.

The human spirit is one of positivity, resilience and hope. We believe this spirit needs fuel. That's why we do our best to provide content that moves you, brings more light into your life and helps you become a wiser, brighter person. If every one of us can foster deeper understanding and compassion towards one another, this world will be a better place.

This service has at its purpose the same kind of mission as does my blog and our book. I am happy I found it and to share it with you folks. From my informed heart to yours, Thomas

Be positively hopeful today and watch it spread all around you to others!

May 22   Take a step back

For most of us, life is a long and winding road. We make so many choices along the way. Some of those decisions seem to serve us and some do not. In truth, all of our choices serve us. However, it doesn't appear that way a lot of the time. When we find ourselves stuck and life is challenging, it is time to step back and do nothing. Allow our higher selves to reconnect with those lost parts of ourselves.

There is a time for action and a time for reflection. Go do something that brings you joy. Even if it is to buy an ice cream cone or take in a movie. It is time to stop striving and trying to figure out what is hindering our progress.

Go do something fun or creative. Often, we find an amazing clarity about how to proceed. We often experience synchronistic events that appear as if magic. It could be some of our angelic guides orchestrating our newest adventure.

Wherever you are right now, do this first. Be grateful. Take a moment and count your blessings. Realize how much abundance you have in your life. Then head off in the direction of your intuitive feelings and you will have a breakthrough.

Those who achieve great things, defeat long odds, and become legends, didn't have anything you don't have. They just kept showing up, expecting a miracle, long after everyone else got practical. Above all don't quit on your dreams and your passion. The world is waiting for a lot of us to keep going and discover our gift, to share with all. From my never quitting heart to yours, Thomas

Gratefully hug yourself and silently love all parts of you – body, mind and spirit!

May 23   Who We Are

As the daily news surrounds us with stories of untold limitation; it is time to have a quick reminder course. After writing this last sentence, I realize that whenever I am encouraging you to keep on going, it was probably me that was stuck. The times that I share some advice for all of us to ponder; it was me that needed that wisdom. And since there is only Oneness, I am always speaking to me. The me speaking is the same as you.

We are all parts of the eternal mind of All That Is. So if someone says "Thomas is always talking to himself", believe it. We are not only the other parts of each other; we also reflect and complement each other as well. So sometimes if you are reading this, and it occurs to you that my words seem familiar, they are, they're yours, speaking to yourself.

This was the message from The Universe today: There isn't a moment in any day, Thomas, when someone, somewhere, isn't better off because of something you've done. And no matter what you do, or don't do, with the rest of your life, you cannot now comprehend the amounts of love, joy, and personal assistance that are already being pressed out to you in gratitude. From t*he Universe - m*y words exactly! Please substitute your name for Thomas, in the message up above.

We always do our best without exception. Sometimes it doesn't look that way, but it always is. It is that sometimes we are under the influence of our self- imposed unknowingness. There are truly, untold amounts of joy and prosperity and love spiraling around Universe, because we chose to share it.

Take a look in the mirror and smile or wink. You don't really have to say anything. Just know that it was us playing together, creating more light around Universe, because it is who we are. And who we will always be! From my Universal heart to yours, Thomas

Amazing what we have created and continue creating - bless us all!!

May 24   More Serendipity

We had three ladies from San Diego visit us last month at our home. Lou Ann encouraged them to join her at her Yoga class. One of the other participants in that class was a lady named Iona. She recently traveled to San Diego and was sitting in a restaurant and a woman in the next table said "Are you from Sedona?" She said she was and they realized they had met in that Yoga class with Lou Ann.

Lou Ann shared this story tonight with a couple of friends here in the Village who hosted us for dinner. They said "We were at your house that day helping you move something and we met those ladies!" What are the odds that all this could happen? One hundred per cent! Universe is always on purpose and loves to show off! We are so blessed to keep seeing the intelligence and love of Oneness.

The more we interact with others of like mind; the more these happenings occur! Maybe you have these things happen as well. Please share your stories of how Spirit is always letting you know it is with you.

Let us all create our days and let Spirit speak to us in its magical and magnificent way! From my serendipitous heart to yours, Thomas

Notice the ordinary miracles around you today!

May 25   Illuminating

We are getting close to the start of this year's festival, which begins next Wednesday. Twenty six films, several reel healings, an incredible healing lounge staffed with local beautiful people with lots of delicious organic food. The amazing Michael Franti is in concert on Sunday June 3rd who recorded the wonderful song "Say Hey I Love You" And so much more.

Today our programming team put the finishing touches to our months of effort and loves in creating this festival. We are honored to have the opportunity to be the liaison teammates, who welcome the filmmakers and celebrate their accomplishments.

We get to introduce their films and moderate a question and answer session following many of the movies. Through this whole process of discovering the films and curating them and meeting these dedicated folks, we have fallen in love.

We have fallen for their passion of doing what they love. We have fallen for their dedication of never quitting their mission, often and against long odds. Fallen for their vision of wanting to make our fragile planet a place of prosperity and love for all beings.

And now all of the efforts of hundreds of talented, totally committed beings of light and love come to the theater. And all of you folks will be the judge at how well we have done our tasks.

Illuminate is conscious cinema. It is created most of all to allow attendees to see what needs to be done in our world, to make it a better place. So if one of you gets motivated to get involved at a deeper level we have succeeded. If one of you finds a space in your own life that begins to heal, we have done our job. If one of you leaves the theater and finds what they love to do, we will rejoice. This is why we do this. We feel honored to have been a small part of this elegant undertaking.

I invite all of you to come to the festival, for any of the films or activities. Your attendance is what keeps it going. Without you, there will not be a festival. In this day of the tremendous challenges of modern life, we often wonder what we can do to help out. This is your chance.

Please join us and stand beside us, as we collectively do what needs to be done. Our children and their children's children will look back on this moment in time and say "Hooray for our parents and grandparents!" They stood up for all future generations of people and the planet's inhabitants and began the creation of heaven on Earth. From my very honored and excited heart to yours, Thomas

See an uplifting film today or any of the ones suggested here!

May 26   Being Happy

Sometimes we work too hard and spend a lot of time trying to create happiness. It may be right there in front of us. I found this list on the internet tonight by Steve Mueller.

1. Seeing the sunrise and sundown
2. Stargazing and philosophizing about life
3. Laughing until your muscles start aching
4. Eating breakfast in bed
5. Tasting something incredibly delicious for the first time
6. The delicious smell in your kitchen when you bake cake
7. Making other people happy
8. Finding money you had forgotten about
9. Heartfelt laughter
10. Eating dessert
11. Running into a friend you haven't seen for a long time
12. Taking a nap in your warm bed during a cold winter
13. Having a movie night with your friends
14. Being totally exhausted after a workout
15. Unearthing something you have been missing for years
16. Making someone laugh
17. Sleeping while the rain gently beats against your window
18. Realizing that a certain setback turned out to be incredibly important

19. Swimming naked

Winning the lottery wasn't on the list. Finding one's soulmate didn't make it either, living in a mansion, not quite up to par. Having the best possible career....nope! No, this list is one that nearly everyone could create in their life. Little things mean a lot. It is true, when we take the time to notice how blessed we are; it is usually the precious little things that mean so much! From my thankful heart to yours, Thomas

Pick a few of the above suggestions and create inner happiness!

May 27 One Soul

One of the challenges for souls that incarnate on planet Earth is remembering who they are. When we take on a body and a brain, we feel separate. We see each other and think that we are not One. We intentionally forget that we are all parts of the same Soul. It is a game of discovery and reconnecting with the One Source, which is who we are.

It is easy to get lost along the way. There is a split in our knowingness. One part totally believes in what it is seeing and experiencing. There is another part that is not encumbered by the senses. It is the observer. It is leading us home.

The beauty of the Earthly dance is the ongoing revelation of the twin parts of our soul's adventure. There comes a time when there may be a discontent. Something about life is not working. There is a place within that feels sort of empty and needs to be filled. This leads us through all kinds of adventures to a kind of coming home. One of our powerful choices sets up a chain of circumstances that lets us know that there is more to life than our humanness. We find our true self.

Welcome home! You have created every moment of your life to find yourself. When this occurs, sometimes all hell breaks loose. Our limited part is almost scared to death! It may take many excursions to find our way back, and it is worth it. When you are going through your days and you feel like things are not going well; it is time to go within. Whether through meditation or study or just being grateful, you can find yourself.

Lou Ann and I were having dinner today and we stopped to remember five things for which we are grateful. Mine were being alive, being with Lou Ann, being aware of being grateful, eating delicious healthy food in a gorgeous place and being happy as we were served by such loving folks at the restaurant.

I invite you to take time along your journey of inner remembrance to find five things for which you are most grateful. It is an awesome exercise. You will think of many more as well. And like us, you may feel such a deep sense of connectedness with the One Source. From my grateful heart to yours, Thomas

Be in gratitude today as much as you possibly can!

May 28   Folks Loving Folks

This morning I went to the local recycle place behind our neighborhood grocery. There are large green containers, where we all put the appropriate materials. A lady was carrying a brown paper bag of bottles and the bottom broke and they fell out and some shattered. I rushed over to help and gave her my plastic bin to put the glass in. We went over and dumped the glass together. At the same time, another lady came over and gave this woman a new plastic container, so that wouldn't happen to her in the future. Love it!

I went inside and purchased a couple of items in the grocery store. At the checkout stand, my total purchase came to $11.08 and all I had was a hundred dollar bill that I made selling a bed yesterday, which, by the way, was generously given to me by a Chiropractor, a while ago; another kind act. The clerk, named Chris, went into his pocket and got out eight cents so I wouldn't have so much change to mess with! A Wonderful Life may not be easy, but it is simple. Just do kind and loving things and we all prosper in the most magnificent ways!

Over the years I have counseled lots of wonderful people. At the time of our sessions, they were stuck in some way. I shared with them the techniques and methods I had learned along the way. However when it came down to it; my favorite and most simple advice is "to follow your heart." What I mean by this is, to follow the love that you feel inside of you. The physical heart is a wondrous mechanism. The spiritual heart is often beyond description. It is not a place of our thoughts or intellect or experience. It is that place that we go when we feel connected to nature, butterflies, children's eyes, puppy's tongues, mother's hugs and all things loving.

The people today, who were kind to each other, were connected to that part of us that cares, connects and includes. May most of our days be filled with these moments of loving each other unconditionally! From my loving heart to yours, Thomas

Celebrate heart connectedness in the simplest of things as you go through your day!

May 29   Remembering

This is Memorial Day. We stop and give honor to those who have given their lives in service to their country. Our country, mostly run by men, has been at war for 224 years of our 241 years since 1776. We have turned our warring nature into a massive machine which uses up a large part of the expense to run this country. This is in no way to demean those who have served our country. I did it, between 1959 and 1963. I was stationed in Texas and my division of the USAF was deeply involved in the Cuban missile crisis. The closest the world may have ever come to blowing up most of the planet. Sometimes, it is necessary to defend ourselves against the tyrants of the world, and many men and women volunteered to do so.

War should be the last resort. It is almost always the result of some men whose personalities are given to fighting to resolve differences. And, so millions of military personnel from all over the world have gone to early graves and today, sadly we remember and cry and pray for our loved ones who bravely served.

All of this has been the result of fear. When we are in a state of fear, we often take actions that we would not do if we were in a place of love.

Today, I would like to focus on the love. It may be said that those who gave their lives did it out of love in many cases. I would like society to find the ways to help young boys be loved in such a way that they do not act out their fear on others. Yes, masculinity has testosterone and it can be a challenge to harness that energy force.

Throughout history there have been those who have found their hearts, like Gandhi and Martin Luther King and many others. Let us find ways for boys and men to discover the beauty of compassion, caring and love. It is time for our country to memorialize those who have served in peaceful ways as well. From my hopeful heart to yours, Thomas

Notice any fears that come up and replace them with love!

May 30   Houston We Have Ignition!

Tonight was our last Illuminate team meeting of the season before the festival tomorrow. There were thirty of us gathered at Danette's house and on line. We tied up some loose ends about the festival. Then we were led in a celebration of all the hard work we had shared, over the past nine months.

Ranjita Ryan and Oman Ken led us. Oman created a song and we all sang it together. The words were about illuminate, our hearts and our love; for truly, one has to love what we are about, to give this much time and effort. Then Ranjita shared with us a ceremony. She gave us gifts that included a pair of white socks covered in red hearts, and a heart shaped crystal. She was using the socks to represent a euphemism to "sock it to them". In a playful way, she meant that now all of this planning and rehearsing was a prelude to sending out our energy in a way that would have impact on the world.

Then we went around the room to many of our teammates and held hands with our crystal hearts in them. We sang words to celebrate the other person and to let them know how much we valued them and their contributions. Then we exchanged hearts with them and went on to another person.

It was a fitting end to all that we had accomplished together. Our team is now ready for takeoff. We may be going where no one else has gone before. Into uncharted territory of conscious cinema, perhaps becoming a more powerful force and even mainstream.

I want to thank all of you who read this, for your support. It has helped me continue to be inspired and to grow deeper in my commitment to create a message of love and support and caring. This is the way the mission will be accomplished. When we walk on Earth like the astronauts walked on the moon. Creating a whole new world dedicated to exploring the best we can be.

Let us take one small step for all of humanity and one giant step for the possibilities of the human soul. From my ignited heart to yours, Thomas

We are all awesome beings! Celebrate it today!

May 31   Push

Two hundred people gathered tonight at the Creative Life Center in Sedona to watch the amazing documentary movie titled "Push". It is a wonderful love story about a couple who have found a way to live powerful transformative lives. They were married in 2009 and one year later, the husband Grant Korgan, was critically injured and became paralyzed from the waist down. Grant was an extreme sports athlete who pushed the limits of competition and crashed his snowmobile, and then his life really began.

He and his wife Shawna began his arduous rehabilitation, often doing ten hours per day of physical therapy and exercise. They were a team of the most dedicated partners. There was no stopping them from creating a powerful life. Shawna has this saying which says: "be firm in where you are going and be flexible in how you get there."

Then in 2011 Grant was given the opportunity to be on an Antarctic expedition in which he and two others would travel a hundred miles across the ice to the South Pole. Grant could only use his arms. There were days when they would only go three miles in several hours. Grant had no feeling in his feet and they had to keep them warm with battery packs. They made it to the South Pole!

Fortunately, most of us will not have to go through such a harrowing life experience. However, we each have our demons and dragons to slay. They may not have below zero conditions and extreme physical conditions but they may test us to our limits. It was encouraging to see folks who never quit, no matter what life hands them. It was inspiring for many of us tonight. For me, it showed me that I can have my heart's desire if I just keep pushing on! From my inspired heart to yours, Thomas

As this couple showed us, we each can let go of our demons inside and move forward with determination and self-care! We can do it!

June 1   What Breaks Your Heart?

We had another wonderful day of conscious cinema at the Illuminate film festival. The films were excellent and the filmmakers shared in question and answer sessions as well as reel healings. We had a program of conscious short films this morning.

The first was Black Star which is a movie about the premature deaths of many entertainers. The filmmakers have formed a healing consortium of different facets to help artists with addictions. The second was Vision: Seeing is believing, about a legally blind artist who has awesome talent and even more persistence. The third was about a fabulous fiddler/singer who has worked through physical handicaps using mindfulness.

Tonight we watched the inspiring movie, Live Your Quest. Then we were treated to a healing discussion with Tom Chi. He is a brilliant scientist and futurist. He said one way of approaching our current planetary dilemmas is to ask "What Breaks Your Heart"?

Mine are: the disappearing rain forest and ocean coral. He said when he was born forty years ago the coral was at one hundred per cent and now it is at forty per cent. Others on my list, is the world's poverty level, with most inhabitants living on a dollar a day. Then there is climate change and disappearance of the polar ice cap. Next is the slaughter of innocent animals both for sport and for food. The world's water ways are polluted. Five hundred million straws are thrown away each day and they are filling up the oceans and harming ocean life; the opioid crises here in the United States. There is our continued dependence on fossil fuels and stubborn resistance to using green energy like wind and solar and geothermal.

Let us all think about what breaks our hearts and get involved and create the most beautiful Earth possible for all of its inhabitants; even if we all take the smallest steps in our own homes or communities. This will be our quest! That we cared enough to heal our fragile spacecraft for all generations to come! From my concerned heart to yours, Thomas

Find ways to help others, one step at a time, even if it is your next door neighbor!

June 2   Instant Karma

When I attended the Black Star movie yesterday; I shared that I had found their movie while sourcing for this year's festival. It brought tears to my eyes and sadness to my heart to see so many young lives cut short by addiction. When the movie was over, the director and producer met me on the red carpet and had pictures taken with me. Then they gave me an original Black Star piece of art work as a gift. I was overwhelmed with gratitude.

Also when I met the visual artist for Black Star, Jim Hansel, I shared with him that my daughter and youngest son both had Stargardt disease. This is an eye affliction that blocks the pupil and you can only see peripherally. You are legally blind. Then Jim gave me his business card and said that the Mayo Clinic was having experiential trials of some new kind of medicine that would slow down the progress of the disease. Now I can share this information with my children.

So my efforts of finding films for our festival created meeting three loving, giving men who shared with me. It seems to work this way a lot. When we simply take actions from a prosperous and loving place inside us, Universe responds. From my very grateful heart to yours, Thomas

Who knows what your kind actions can create?! Amazing results happen when we come from our hearts!!

June 3   Notes from the Edge of Paradise

Another full day filled with incredible experiences to fill my soul. I started the day moderating a film and a discussion afterwards. The movie is titled The Edge of Paradise. It is a poignant story about a group of young people who gathered on the island of Kauai and lived there from 1969 to 1977.

First there were thirteen hippies living on the beach that got thrown in jail for just hanging out naked. The brother of Elizabeth Taylor, Howard Taylor bailed them out and let them live on his seven acres just up the coast. They named it Camp Taylor. Soon many others gathered there. Some were soldiers that had fought in Viet Nam. Most were just young people who were tired of the war and the toxic world we were creating.

They were unclothed most of the time and lived in tree houses and enjoyed their new found freedom. They formed families, had babies and created community. The film was touching in a lot of ways. They wanted to live somewhere where it was safe and they could be themselves.

The contrast between the graphic pictures of that horrible war and the love and caring they found made me weep. I cried for all the young men who had lost their lives, cut short by a war that should never have occurred. I cried tears of joy for those who found their paradise. They were my tribe. The local people eventually became jealous of the Taylor campers and created laws to force them out. The filmmaker interviewed many of the former campers and most of them said it was the greatest time of their lives.

Later in the day, the director gave me a huge coffee table book titled Camp Taylor with all the pictures from the movie. He knew that I had something to do with getting this movie in our festival and wanted to thank me. I cried again for his kindness. From my very blessed heart to yours, Thomas

Live this life from a place of constant wonder!

June 4   I Am the Sky

Today I moderated at a film, titled The Way Home. The title is referring to all of us souls on Earth, remembering Who We Are! It means that we have often been unaware of our true nature. The movie is about the life of a spiritual guru named Mooji. He is self-realized! He knows that he is the Eternal Presence. That he has awakened to his Divinity.

Mooji is from a long line of spiritual men and women who have taught about reconnecting with our essence. He does this by sitting in Satsang. The meaning of *Satsang* is 'company of the Absolute Truth' where 'Sat' *means* the Absolute Truth i.e. God and 'sang' refers to the company of seekers or Saints.

The movie shows the wide variety of gifts that Mooji has. He is also an artist who paints, sculpts, does woodwork and cooks. However it is in Satsang that we greet the Mooji that shines even brighter. The Satsang is a quiet meditative event. Attendees gather and sit quietly awaiting the guru. When they enter, they usually sit in a chair and meditate as well. Then in a few moments, they awaken and begin speaking softly about the Nature of God or Spirit.

The energy in the room becomes even more peaceful. When the guru looks at me, I feel loved, cared for, and complete. There is nothing missing in my life at that moment. Whatever concerns or cares that I brought into the room have melted away and I am in bliss. The words that are shared are immediately recognized as true to me. I feel at one with everyone and everything.

Mooji shares an analogy. Our essence is like the sky. The sky is always the same. The clouds that drift by are like our thoughts. They float on by. Sometimes they get angry and filled with thunder and lightning and can be destructive. But the sky remains the same above those clouds.

Mooji teaches us how to access that part of our being, beyond our thoughts. This place is always the same, has no limitations, doesn't age, has no gender like male or female, has no dimensions, and has no personality. It is One, always has been, always will be.

Sitting in Satsang is a unique experience. Unlike any other that I have experienced. I still feel peaceful about this morning's session. Something has shifted. My Center is still the same. My outer is discovering The Way Home! From my blissful heart to yours, Thomas

Be like the sky today and let the angry or uncomfortable thoughts float by like clouds! Be who you really are, grounded in light and love!

June 5 Stay Human

Michael Franti rocked the house last night at the Sedona Performing Arts Center, here in Sedona. It was the swan song to this year's festival. I did not know who Michael Franti was. However, our daughter Uma has been singing one of his songs for quite a while titled *Say Hey*.

Michael Franti just made a movie titled *Stay Human*. It tells the story of an amazing midwife, Robin Lim who is in the Philippines. When babies are born she leaves the umbilicus attached for quite a while, so that the new born feels a continued connection with the mom. She believes that when we immediately sever the umbilical cord there is a trauma that stays with us through our life in some way. She believes that the world would be a more peaceful place if we nurtured infants in this way. CNN nominated her for their hero of the year award in 2009.

Then Franti discovered Arief Rabik who is a sustainable bamboo farmer. The founder of Indobamboo, Arief, is a second generation bamboo specialist, following in the footsteps of his mother Linda Garland, who founded the Environmental Bamboo Foundation.

Linda is well-regarded for putting in place the ground work that made many giant leaps possible for industrialists, designers and scientists focused on bamboo, helping push the international development in bamboo industry.

Arief is an environmental scientist in his own right with over 15 years of experience in bamboo forest management and production. They are saving lots of forests by harvesting fast growing bamboo.

Then in another film segment, Michael met Steve and Hope Dezember of Atlanta. It didn't take long for Hope to fall for her now-husband, Steve. "He charmed my socks off on our first date. He had candles lit, he had Frank Sinatra playing and he cooked crab legs," she tells People Magazine in August 2011, four months after their first date, the former engineering recruiter, then 28, was diagnosed with ALS. Steve proposed to Hope two days later. Steve is still going as of this writing and his wife Hope has dedicated her life to his wellness and care. Find out more about his work and their story on their website hopeforsteve.com

Michael Franti is a beautiful soul with a mission; to help folks in need all over the world. These stories are some of the amazing experiences in his life. If you get a chance, watch his film, Stay Human! You can find his film on YouTube: https://www.youtube.com/watch?v=0fRv2waokzo His music is penetrating and upbeat. He captured the hearts of the large crowd here in Sedona with his music and giant heart! Let us all stay human together and help everyone who needs us! From my hopeful heart to yours, Thomas

Use your gifts today to help others, even the love inside you!

June 6   Grateful

Life is so sweet and I am so thankful for all of the gifts I have been given in so many ways. I was chosen to be in the Illuminate Film Festival Film Lab following the festival.

There are fourteen of us gathered here for three full days. We are learning what it means to create, produce and market a movie or some other visual presentation. Paola and Peter are our inspirational leaders. Not only are they successful filmmakers, they are deeply spiritual and loving. We gather together and do some Kundalini Yoga and they use a Tibetan bowl to bring us in focus. They have lots of experience in creating conscious cinema. We are learning what it takes to be mentally and spiritually prepared to create our projects.

Twenty years ago, we created The Positive Place Talk Show for television. The program was about the wonderful things that were occurring all over the planet. There are countless people around the globe reducing climate change, saving the rain forest, saving endangered animals and many other worthy causes. These folks are our modern day heroes. They work tirelessly for the good of all.

Our talk show's mission is to show these incredible stories of service and courage. I presented my updated version of the talk show and it got a wonderful response from the lab facilitators and a successful documentary director who said he wants to help create my show.

I am scared, thrilled and humbled at the opportunity, to once again renew my dream and produce a television program that will make a difference to all of our planets' inhabitants. Wish us luck! Of course Lou Ann will be right there with me, as we live our dream together. From my very grateful heart to yours, Thomas

Be peaceful inside as you go throughout your day and let your light shine!

June 7   Out into the World

Our Illuminate film lab is over. The attendees, most of them filmmakers, have wonderful narrative and documentary movies that they are making. It is conscious cinema. They are making statements about the current status of our planet. There are billions of people and animals suffering from hunger, wars, poverty, climate change and disease. We in the affluent West are among the wealthiest in the entire world. There is plenty of food and abundance for each human. And yet we are faced with a world of unparalleled pain and anguish.

Who will answer the call? These filmmakers that I have had the honor to learn with will be the storytellers that perhaps will make a difference.

Our creation of Heaven on Earth will not be created from the top down. It will be all of us who are working two jobs or retired on social security, barely making ends meet, sometimes. This is a revolution of those in the trenches of life, gathering their hearts, their souls and their spirits to build a new planet. I am inviting all of you who read this, to get involved. Volunteer wherever you are able. Donate your time, energy and money to the cause that breaks your heart.

In the resurrection of our television show, we will begin in our local city of Sedona and the surrounding Verde Valley. We need help filming shows with technicians and creatives that can lend a hand. We will need stories with inspiring themes. I am sure there are folks all over the area who are doing good works. Their story can make a difference and encourage others to get involved.

Please call or text me at 808 557-8830 or private message me on Facebook. Whatever way you can support the mission, please let me know. Lou Ann and I cannot do this alone. We will need all the love and support possible. Our future generation's lives depend on it! From my very committed heart to yours, Thomas

You can make a difference today, even showing kindness and caring with someone you work with or your children. There are endless possibilities!

June 8   Fruits of Our Labors

We were watching an old demo tape of the Positive Place Television Talk Show from 1997 with a filmmaker, who may help us make our show. We filmed three segments back then. The first was right here in Sedona with the marvelous musician and singer Carl Anthony. He led a group of children singing songs about loving themselves.

The second segment was filmed at the Best Friends Animal Sanctuary in Kanab Utah. Their facility had rescued 1500 animals from all over the world. Lou Ann did a wonderful segment, celebrating the animals. At the time, Best Friends rescued any animal that was homeless or needed care and love.

The third segment was an interview with Larry Tucker, who was nominated for four academy awards for his work on Bob, Ted, Carol and Alice. He and his wife Marilyn were madly in love and Larry was bedridden at the time we interviewed them. He said his definition of true love was when the reality of the relationship was better than the fantasy!

I read a Facebook post of a local young woman who is moving into her own apartment with her toddler. She has no furniture or any household goods of any kind. Within a short period of time a couple of dozen people responded on line. They were giving them a dinette set, a bed, clothing, food, pots and pans, silverware and practically everything they would need to set up a home. I had tears in my eyes and was thrilled how kind folks will step up when others are in need.

We do have good hearts that really shine when it counts! I also realized, that this would be the kind of a feel good story that our new TV show would feature. Life never fails to surprise and amaze me! I invite you to share inspiring stories with us that you know and perhaps we can put them on our show in the future! From my wide open heart to yours, Thomas

Send us a story of someone you know where you live, who is making a difference in others' lives. If you don't know anyone, who is, become that person!

June 9   Universal principle #11: Purpose

"The Universe's purpose for each of us is to direct us to Oneness. When we align our individual purpose, what we love to do (our talent), with the Universe's purpose, the flow of Divine Power fills what we love to do with passion. This prepares the way for achieving fulfillment in career and relationships."

Most of us are not doing what we love to do. Many of us have gifts and talents that are not being used. We choose to get employment and earn money to meet our obligations. We seldom find the juice that fills our heart with passion for doing what we love. The world needs your passion for your magnificent expression more than ever!

The other night I had this dream in which I was encouraged to sing. When I began, an enormous amount of energy was available. A stream of powerful light flowed through me and I was able to sing as loud as I chose and as long as I chose without taking a breath. It felt like it could go on forever. I was amazed, as were others around me who heard me singing.

I awakened and was so excited! Then these thoughts came to me: life has always been about love. There are no them, only us. Let us all be for all of us. We are the human race; we are not in a race. Slow down. We are limitless beings. We are one. Focus on the love. Bring all of your love to everything you do. Stay present without judging. Now is the time–this is the time we have all agreed to come together and shine our light. There is no darkness, everything is light and love...that is all there is.

All infinite beings throughout creation are invited to join us now in bringing forth the truth of our unlimited love, prosperity and joy. We are here to serve in any way we can. Thank you for everything—-I love you! From my heart to yours, Thomas

Slow down today as often as you can and recognize the love inside you and in all!

June 10   It's In Everyone One of Us

In 1975 David Pomeranz wrote this wonderful song:

It's in every one of us
To be wise
Find your heart
Open up both your eyes
We can all know everything
Without ever knowing why
It's in every one of us
By and by It's in every one of us
To be wise

Find your heart
Open up both your eyes
We can all know everything
Without ever knowing how
It's in every one of us
Here and now
It's in every one of us
I just remembered
It's like I've been sleepin' forty years
I'm not awake as I can be
But my seein's better
I can see, through the tears
I've been realisin' bad
I bought this ticket
And watching only half of the show
But there is scenery and lights
And a cast of thousands
You all know (you all know) what I know (what I know)
And it's good
That it's so

To hear this wonderful song go to:
https://www.youtube.com/watch?v=xd1QnNBZQ2A

The lyrics say find your heart. They don't say find your mind. He encourages us to open up both our eyes. That means to me, not to ignore what is going on in our world. And it is time to wake up. It is like we have been sleeping for years, more like centuries. Our wisdom and good is not just in some of us. It is in everyone one of us. Some are in such pain that they have hidden wisdom and love and they have not awakened. It is up to us who have begun to awaken to the goodness of life to celebrate and share our wisdom. From my awakening heart to yours, Thomas

Place one or both of your hands on your heart and know it is in every one of us – notice with each breath – wake up to the truth inside you!

June 11   The Show Must Go On!

In the Illuminate film lab there was a man named Larry Rosenberg. He is a delightful, articulate, entertaining and loving being. He has a gift of making up songs in the moment about whatever we might be saying. He is two years younger than me and three years older than Lou Ann. They are both on the cusp of the baby boomer generation. Larry has created a musical show, titled The Larry Show. He had us over to his home tonight and he is also a gracious host and wonderful cook, a man of inexhaustible talents!

His show is about his life. He blends many famous tunes and dance into the fabric of the story. It is a happy, joyful, sad and endearing tale of a person who transcended his environment and early life. He has risen to the top of several career paths. However, he has found his treasure in telling his life story. And he has a message for all of us who are of the same generation or even older. It is never too late! Never too late, to find the spark that lights up our eyes, quickens our pulse and brings joy to ourselves and others.

I am encouraging any and all of you to find your song, your story, your passion, your joie de vivre! We are not all musically talented like Larry. However, there may be some of us who have left behind a dream. We are retired or just tired. We have a story to tell that is uniquely ours.

Take a moment and think about what might give us a renewed joy of life. It may be something from decades ago that is still simmering on life's back burner. It may be time to turn up the heat and let it cook!

Please join us happy septuagenarians and let your freak flag fly! Meaning, don't judge that hidden gem of expression that you have been holding back! The world needs it! You may need it! From my ever expanding heart to yours, Thomas

Let your gift out and share it – begin today with tiny steps to create it!

June 12   Phone Home

Thirty six years ago E.T. was released today. It was a transcendent film for many of us. So many films from the 1977 Star Wars the Lost Hope, to Close Encounters of the Third Kind (November 16, 1977) and Raiders of the Lost Ark (June 12, 1981) stimulated our imaginations. Even Superman with Christopher Reeves in December 1978. It was a magical time for movie goers of all ages.

Of course we are all E.T.'s, the Earth is not our real home. We have been traveling here for many lifetimes. The challenge, when we get here, is to turn on our heart light and keep it glowing. We sometimes hide our lights under our fear. When the light goes out, we lose our way. Remember that our greatest fear is how bright our light is! Not how much darkness is in us. Remember some of the words in the Neal Diamond song: *Turn on your heart light; let it shine wherever you go let it make a happy glow for the entire world to see.*

Let us be planetary citizens who take care of this fragile Earth space craft. There may be millions of planets like Earth in the cosmos. We may someday visit many of them. Right now, this is our temporary place of travel. Each of us can assist one another, in discovering our light inside. We can love each other so much, that we can be seen all over the galaxies!

I would encourage all of us to re-watch those wonderful movies of four decades ago and discover an innocence of heart in their making and design. When we do, we may get reconnected to our purpose for coming here again. And don't forget to follow the trail of Reese's pieces home. From my extra-terrestrial heart to yours, Thomas

BE the light that is shining in and from your heart in all directions!

June 13   Love is in the heart of the observer

There is an old saying that "Beauty is in the eye of the beholder." Margaret Wolfe Hungerford is said to have first coined the phrase. This is to say, what we see, feel or think, is our personal perspective.

Somehow, we humans have come to an agreement that beauty should look a certain way. Billions of dollars are spent each year attempting to keep our physical youth. Wrinkles are to be dreaded. Gray is to be colored, black, brown, blonde or red. Slim is to be preferred over heavy. We hitch up our pants, tuck in our shirt, straighten our blouse or tie. To be neat is ranked higher than not so. I am not here to say, which is preferable.

I was looking in the mirror a while ago and saw all the wrinkles of too many years in the sun. I have always loved wrinkles. The actor James

Whitmore had one of my most favorite faces. His heavily lined face told so many stories. Perhaps we could see wrinkles as a badge of honor; images of a life well lived, rather than always trying to hide them.

I just took a nap and came back with this thought. Sometimes I look in the mirror and think "I am getting old looking". Wrinkles are also a sign of aging. We may associate wrinkles with the end of our life. So there may be a built in fear of these creases, being the sign of our demise. However, we could also look at our crevices and say "wow"!

Our face is a symbol of the journey of our life. A snapshot, perhaps of all the adventures we have taken along the way. I would rather have us focus our minds and hearts on our inner beauty.

Let us celebrate the beauty of our life's pathway, and look in the mirror and say "Thank you" for every moment! We all have ESP, extra sensory perception. I also believe we have, Eternal Spiritual Perspective. Our souls see through our blemishes, scars, brokenness, only to see the real beauty, from my observing heart to yours, Thomas

Observe today your eternal and internal youth of your soul!

June 14 We were born to love

We are all so blessed to have so much information at our fingertips on how to live a loving, transformative life. I have been reading Tom Shadyac's book *Life's Operating Manual* lately. He shares that Charles Darwin used the term survival of the fittest twice in *The Descent of Man* but used the word love ninety five times. It is interesting that most scholars focus on the reference, of survival of the fittest, rather than our love for each other.

Darwin went on to say that human kind's ability to cooperate and sympathize has allowed us to adapt and become the most prolific species on the planet. Then, Shadyac also shares that Jeremy Rifkin, in his book *The Empathic Civilization*, chronicles our history from a very different perspective. We are not a species wired for violence, aggression and war. We are a species that is wired for love, kindness and compassion.

Rifkin points out that when we see the airwaves filled with war, violence and crime that they are the exception, not the norm. If we watch the news too much, we assume that what is reported is occurring the most. It is actually the opposite. The news does not report, every door that is opened, every thank you shared, every kindness observed. The amount of goodness and love is almost incalculable, like grains of sand. Right now, as I share this, there could be millions of wonderful exchanges of loving acts happening!

This is why I have been writing for nearly a year. I want all of us to focus on and celebrate the magnificence of the human spirit. And this is also why a group of us are gathering tomorrow night in our home, to brainstorm about creating a television show that does just that. From my excited heart to yours, Thomas

Today be empathetic whenever you can! Love is everywhere!

June 15   Dream your biggest dream!

Six of us gathered at our home tonight and brainstormed about the possibility of creating the Positive Place Talk Show. We were led by Nick Conedera the director of the inspiring Miracle Morning movie. Here is a link to this film either on Amazon Prime Video or Vimeo on demand: https://miraclemorning.com/movie/

He showed us a system called Appreciative Inquiry. It has four phases or elements. They are discovery, dream, design and destiny.

We all looked at our relationship in the past with media and cinema through journaling. Then we dared to dream of the fruition of our labors and involvement. Then we used sticky notes to design the show in four segments, including funding, content, production and distribution. It was three hours of exciting contributions by all of us. The destiny part will come later.

In the dream phase of the brainstorming, here is what I wrote. 'On the February 2028 cover of Time Magazine was a large red heart. Here is the story. *The Positive Place Television Show has changed television in an amazing way. Ten years ago, six people met in an old house on the outskirts of the city of Sedona Arizona and dared to dream. Their mission was to help the world be a place of love, compassion, caring and abundance for all.*

This is where the Positive Place became a transcendent program. They donate every dollar of net profits to sustainable organizations all over the world. They fund climate change, clean water for families in third world countries. They have created their own non-profit centers to help eliminate poverty. They have partnered with other philanthropic organizations to fund inner sustainability. Inner sustainability is helping people get healed in their personal lives.

When folks are healthy, mentally, physically and financially, they make choices that create outer sustainability. They recycle, use alternative fuel, become carbon free, and eat a life sustaining way and shop sustainably.

The Positive Place has put the love of all beings in its mission. And it has put the heart back into show business. We honor them with the Time Magazine most influential award of the year!'

I encourage all who read this to find a project that will have you dream. Even if this show does not unfold like we want it to; it creates energy for other souls on the planet to get involved in making a difference. When any one of us takes a stand for the good of all, positive change happens sometimes in miraculous ways. From my dreaming heart to yours, Thomas

Feel the joy of creating your dream today as you visualize it as if it has already occurred!

June 16   If

Lou Ann just called me about a meeting she went to with many other women who are using their power in wonderful and supporting ways. She was so enthusiastic about it! Then later I thought, that's the way she is about most everything in life. She brings so much excitement to even inconsequential events that they take on more meaning in our lives.

The other day I was feeling kind of low. Nothing in particular, just tired. I recalled the lyrics from one of my favorite songs titled, If. Here are the lyrics by David Gates of the musical group Bread In a YouTube link:
https://www.youtube.com/watch?v=5a_4fBH_7dk

The line in the song was how I was feeling the other day: "And when my love for life is running dry, you come and pour yourself on me." This is how Lou Ann's enthusiasm for life appears for me. She pours herself on me and I get renewed.

Let us find ways to pour ourselves on each other so that our love for life won't get too low. We can be each other's Gunga Din! From my filled up heart to yours, Thomas

If we each knew how precious we each are today and every day!

June 17   Universal principle #12: Comfort and Discomfort

"Our bodies are magnificent instruments that we create to support us in having the experiences we come here to have. Our bodies are created and maintained in consciousness. They mirror the state of our consciousness, beliefs in how to look, act, age and die. Unencumbered by beliefs, our consciousness is unlimited. The natural state of our consciousness is perfect ease, as is the natural state of our bodies. The beliefs we have about our bodies are there to love and embrace just the way they are. The resulting expansion of consciousness shifts the bodies' state from that of un-ease to ease."

We don't live long enough. We have the ability to live longer, healthier more productive lives. We eat foods that don't support our health. We think thoughts that keep us impaired. We don't exercise enough. We work sedentary jobs. Those are all a recipe for a shorter, less healthy, less joyful life. Then there is stress. Stress causes almost all illness on some level.

How can we de-stress? Begin by assessing where you are right now in terms of what you want to create in your lifetime. Find people to love and spend more time with them. Find a vocation that gives you passion.

Get up out of the chair and walk at least three times per week for at least a half an hour. Do Yoga. When your spine is flexible it will add years to your life and life to your years. Learn to meditate. Volunteer your time.

Eat a mostly whole food plant based diet. Make a grateful list and add to it every day and re-read it daily. Thank all of the people in your life that are doing something for you.

Ask your food server, hostess, attendant, check out person their name and let them know how much you appreciate them. Rescue a pet. Get out into nature and spend time in a quiet setting.   Write your memoir. Travel to other cultures. Become an activist for the planet or a cause you love. This may be the only life you live. Live every moment as if it were your last. From my heart to yours, Thomas

Be in a natural state of ease! Breathe in and out and relax your shoulders! Ahhhh!

June 18   Fathers

My dad was addicted to alcohol before I was born. When he was sober, he was a decent man. He was in so much emotional pain, he was hardly ever sober. He drank himself to an early death. Here is the irony.

When I was a teenager and I was asked what I wanted to be when I grew up. I replied "I want to be a father", not a baseball player, astronaut, president or movie star, a father! When my first wife was pregnant with our four children to be; I knew who they were, before they were born. We didn't even have any alternative names.

I adored my children while they were growing up. Alas, I made choices that had me leave them when they were quite young. I often ask myself what is the difference between an alcoholic father and a father that leaves? My heart says, not much. The deepest pain that I still carry today is not being with my children as they grew up. I could share with you the reasons of my heart, as to why I made the choice. However, I will not.

Two of my sons have grown up to be excellent fathers. I am proud of them. My third son has never chosen to experience fatherhood. My daughter is a wonderful Mom and so is my step daughter! So, on Father's day, I am often sad. Three of my children and my step daughter do call and wish me happy father's day. I am thankful for that. I always want this post to be an uplifting one. I will leave you with this.

Parents always do the best they can do. My dad and I were suffering inside in a way that didn't support the ones we love. I hope that many of you have paternal parenting that has helped you become the wonderful persons that you are. I will close, in saying to my dad:"I hope that you are experiencing total love and joy and freedom wherever in the Universe you are! From my tender heart to yours, Thomas

Life has sad parts to it. Choose focusing on the happy parts when you can! It's all part of the fabric of our lives.

June 19   Ye Olde Sayings

Lou Ann loves to have her back scratched. Last night after doing that for her, I thought of the saying "I'll scratch your back if you will scratch mine." It is nearly impossible to scratch one's own back. So when we make the agreement to exchange back scratches, we are doing something for someone they cannot do themselves. That feels like a very loving thing to do for each other.

Then I was lying there in bed and other old sayings began to pop in my head. "Do unto others as they would do unto you!" This is the essence of the Golden Rule. I guess we gave it the name golden, to show that it is of the highest value. It really is a wonderful way to go through life. When making a decision, we consider all the ramifications of that decision upon others.

"There's a bridge between your heart and your mind!" This is a line from the theme song of The Positive Place Television Talk Show. A former mentor used to say: "The mind is a wonderful thing, waste it!" He was being sarcastic to make a point. He teaches a course called Radical Honesty. In the eight day seminar he encourages folks to begin noticing. Then, not analyzing what we notice. He invites us to get in touch with our feelings. And to see how what we notice, affects us.

We humans are meaning making machines. We attempt to put a meaning about almost every life event. When we do that, we often get stuck in our minds and judgments. Then it is difficult to allow ourselves to open up to a new paradigm.

Back to the bridge between our hearts and minds; it is when we make the eighteen inch journey from our thoughts to our feelings that we discover the magic of living. Here are more lyrics from the above theme song. *"Look inside yourself and you'll find, there's a bridge between your heart and your mind. There's a positive, there's a positive place."*

I encourage you folks to make that journey from your mind to your heart. When you do it often, it will change your life in marvelous ways. From my positive heart to yours, Thomas

There is magic in the air when we travel from our minds to our hearts!

June 20   Universe did it again!

Today, I thought Lou Ann and I were just going to have lunch with three other friends. We met Ranjita, Gloria and Devin at the Indian Gardens. However, there was magic to occur! When we went to Ranjita's house, gathered in a circle, and through her leadership, began to support each other in creating our dreams.

We began by focusing on what might be blocking us. I shared that often in my past, I have created a variety of ways in which I get "too busy" and my desires remained unfulfilled. Then Devin looked at me with his eyes completely focused on mine. I will say in my words what he shared. "There is nothing that can stop you from creating what you desire. You are Oneness expressing itself through you. You have no limitations. You are completely loved!"

I was stunned. It was the same kind of feeling I had experienced a year ago when I was encouraged to begin writing. Something was different when he spoke with me. I knew that I was an unlimited being at a deeper level, than I had ever felt before. We embraced. I felt unconditionally loved by All That Is!

Once again, Beautiful Oneness created an amazing day filled with love, connection, compassion and clarity. My wish for all of you is to continue to say yes to Life and see what happens! From my ever thankful heart to yours, Thomas

Each of us is Oneness expressing itself! Really breathe that one in!!

June 21   The Nature of Our Being

Yesterday I mentioned that Lou Ann and I were with Devin. His full name is Devin Mikles. He is a gorgeous soul. He has been a practicing medical doctor for some thirty four years. Until yesterday, I did not know the extent of his awareness and deep spiritual knowledge.   He channels or writes poetry that I would like to share with you. Here is the first.

The Rebirthday Room

In every moment we die and are reborn into the void from

A nothingness that is the fecund, all pervading

Indivisible, preexisting, always perfected emptiness,

That is undeniably complete and total love-bliss consciousness.

Only in the room of the Divine Heart of this constantly appearing,

Revealed true nature of eternal, infinite, immutable happiness,

Can we find a refuge authentic enough to shed the hard

A skin of the ego's I, and make the translation to the truly real.

Let us embrace the icy fingers of the valley of separate death

That we may be reanimated beyond the shadow of seeking, fear and longing

Into the bright heart of devotion, compassion and endless

Forever now in recognition of our One and True Reality.

May we always know the Beloved on sight fully in every

Human, hill, animal, plant and stone, forsaking all illusions.

And may the peace that passes beyond our understanding

Be the walking path of our Sadhana reaching ever to the Star of Isness.

Peace.

Please read this more than once to get the full depth of this wonderful sharing. His poetry book is now published! It is New Horizons by Devin Alaric Mikles

We are a vital part of the Oneness of everything. We are not separate in any way. We have all-knowing in our soul. It is time for us to reclaim our awareness of our Divinity.   If we stop and take the time to realize that everyone and everything in Universe is the same, it can give us peace. We can perhaps relax and move through life with a different way of being. No more hectic exploration. No more fearing death. We can breathe into our present moment and let our Divine connection, lead us through this incarnation. Welcome to planet Earth beautiful beings of light and love. Enjoy the ride! From my eternal heart to yours, Thomas

Reclaim the awareness of Divinity in you!!

June 22   Solstice

We folks in the northern hemisphere refer to this time of year (June 20-22) to be the summer solstice. It is when the Earth reaches 23.5 degrees in the Zodiac sign of Cancer. In the southern hemisphere this occurs six months later when we experience our winter solstice in the north. The word solstice comes from Latin meaning sun stoppage. The Earth is tilted on its axis and as it makes this rotation around the sun in an elliptical orbit, it appears to stand still at the summer and winter solstice point.

So this may be a time for us to take a small break and shift our focus a little. While the Earth appears to rest, it might be advisable for its inhabitants to take a deep breath and relax. Our culture appears to be driven. We feel like we are going to run out of time. Perhaps there is an internal clock prodding us to do as much as we can in the span of a lifetime. However, there is also an eternal clock that is not ticking. It has never kept time and has no hands to go around its face, like our timepieces. It sits at zero and will remain there.

However, back on Terra firma; we can take this time to be grateful for the sun in our solar system. It gives everything life in the physical form. It is about 4.6 billion years old and will be in the same form for some five billion more years. Enough time for you and I to get in a bunch of incarnations. The sun is like our souls. It breathes life and light into every particle on Earth. Our soul breathes spirit into our physical being and makes it a glorious life experience.

It might be an excellent time to give thanks to the sol and the soul. They are who we are in spirit and in form. Each day we can remind ourselves of our connection to light. It is who we are. Happy summer solstice to everyone and everything. May we go into the next phase of this year with a peaceful heart filled with the gratitude of shining our light so that all creatures of Earth know they are loved! From my shining heart to yours, Thomas

Be aware of your soul and the glorious experiences you are having!

June 23   Staying Young

We usually have popcorn on Friday night at home, while we watch Real Time. We are working on creating the next phase in our life. We are involved in several projects including the possibility of creating a TV show. It feels completely normal to be creating it; like we have been preparing for it, a long time. We are working on permaculturing our land around our home. This is planting a variety of organic fruits, vegetables, herbs and spices in the way nature would do it. And we have lots of vacation rental guests coming to our home. Life is busy and sweet.

We probably will never retire in the classic sense. We love being involved and making a difference when and where we can. The irony may be that Lou Ann is 75 and I am 80 and it feels like we are just starting out on our life adventure! I am sharing this, only to say, if you are a baby boomer or older like me, life is not over by any means.

Sedona is filled with septuagenarians and older, who are living passionate, committed lives of consequence. My wish is for everyone to awake in the morning with a sense of purpose and a feeling of being young at heart.

Most of us do not know how long this particular life journey will last. Please make the most of it for yourself and for all the creatures on spaceship Earth who need your love, talent, experience and energy! From my young heart to yours, Thomas

Be young at heart on spaceship earth no matter what your age!

June 24   Thank you God!

Yesterday I was playing tennis in a men's doubles match. One of the opposing players hit a winning shot and exclaimed "Thank God". It occurred to me that I have never heard him say "Thank God" when missing a shot. It is easy to thank higher powers when we are winning at life. Not so much when things are going the other way.

We are eternal particles of God's energy and we are creating everything. We get to take the credit for hitting or missing our goals and dreams. Tennis feels easy when a player is in the flow. We seem to hit most shots well and find an empty space or the opponent doesn't return the shot. It is usually not that easy in other parts of our soul's journey

In life, there are so many factors that go into each experience; our mood, our health, our environment, our ancestry, our upbringing, our mind, our judgments and our feelings to list a few. I think it is helpful to thank God for every life experience. Whether it is what we may have intended or not. Of course when we are in the middle of a tragedy, it is hardly ever easy to see the good or sometimes the God.

It has been my life experience that often those events that I felt the least thankful for when they occurred, turn out to be the most profound. Most life events don't have life and death outcomes however. We make choices and the results we create can be celebrated because we are Divine and we are part of All That Is and that makes them sacred. Whether we like the outcome or not. To be alive and awake to know we are spiritual beings is enough to say "Thank God" From my thankful heart to yours, Thomas

Know you are a part of All That Is – the Divine!

June 25   Magic

Lou Ann and I were watching *Fantastic Beasts and Where to Find Them.* It is another J. K. Rowling rollicking, fun adventure. One of the main characters is called No-Maj., meaning he doesn't do magic. In the wizarding world, in the Harry Potter books, they were called Muggles.

It reminds me that all of us have some of these qualities in us. There are definitely times when I feel like a No-Maj and things are an effort to accomplish. And then there are times when it almost feels like I could cast a spell and make my dreams come true. Far fewer of those, so far for me.

Then I recall, many years ago, I learned how to do personal treasure mapping. We would gather up all sorts of pictures, written articles, symbols and put them on a white poster board to create our life dreams. It was fun going through all the material and create a gorgeous display that was often hidden in my heart. Just the act of placing them on a board in living color, gave me a lift. Then life would get in the way, meaning me! I would stash them away in some closet out of sight.

Then we would clean out that closet or get ready to move and discover it hidden, rolled up and dusty. Then the magic part of us would appear. When we opened them up and flattened them out, we would cheer! So many of the things we desired to do had manifested, not all but a lot! Then I would realize that some part of me was working on my life almost like magic. A part of me that was a wizard at doing what my soul intended was smiling.

If you have not done treasure mapping; I urge you to do so. There is enough "No-Majing" going around. Let us discover the amazing talents and gifts we keep hidden and create magnificent lives! From my magic heart to yours, Thomas

Treasure mapping is fun and magic – try it!

June 26   Ebb and Flow

Sometimes I sit in front of this screen and wonder what to share. Sometimes I sit for a long time. I believe I have told you, that I try to never say the same thing in exactly the same way. I am not sure why? I get bored hearing the same thing. I am writing to myself along with you. You probably have more patience than I? Right now, it is ebb time. Mostly, it is flow time.

I know that I share the same subjects. It is when my mind gets in the way that there is less flow and more ebb. I am writing like Julia Cameron suggested many years ago in her wonderful book *The Artist Way*. I am writing whatever comes to mind without being focused on a particular subject, except the movement of the tides, I referred to earlier. I am now pausing and allowing my inner self to share.

We are life expressing in a very unique way. No two things are completely alike. No two humans writing or reading understand them exactly the same way. I know that I love expressing my experience of what I know of Spirit, with you. I don't claim to be an expert or all knowledgeable. I am just another spark of Oneness reminding me and you of our incredible journey.

It is awesome that we have minds along with our souls to be able to think and to speak. I appreciate every one of you who take the time to be with me through these pages. There are a lot of things to do in today's world. I am honored that you choose to be here whenever you do.

When you find yourself kind of stuck like I am tonight, take a deep breath. Relax and let life come to you. Let that part of you that is timeless and all-knowing take the reins of your life. Surrender to your innate goodness and all will be well. From my flowing heart to yours, Thomas

Check out the spark (or sparkle) of Oneness on your journey!

June 27   Love the Life you're with!

A friend was sharing a story about her life. She was creating a way of living that felt natural and supportive. Then she said "Life got in the way." I have said the same thing and perhaps most of us have. We have this dream or idea and we get excited about it. Then we "have" to make a living. Then the passion often gets put on the back burner. And many times it never makes it to the front burner and gets completely forgotten.

Remember the song "*Love the One you're with*" by Stephen Stills? That song came to me, as my friend and I were talking. I said it feels like life has to be a certain way for us to be happy. What if we allowed Universe to take over our dream and we then love the life we have created.

I know sometimes our life creation doesn't feel so hot! However, even when we are stuck in a place that doesn't appear what we have intended. We can sometimes find a small bit of cheerfulness under the mess.

There is a wonderful article in the current July issue of Oprah. Molly Simms and thirty one other Oprah staffers attended a month long course on being happy. It was taught by a Yale Psychology professor, Laurie Santos. Santos taught this course in the spring of this year, titled Psychology and the Good Life. Twenty five per cent of the undergrads signed up for it! Making it the most popular in Yale's history! That is thrilling to think, that our young adults are not just focused on what they desire to achieve. They want to be happy as well!

If we can't have the life we think we want, let's love the life we have created. David Steindl-Rast said "It is not happiness that makes us grateful; it's gratefulness that makes us happy."

Let us take a moment each day, as we arise or when we are going to sleep are two good times, to make a gratitude list. There is a double gift we receive when doing this practice. We get to recall what actually occurred to bring us happiness and the immediate pleasure of reliving it again. So, if you can't be in the life you want, love the life you're with! From my happy heart to yours, Thomas

Take a moment right now to be grateful and love the life you are having!

June 28   It's A Wonderful Thing to Be Me

This is the title of a song that Lou Ann and I used to sing with the Canyon Singers here in Sedona. It was written by Don Besig and Marcy Henchen. Here is a delightful performance by a youth choir in 1980 and joined by some familiar characters that always help us to feel wonderful. This clip has two songs on it, the first half is the song I want you to enjoy!
https://www.youtube.com/watch?v=5QUkvDA7xY4

I have tears in my eyes as I remember singing this song with that wonderful group led so lovingly by Sandy Reid for some twenty five years. The words are universal for our lives and our time. There is so much stress and tension these days, if we watch TV or listen to the news. Lou Ann I were organizing a bunch of music and I found this song. The words immediately take me back to a time of my youth when I spent almost all day, outdoors.

I wish for all of you a new day coming, where you can wander through the meadows and the fields and connect with nature. Take a deep breath and sing this refrain: It's a wonderful thing to be me and to be free! From my nostalgic heart to yours, Thomas

Go out in nature if you can and feel its wonder!

June 29 Serendipity Once More

Earlier today, Lou Ann suggested to me to work on the business plan for our television show. I shared with her my concern for our personal cash flow and thought I should focus on that. She reminded me to follow my heart and Universe would take care of the details.

This afternoon, I was lying down thinking how to create more personal income so that Lou Ann and I could continue to do the wonderful conscious work we are honored to do. (I know, sometimes I don't listen very well!) As I browsed through the options in my mind, my phone rang. A wonderful lady named Hope called me and was thanking me for encouraging her to go to the complete Illuminate Film Festival four weeks ago.

She said she had driven up to the Performing arts center and had gone inside and purchased a couple of event tickets. When she went outside to get in her car, it was dead. She called a repair person. She came back inside and happened to speak to me while I was working at the Love and Support desk. She said I told her to attend the entire festival because it would serve her. She purchased an all access pass and went to the entire festival and it inspired her significantly. She went back outside to greet the repair person and the car started without repair! She is a filmmaker and met other filmmakers who will help her with her next film. She thanked me so much for encouraging her to go all the way!

I am smiling right now, because this kind of thing happens all the time when I get out of the way and just serve! Now I will spend some time tonight working on the TV show business plan and allow it to unfold as it desires to do. And Universe will handle the details of the rest of my life! From my very humbled heart to yours, Thomas

When we get out of our way, magic happens!

June 30   Signs

Well behaved women rarely make history.

Peace

Vegan

No GMO

Renewable Energy, Sustainable Peace.

Vegetarians make better lovers.

Think good thoughts, do good deeds!

Love animals, don't eat them!

Commit random acts of kindness and senseless acts of beauty.

We are all in this together.

Peace and love on our planet.

Zero emissions.

Respect

Coexist

Real men are kind to animals.

No fur.

Peace is possible.

Eat organic.

Those who make you believe absurdities, can make you commit atrocities!

What wisdom can you find, that is greater than kindness?

Lou Ann and I came out of the local Natural Grocery and this shiny new car was parked next to us. The signs above were all attached to it. It was a Tesla! Times are a changing'! From my sign loving heart to yours, Thomas

Pick one of the signs and embrace it fully today!

July 1   No Passing Zone

Lou Ann and I went to the "Families Belong Together" rally today in Flagstaff Arizona. I was driving up the highway and noticed a No Passing Zone sign, along the highway. That sign reminded me of how I used to drive. In the past, I was a fast driver. Not reckless or impolite but in a hurry. Last October, when we were traveling back east with a trailer hitched to the car, I slowed down to the speed limit. I did it to save on gas. I discovered that there were other benefits as well. I could relax! I didn't have to look around for police cars because I was no longer going ten miles over the speed limit. I also noticed the lack of tension inside me. I actually felt free!

I thought about this as a metaphor for life. How many of us are hurrying through this incarnation? After the rally, which I will share later, we went to the movies. We saw It's a wonderful Day in the Neighborhood. It's the life story of Mr. Fred Rogers. For more than thirty years beloved Mr. Rogers shared these concepts to millions of children:

"When I was a boy and I would see scary things in the news, my mother would say to me, "Look for the helpers. You will always find people who are helping."

Play is often talked about as if it were a relief from serious learning. But for children, play is serious learning. Play is really the work of childhood;

Knowing we can be loved exactly as we are, gives us all the best opportunity for growing into the healthiest of people"

I encourage you to see the movie. It is a rich documentary of an iconic man whose life was full of love for everyone. It felt to me that Mr. Rogers wasn't rushing through life like many of us do. He found a way to be his authentic self and settled in to a transcendent television career. I wish that for all of us.

Not only do we stop and smell the roses, we take time to water them, prune them and care for them. And to do this with all the other parts of our lives. Let us take the time to enjoy every precious moment. When we do, our lives will be rich beyond measure. From my relaxed heart to yours, Thomas

Give yourself a free pass to slow down today while doing simple things like washing dishes or folding clothes or you name it! Breathe and enJOY!

July 2 Yes, cry!

There were many wonderful speakers at the 'rally for reuniting families' yesterday in Flagstaff Arizona. One woman, who is a Hispanic immigrant, spoke passionately about her life experience. At a certain point, she began to cry. She was speaking of the current actions of children being ripped from their parent's arms. She said: "Forgive me for being so emotional. Wow! Forgive her? Let us celebrate her! She was sharing from deep in her heart about her own personal struggles as an immigrant in our society.

Then the mayor of Flagstaff spoke to the crowd. She was articulate, passionate, inspiring, knowledgeable and on fire! She encouraged all of us to get out and vote! This being of light is going places; maybe even President of the United States!

Life is about a whole range of emotions; fear, anger, sadness, joy, love, surprise, envy, guilt and others. When we experience many of these, we often cry. Have you ever noticed that when people cry in public, they often make excuses for the tears? We often say," I'm sorry", for doing so. We wipe away the tears. Someone leaps to our rescue, with a facial tissue, to wipe up the tears. Why?

Why are we embarrassed about shedding tears? Why don't we honor them? Let's celebrate them. Not necessarily the occasion for the tears, but that we are human beings with feelings. Sometimes we cry when we are sad and sometimes there are tears of joy. One is not better than the other.

It is preferable for us to be joyful rather than sad, of course. However, the tears we create say something wonderful about us. They say, "We care." We have compassion. We have feelings for ourselves and others. We care about people, animals, life, death and thousands of life experiences that touch us deeply.

I say yes to tears. May most be those of joy and celebration! And when they are tears of sadness and grief, they are just as valuable and are to be treasured. From my compassionate heart to yours, Thomas

Give yourself permission to really feel your feelings today and cry without judging yourself!

July 3 Falling in Love with Life

In a dream I had fallen madly in love with another woman. She was everything I could ask for, beautiful, talented, caring, sensitive, expressive and physically loving. I knew I had to tell my wife Lou Ann about her. When I met with Lou Ann in the dream, I realized I already had these things in her and I didn't need to leave her to have it. When I woke up, I knew the title of a book I might write. "Falling in Love with Life." a book about our whole process of discovery of the truth about who we truly are!

We are spiritual beings who express ourselves as humans on planet Earth. Our core life purpose is the reawakening to our divine nature. When we see life from this perspective, everything shifts. We no longer feel separate and needy. We no longer feel competitive. We simply know who we are and what everything and everyone else is as well.

Life is a process of waking up. It comes to us in bits and snatches. Some days we get it and some days we don't have a clue. Each time we have a connection with our divinity, we add a layer of knowing which accumulates until one day we wake up and there is no longer a belief but a certainty of who we are.

Everyone is somewhere in this process of discovery. Those who have more realization of our true nature are not better than those who do not. To continue the sleep analogy, some are still in bed, some are dreaming, some are wiping the cobwebs from their eyes and some are wide awake and leaping out of bed.

All of our life experiences, the joyful, the bitter, the amazing, the sad, the loving are part of such a rich tapestry of love. I wish for all of you to fall in love with life and have each day be a loving, wonderful, joyful, abundant magic carpet ride! From my heart to yours, Thomas

As often as you can today, reawaken to your divine nature, which is your core life purpose! Celebrate YOU!

July 4   Patriotic

Lou Ann and I grew up like many of you. We celebrated the Fourth of July, with lots of fireworks and delicious unhealthy food. I have been stirred by many of the patriotic songs. You're a Grand Old Flag, God Bless America, Yankee Doodle Dandy, America the Beautiful and others. I knew all the lyrics, and sang them with pride. I was innocent like many, who sang these inspiring words. Now something is missing for me. Maybe it has been missing for a long time for a lot of us.

I believe in the epic words of Thomas Jefferson. We hold these truths to be self-evident: that all men are created equal; that they are endowed by their Creator with certain inalienable rights; that among these are life, liberty, and the pursuit of happiness. Of course the term 'men' refers to everyone. All people are created equal. All souls are spiritual and eternal and they get to choose whatever they desire. However, many of us do not know this.

The Declaration of Independence is about freedom, the freedom to choose our life. The challenge is, when I make my choice for freedom, does it infringe on someone else's choices, therein lies the rub. Perhaps never before in recorded history has a country taken on such a tremendous challenge.

I don't think it is necessary to be loyal or patriotic to a place, a flag, a history or any other thing. The dictionary definition of patriotic is "showing love for your country and being proud of it." Right now there are a lot of things going on in our country that I am not proud of.

Now, when I hear the National Anthem, I feel sadness inside. I totally agree with the quarterback Colin Kapernick who knelt at the playing of the anthem last year. To me, he was saying he didn't feel free and millions of others in our country weren't free either. He was asking the question about how we can have freedom for all of the people of the United States.

I am patriotic to an idea, the idea of freedom for everyone. When there are those of us who are not free, for whatever reason, it is our duty as Americans to find a way for them to have freedom as well. Freedom to have life, liberty and the pursuit of happiness.

It is nostalgic to listen to these old songs and marches. However I believe we need an anthem for a new age, one that is not about bombs bursting. It would be an anthem that is about love and caring and compassion for all people of the Earth; a world anthem without borders that brings us all together. The God in us loves everyone and everything equally. Let us be the generation that finds a way for freedom for all the people and beings of the Earth. From my free heart to yours, Thomas

Visualize freedom and equality for all and feel the gratitude inside for it!

July 5   Freedom

One of the reasons I like the song "I Love Myself the Way I Am" is that it reminds me that I don't often do it. I just finished a five mile walk. I walked at 15 minutes per mile. It is a hundred degrees outside. We are at 4000 feet altitude. During the walk I would occasionally pass a bike rider and I would speed up my walk lest they think I wasn't walking fast enough! Yes, I just described a walk which ninety nine per cent of my neighbors were not doing and I was concerned about what someone else might think of me if I was walking too slowly. I spend way too much time thinking about what others might think. And I am not free!

Let's look at freedom from another perspective. None of us are free to the degree that we keep ourselves imprisoned by our own thoughts and words and actions. As you can see I am not free of my own mind that somehow compares me to others and what they might think. So today I declare a world holiday for freedom for all of us. Not just one nation under God but all nations in God. We are truly one and if we are ever to be free, we begin by accepting and loving ourselves and then others as ourselves. No boundaries, no borders, just one planetary race of people celebrating freedom for all, from my heart to yours, Thomas

Notice your thoughts today and if they aren't in alignment with who you really are, love yourself and let them go!

July 6   Indispenzable

We first saw Dr. Dispenza in the *What the Bleep* movie. That movie had many brilliant minds sharing what they understood about consciousness. Dr. Dispenza was no exception. In fact, for me, his explanation of spiritual concepts which had been confusing to me, were made crystal clear.

I have shared with you before; it is called "I create my day." Here is what Dr. Dispenza shared: "So if we're consciously designing our destiny, and if we're consciously from a spiritual standpoint throwing in with the idea that our thoughts can affect our reality or affect our life — because reality equals life — then I have this little pact that I have when I create my day. I say, 'I'm taking this time to create my day and I'm infecting the quantum field.

Now if (it) is in fact the observer's watching me the whole time that I'm doing this and there is a spiritual aspect to myself, then show me a sign today that you paid attention to any one of these things that I created, and bring them in a way that I won't expect, so I'm as surprised at my ability to be able to experience these things. And make it so that I have no doubt that it's come from you,' and so I live my life, in a sense, all day long thinking about being a genius or thinking about being the glory and the power of God or thinking about being unconditional love."

More Joe: I often hear people questioning why it is that what they are intending to create has not manifested. Normally, if we find ourselves asking such a question, there are only a few reasons. One is that we're feeling separate from our creation, and if we're feeling separate from it, we're living in lack. This means we're feeling and living from emotions that are not based in wholeness or gratitude, such as fear, anger, frustration, and so on.

This is why it's so important to do the work every day—to consistently condition our body to the feeling of that future experience or creation. When we successfully do this enough times, we won't feel separate from our creation and we won't feel lack. We'll feel like we've already connected to it, and this in turn creates more feelings of wholeness. If we understand that we are whole—and that in the state of wholeness the thought of our creation brings it closer to us—then rather than thinking of our creation as something separate from us, it already is a part of us. This is how we begin to create outcomes in our life.

The work is meditation. It is not new. Dr. Dispenza takes us into a new paradigm however. He is inviting us to move from lack to wholeness through his meditations. Please go to mindmovies.com and sign up and get involved on creating everything that is desired. It is time for those of us who want the world to be a glorious place to learn this powerful tool. From my meditating heart to yours, Thomas

It's so fun to do what Doctor Dispenza suggests and watch the ah-ha moments abound!

July 7   Universal principle #13: Abundance

"Abundance is our natural state. Everything we experience is an aspect of the abundance. When limitation appears, we are seeing a reflection of our beliefs, a resistance we have created to knowing we have it all. Opening these beliefs provides us with a clearer view of the abundance that is all around us awaiting our feeling of gratitude. Feeling gratitude for what we presently have opens us to knowing we have it all."

How do you define prosperity? Is it how much material substance we have created? Is it the size of our annual income? Is it the amount of our estate? Is it material at all? Someone once defined abundance as being able to do whatever one desires whenever one desires to do so. Here are my definitions of abundance:

I believe you are abundant if you are willing to give away everything you possess.

That you realize you do not own anything and you are only borrowing it for a lifetime or less.

You focus on what you do have and are truly grateful for it.

When you love yourself and love others as yourself.

When you know who you really are, a divine being.

When you know that nothing is missing.

When you believe it!

Underlying the belief of abundance is the principle of giving and receiving and the principle of what you focus on expands. The more we give the more we receive. In fact they are one in the same. When we give to others we realize that it is ourselves who are being enriched. When we receive from others we are giving them a gift. It is the natural flow of the Universe. The giver gets the greatest gift! From my abundant heart to yours, Thomas

What we focus on expands, our life is in our own hands (hum or sing it to 'Twinkle, twinkle little Star)! Do this as often as you can today!

July 8   The Sweetness of Life

Lou Ann and I have been traveling down to Galveston Texas for the past thirty five years. We got married on December 31st 1982. We went down to Texas in October of 1983 and I officiated at Lou Ann's youngest sister's wedding. That is when I met most of Lou Ann's family. On nearly all of our trips there, we stayed with Lou Ann's younger sister Marilyn and her husband Jay Royer.

We have camped out at their home and have been treated royally over the years. They have housed us, fed us, entertained us and have given unconditionally. We have been so blessed to be a part of their life. In a word, it has been sweet. There is no way we can ever thank them enough for their love and caring. They are two dear people!

I wish this kind of life experience for everyone. It is simple in concept. Just give from our hearts and everything else will work out. Let us all focus on the sweetness in life. We spend way too much time in judgment of each other. Let us give others the benefit of the doubt when they might not be feeling loved or loving. We have all been stuck in an emotional or mental space that does not serve us or others.

Here are some ideas for creating kindness:

1. Leave money on vending machines for someone
2. Bake cookies for the elderly
3. Serve at a homeless shelter
4. Do a 5k for a good cause
5. Help at a veterinarian office
6. Pick up litter on the beach
7. Let someone go in front of you in line
8. Give a stranger a compliment
9. Make dinner for a family in need
10. Insert coins into someone's parking meter
11. Buy flowers to hand out on the street
12. Leave letters of encouragement on people's cars

I believe with all my heart that we can actually change our world and make it a more loving place by being kind. It doesn't require a lot of money or time. It only requires us to show up and give when we can. From my very grateful heart to yours, Thomas

Which of the kindness ideas can you do today?!

July 9   Love in!

Today more than a hundred people gathered in a small town in between Houston and Galveston to celebrate one person. Her name is Sadye Maxwell Dudley and everyone calls her "Sissy". She is one of five siblings, born in a little home in Galveston Texas. She will be eighty years old on Wednesday. She was second born to Sadye, her mom and Charles Wallace, her father. She and her husband, Harry had six children, four girls and two boys. You can see why there were so many people at the party! Her sister Marilyn baked one of her gorgeous gigantic cakes; her daughters, created memorable displays of her life in photos on a large board.

I was there because I am married to Sissy's sister Lou Ann, the middle child of the Maxwell family. So many folks pitched in to make this party a huge success. Marilyn's husband, Jay worked tirelessly in the kitchen with his family who volunteer to do special events like this. They usually do this for Light House Charity and situations of helping folks during floods and storms. Lou Ann and I helped a lot with setting up tables and with food and anywhere else that was needed.

Most of these folks have known each other for years, if not decades. I watched them as they laughed and hugged and renewed their relationships. It was a big love in! I suppose this kind of celebration goes on all over the world. As I reflect upon it, I am touched by how much love and caring is shared for a mom of six children.

Sadye (Dudley) her married name, is not famous. She didn't invent some gadget. She didn't write a bestselling novel. She didn't get a secondary education and receive advanced degrees. She is a mom who loves her children and so many grandchildren and great grandchildren. And she lives in a family that celebrates that! They are one close, caring, loving family who make a difference by being there for each other; whether they live in close proximity or not. I was honored to be there and see and feel the love! My wish is for all of us to have this kind of love and support! From my grateful heart to yours, Thomas

Celebrate your family or extended family today with a call, text or note and let them know they are loved!

July 10   Confucius Say!

We were at dinner with Jay and Marilyn Royer this evening, at the Asian Fusion restaurant. They have wonderful food and even more wonderful, generous, caring management. When the meal was finished we received Fortune Cookies with these messages. *Be kind, for everyone you meet is fighting their battles too! Business is a lot like tennis, if you don't serve well, you lose! Compassion will cure more than condemnation! Actions speak louder than talks!*

There is almost no substitute for being kind. When we get irritated and raise our voice or become sarcastic, it hurts ourselves most of all. And as we have said so many times, it is difficult to know what is occurring inside someone else. We have not had their life experience. So when someone acts rude in traffic or is acting in an unloving way; we cannot know what has happened for them to be that way.

I play tennis a lot and my serve is the best part of my game. It makes the game easier because a strong serve can win a point in one stroke. Of course, this fortune is perhaps well said inside an eatery. Even if the food is good and the service is poor, they would not do well. And the metaphor implies that in life, how we serve, determines a lot of how our world will turn out. There are so many unselfish folks serving all over the globe, and we all benefit by their selflessness. So, by serving well, we all win! Even in tennis!

I can't imagine when condemnation ever supported humanity. Even if people break a law and are "condemned" to serve a prison term; we as a society have lost. When any of us do something that deserves that kind of punishment, it is a sad day. Perhaps we can all be more loving and supportive of each other and these kinds of events won't occur as frequently. Let us all be more compassionate!

Teddy Roosevelt said *"Speak softly and carry a big stick."* He, of course was referring to international diplomacy. It meant to negotiate peacefully, with the knowledge that if things went wrong, our country could defend itself. I propose a new saying. "Speak softly and have a big heart." Our actions do speak louder than our words. What we do carries the truth with it. What we say can always be interpreted or can be misinformation. We will all be remembered for what we did, not what we said! From my fortunate heart to yours, Thomas

Serve others today with a caring smile. Whichever way you do serve, be kind as each is fighting their own battle.

July 11 Universal principle #14: Giving and Receiving

"Giving and receiving always occur in balance. It is natural to receive gratefully and to give generously: an expression of appreciation for the gift we have received. The corollary to the principle of giving and receiving

is that we give only to our Selves knowing we already have it all." This is because there is only Oneness and it can only give to itself.

The more we give the more we receive. In fact they are one in the same. When we give to others we realize that it is ourselves who are being enriched. When we receive from others we are giving them a gift. It is the natural flow of the Universe.

I love Christmas at our home when we exchange gifts. I love to see the faces of other loved ones as they open their gifts. That is when I discovered that the giver gets the greatest gift!

I notice that I am sometimes a conditional giver. There are people in my life that I find I do almost all the giving and they do not thank me or seem to appreciate my gifts. It is then that I have a tendency not to want to give to them. There are others in my life experience who give equally or perhaps more than I. I then feel like giving to them more often. Just noticing my limitations! My loving wife Lou Ann is an unconditional giver and I am so in awe of her gigantic heart that just keeps on giving!

Dogs are givers! They are amazing in their ability to continue to give love even when they are abused. Be sure to see the movie A Dog's purpose; A training manual on how to love unconditionally! May we all get to be dogs someday! From my heart to yours, Thomas Woof! Woof!

Give unconditionally today without expecting anything in return! When we breathe in, we receive. When we exhale, we give! Let our breath remind us to give to another in some way today!

July 12   Would you rather be happy or right?

Sometimes we learn a pattern in our lives that ultimately doesn't support us. Early on, we are taught to be right, rather than wrong. In school, we are graded by how many right answers we get on exams. As students we learn to avoid as best we can, the embarrassment of being wrong. Getting the right answer becomes the primary purpose of our education. Isn't it regrettable that this may be inconsistent with actually learning? Can you imagine the generative and exciting learning environment that would result from a class that rewarded asking the best questions?

As a marriage counselor I often ask people if they'd rather be right or they'd rather be happy. Although nearly everyone says they would prefer happiness, the battle continues over right or wrong. If you pause and consider it, it's really not helpful is it? The very fact that we'd mindlessly choose to win an argument at the cost of damaging our relationships points to something terribly amiss. This compulsion to be right sidetracks our lives and impedes our learning and happiness. An article in a health magazine says

"People who always need to be right tend to have fragile egos," When they feel as if their self-image has been threatened, they want to make themselves look bigger or smarter, so they blame others. It's a coping mechanism to deal with insecurity. Being right affirms and inflates our sense of self-worth. This will help me be more patient with folks who love to be right, including myself. In some way we feel threatened or don't feel good about ourselves. We can help each other by loving each other unconditionally! From my open heart to yours, Thomas

Even though being right was taught to us when we were children, give that one up and choose humility, compassion and happiness!

July 13   Travel and Change

We had a nice visit with Lou Ann's family and now it is time to be back home again. The John Denver song is ringing in my memory. "Hey it's Good to be back home again." We live in a forty seven year old house at the top of a hill. We have been there eight years. It feels like we have been there longer. It has become home. "Sometimes our old house feels like a long lost friend!"

Living and traveling with Lou Ann is the sweetest thing I know of. And it is all the little things that she does in our life that makes it so sweet. So, tonight when we finally lay down in our bed next to each other. I will experience the "kisses that I live for", "the light in her eyes that makes me warm and totally feel "the happiness that living with her brings me."

I wish for the whole world to feel that loved; not only by another but by oneself as well. We all go through a lot of travel and change. May your travel enchant your heart, and may the changes awaken your spirit, and may you find a love that makes you warm! From my filled up heart to yours, Thomas

Home is truly where your heart is, so when you travel it goes with you!

July 14 The Mirror

Everything we see and feel is a reflection of the state of our own consciousness. Every person we attract into our lives is showing us a perception we hold about ourselves. Every feeling expressed by another to us, mirrors a feeling deep within us. This reflection is a gift, for it allows us to be aware of the beliefs we hold, and the ways we have blocked the free flow of Divine Love through us.

In the series of experiences that make up our life there can be time for reflection about the whole purpose of it. We are so busy in doing, that we have little time for being, which is after all what we are: human beings not human doings. Many of us stick to the script; we see life as a one-time event of some four score and two and then hope there is an afterlife.

Then what? Perhaps if we played our hand right, we get a heavenly home, if not, a horrible fate. Then there is the possibility that we are here many, many times before exiting stage left. If we are eternal souls who have a consciousness that endures in some form, then why not keep coming back?

The gospel means "good news." The good news is, we are here and experiencing life. However, the planet is a mess. The human inhabitants use up its natural resources and even kill each other a lot.

The Earth is a reflection of who we all are. Right now we are not doing such a good job of caring for our planet. It is up to each of us while we are here to do all we can to nurture and love our amazing planetary home. Recycle, become sustainable, and treat everything as sacred, because it is. So before our own journey to our spiritual home, let's make this one the best ever! From my reflective heart to yours, Thomas

Treasure this moment and this place called Mother Earth as much as you can today!

July 15   Beautiful and Prosperous Life

Lou Ann and I were headed down to the Phoenix area this morning. I said a little affirmation that our day would be filled with beauty and love and joy and prosperity.

We first drove down to an area north of Phoenix to pick up a utility trailer to help us with our garden project. When we arrived at the place the seller showed us his trailer and shared that one of the almost new tires had a slow leak in it. He said the local tire company where he purchased it would fix it up for us for free.

We drove about a half an hour further south into the Valley of the Sun and a car was passing by and waved frantically at us. I looked in the rearview mirror and discovered the right side of the trailer had sunken down. We pulled over and discovered that the "slow leak" had other intentions. Just at that moment a police officer pulled up behind us, with his lights flashing.

He asked "Do you know why I pulled you over? I replied "the tire!" He said "no you went through two stop signs when exiting the freeway!" He shared that a lot of people from out of the area do not see the signage. He said he was just giving us a warning. Then he offered to stay behind us for safety as we pulled into a large parking area.

We got out and went into our own car to get a lug wrench to loosen the nuts on the wheel so we could put the spare on. We discovered that our lug nuts were much larger than the ones on the trailer. Lou Ann was inspired to go into the closest grocery store and ask for help.

She inquired at one of the check-out lines as to whether anyone there had the tools we needed to pursue our task. A lady several feet away heard her inquiry and shared that she had a whole adjustable wrench set with a bar to turn the sockets. We discovered she was a Naturopathic physician here from Wisconsin. A few minutes later with her help, I was able to take off the old trailer tire and attach the spare.

Then we went to the tire shop to get the damaged tire repaired and they said they could not do it because we were not the person who purchased the tires. It had to be the original purchaser. I then called the gentleman who sold us the trailer and he offered to give us forty dollars to get it repaired which is about twice what it would cost to do so.

Then we headed home and I reflected on my morning affirmation. It was true that we discovered a flawed product which was concerning. Then we had the tire fail at high speeds on the highway. Then we were admonished about running a stop sign by an officer of the law.

However, we would not have met the angels in the grocery store who rescued us. We would not have met a man who was honest about the possibility of the tire on the trailer. And then gave us a portion of the sale back to help us out.

For me, I feel abundant about the monetary gifts we were given. Even more about the gifts of love and caring we also received. The day did not unfold as my conscious mind had envisioned. The Universe had a better plan. I truly feel like it was a "beautiful and prosperous" day.

May all of you discover the wonderful gifts of life that come in perhaps mysterious ways. Let us celebrate the magic of Oneness and how it opens up blessings for us each day! From my beautiful and prosperous heart to yours, Thomas

Open yourself to all the wondrous and bountiful gifts the Universe has to offer you and allow them to flow through you now!

July 16   Make Someone Happy

Lou Ann and I watch the Hallmark television station. We watch all the romantic movies throughout the year. We especially love the Christmas movies, which we record and watch several times. The movies are sentimental, loving and follow a familiar theme of couples finding their life partner. The writing is corny and obvious. We have seen so many we could write them ourselves. It would be easy to be critical of the sameness of the plot and the writing. However, for us, the love shines through!

There is another series on the Hallmark channel called "Signed, Sealed and Delivered." It has a whimsical story line of four United States Postal service employees. They work in the Dead Letter Office at the Denver Colorado postal facility. Their mission is to attempt to deliver packages and letters that have become undeliverable. They gave themselves the nickname "The Postables."

The four workers head out of their office to deliver mail that can save lives, solve crimes, reunite old loves and change futures. The group includes leader and charming postal detective Oliver O'Toole, technophile Shane McInerney, free-spirited Rita Haywith, and master researcher Norman Dorman. Together, they work to get the mail to its destination, and although late, in some respects it often gets there at just the right time.

Lou Ann and I laugh at their antics and cry at their foibles and personal victories. I highly recommend you watch it, if you desire to have your heart warmed. The series was created by Martha Williamson who also created Touched by An Angel, so you know you will be inspired and shed some tears.

The episode tonight ended with the song "Make Someone Happy". Here are the lyrics, it was first sung by Jimmy Durante in 1947. Here is the YouTube link: https://www.youtube.com/watch?v=fznw-AGoENo

This is sung from a boy to a girl, but it could be sung to our self, our friends, our lovers, whoever makes our heart smile. My favorite stanza is "Fame if you win it, comes and goes in a minute. Where's the real stuff in life to cling to?" The answer for me is always love.

In truth we cannot make someone happy. However when we come from a deep place in our heart and connect with another soul; there is a good chance that they will smile and their heart will glow! From my happy heart to yours, Thomas

Give unconditional love to others and to yourself today, so the glow of it will fill your heart and emanate out to others!

July 17　Now

Our Grandson, Ganapatiye, is thirty years old. He is working toward becoming a traveling nurse. He will be a great one. He has been practicing Aikido for more than half his life. He has a good heart. He shared with me that sometimes life is a challenge. I agreed that it is.

I encouraged him to be in the moment. I know this can be a trite or nebulous saying that we have heard often. However, there is no other time. Yesterday was used up and tomorrow may never arrive. There is only now, and that is where all the power is! Our monkey mind will do its best to keep us locked up in fear. It will constantly remind us of our limitations. It will refer us to the past and the future, of which there are none.

The more time we can spend in a quiet place and begin to meditate, we will find the power of the present. Once our mind slows down and we begin to have no thoughts at all, we will find our joyful center.

Here is a quote from Mooji: "There is a presence, a silence, a stillness which is here by itself. There is no doer of it, no creator of this stillness. It is simply here in you, with you. It is the fragrance of your own self. There is nothing to do about this, it is naturally present. This fragrance of peace, this spaciousness, it is the fragrance of your own being."

It is nice to know that there is nothing to do. Just be. Yes, we get to do all we desire in life and reap the results of our choices; however those actions and choices are not who we are. We are that still place in the midst of our soul that has always been and will always be. We are the light that shines brighter than the sun! We are One and we are home and we are now! From my present heart to yours, Thomas

Breathe more fully into the present moment as often as you can today! The nectar of that gift is the 'present' that we give to ourselves!

July 18　No Regrets

Lou Ann and I have been watching the Hallmark Channel, Christmas in July, programming. There were two different movies with the same theme among the mix. In both cases, two workaholic women have tragic accidents that have them in a coma. They go to the other side and meet an angel who gives them an assignment to help another human. The new lady angels realize right after their death, that they have regrets about the way they lived their lives. They were driven and materially successful. They had few friends and mostly ignored their families. Then they got to see what was missing in their life.

Most of us do not get this opportunity. We don't get to see our lifetime from an angel's perspective. When we reach the end of our life, many of us will be able to look back and see how it went. Will we feel good about the journey? Author, Travis Bradberry lists five things that most of us will contemplate.

1. *We wish that we hadn't made decisions on what other people think.* Please take the time to make choices that empower and celebrate who you truly are! Your life will be so abundant if you do.
2. *They wished they hadn't worked so hard.* I think a lot of us, like the women in the above two movies, get trapped in this one. Please find space in your work week where you can feel the connection to the vital parts of your life! Do something you love every day!
3. *They wish they had expressed their feelings.* I have seen so many people in committed relationships swallow their feelings. It creates stress in their lives, leads to disease and damages the relationship. Find ways to get the training that will allow you to speak the truth to the people you love. We can create heaven on Earth!
4. *They wish they had stayed in touch with their friends.* Let's all take the time to reconnect with our dear friends. Call them, text them, Zoom them, Skype them. Better yet meet them and hug them if you can. Even if for a minute, let us share our love and lift each other up!
5. *They wish they had let themselves be happy.* Happiness is a choice. It comes from within not from the outside. We have the personal power to create a happy life. Find things that fill up your heart and go do them!

Don't wait until it is too late. Take the time now to put these five suggestions into action. Then perhaps most of us will have fewer regrets. We will look at our life and smile about the choices we made to make the world a better place. From my happy heart to yours, Thomas

If you can today, set these 5 suggestions into motion! EnJOY!

July 19   Don't Forget Mother Nature

Here in Sedona we have a Sustainability Alliance created by Darcy Hitchcock. She has created a forum for all of the upcoming City of Sedona candidates. They will have to answer questions about how they are going to make the city more sustainable. Her Sustainability Alliance has a form for all local businesses to fill out and see how green they are. There are three levels of sustainability that these businesses can advertise to let us know they care about the environment.

Here is how you and I can be more environmentally conscious. Here are nine things we can do as listed by Courtney Sunday from Canada.

 Stop eating meat (or at least reduce it).

The Environmental Working Group found that red meat is responsible for 10 to 40 times as many greenhouse emissions as common vegetables and grains. If the grain fed to livestock were fed to people, we could feed 800 million people! Reduce your footprint and go meatless.

Stop eating dairy.

This has some of the same bleak statistics as mentioned in point one, as well as the fact that it takes a lot of feed to keep a dairy cow alive. 66% of all crop calories go to cows, and cow farts account for 28% of all methane emissions related to human activity. Yes, I just wrote cow farts.

 Change your car driving habits.

We don't all have the luxury of walking everywhere, but vehicles are the biggest compromise to our air. Those tailpipes are at street level, where we can inhale the polluted air directly. Consider a world where you carpool, Uber, walk, go electric or take public transit more often.

Notice how you use water.

We have a lot of water in Canada, but we also use a lot of water, and 65% of what we use is in the bathroom. Have shorter showers. Don't leave the tap running when you're brushing your teeth. Buy an energy efficient showerhead. It all helps.

Reduce the amount of paper in your life.

Do you know that **40% of the world's commercially cut timber** is used for paper? This endangers natural habitats and uses a ton of water. Since it has become inexpensive to print, we do it without thinking. And lest you think you are paperless, think about your bank statements, the paper towels you use to clean the countertops, the junk mail you haven't opted out of and the way you wrap your Christmas presents. There are many areas where each of us can help to lessen paper production.

Use a refillable water bottle and reusable lunch containers.

Bottled water and throw away packaging is wasteful. **Landfills are overfilling with water bottles alone.** It is also estimated that 3 liters of water is used to package 1 liter of bottled water. It is time to splurge on bottles and BPA lunch packages that will last. Failing that, a mason jar never hurt anyone, except perhaps your desire to not be seen as a hipster.

Be mindful of what you throw in the trash.

From kitchen scraps that can be used to make stocks to **items that can be recycled**, our trash should be less full the more aware we get. Channel your inner grandmother and see how many times things can be reused or repurposed rather than simply thrown away.

Bag it yourself.

Before venturing out on your next shopping trip, make sure you've some reusable shopping bags with you. Plastic bags are a huge threat to marine life, and they're an **inconvenience to the environment.** Reusable bags are the way to go!

Borrow or fix rather than buy.

Buying throwaway fashion is detrimental for the environment – **1 kg of fabric generates 23 kg of greenhouse gases!** Start thinking about keeping what you own and become more discerning. Darn your socks and sew on new buttons. Borrow clothes if you find you are in between sizes.

This is the only planet we have. Let us think about our grandchildren and their grandchildren. What kind of Earth do we want to leave? Each of us can do many of these simple solutions to help Mother Nature. From my sustainable heart to yours, Thomas

Choose a few of these ideas to start doing today!

July 20   Rainbows

A couple of weeks ago, a couple stayed at our home in Sedona for just a night. We enjoyed them and they promised to stay in touch. We had several things in common, regarding personal development. The lady named Hyacinth is working on women's empowerment. A couple of weeks later they connected with us on Google Hangouts on our computer. We discussed our television show and how we could possibly get it produced. We made an appointment to meet with them today in south Phoenix.

We discovered a bustling business of folks all volunteering to help people with their businesses. The lead person is a man named Perry Ealim. He is an ex Los Angeles Rams football player. I have cheered for the Rams for seventy years. He is a savvy business entrepreneur. He has been on Oprah twice. He has a huge heart and a deep financial background. He helped us incorporate and create an EIN number for our new business. Our corporation is named Enriching Life Forever and Lou Ann is the CEO!

Perry also looked over our business plan and made several suggestions for improvement! I mention all this because once again, a serendipitous event created the possibility for an amazing future for us and our TV show. Hyacinth randomly chose our Airbnb.

When she arrived we made a connection and now the Universe is once again working its magic. I realize that all of this may not manifest as I picture it. It doesn't matter. What matters to me is that we keep moving forward in the direction of our dreams.

I encourage all of you to keep following your dreams as well. Keep on doing what you love or find love in what you are doing and let your treasure manifest! On the way home, there were several rainbows in the magnificent sky.

I think about the colors of the rainbow and the colors of all the beautiful people we met today. There are seven main colors in a rainbow. There are an infinite amount of colors of the people of the Earth. Louis Armstrong said it well it his famous song: "The colors of the rainbow so pretty in the sky are also on the faces of people passing by."

Rainbows speak to me of miracles. We are all miracles made manifest by our eternal souls. On days like today, we get to feel this divine connection in the beauty of the colors of the human race. From my colorful heart to yours, Thomas

Treasure all the messages from the Universe and allow miracles to happen!

July 21   Channeling the "Lou"

Most of my life I have been a type B personality. People with type A personality traits that can be assertive, ambitious, highly competitive, preoccupied with status, workaholics, and lack patience. People with type B personality traits are relaxed, less stressed, flexible, emotional and expressive, and have a laid-back attitude.

I have accomplished a lot in my life and there is a lot I did not do. A part of me is actually okay with my less than aggressive style. Another part of me wishes I had been more assertive and ambitious. Maybe you folks have that same dichotomy? There are times when I am driven but not nearly as much as the times I am relaxed. I have looked at folks who society says are successful. In some ways, I have some regret for not doing as much as I could do. However, society's measure of success is no longer my goal.

And through it all there has been an inner perseverance. Some part of me that has not quit. Lou Ann, my divine partner and wife has a larger perseverance gene. She does not often give up. We have fun with this trait now. When I keep attempting to complete something and finally do so; I say that I am channeling the Lou, 'never quit' DNA. She has been such an inspiration to me!

I encourage myself and you folks to keep on going. And do it at whatever pace your inner guidance allows. It is possible that we incarnated here for a specific purpose. Even if we have not connected with that purpose, it may be helpful to persevere. Something inside of me lights up when I continue on and discover a way to finish a project.

Let us love ourselves unconditionally through our passage in this incarnation. And know that whether we do it in an ambitious or relaxed way, our soul is okay with it! From my relaxed heart to yours, Thomas

Persevere in whatever you are doing or being today! Happy channeling!

July 22   True Abundance

Wherever we place our energy is what happens to us. We are often unconscious about our creations. Most people on our planet are in survival mode. There are billions of us who do not know where the next meal is coming from. There are many of us who are addicted to the chemical reactions in our physicality from stressful living. It is a challenging time to be alive. We have given our power over to our material creations.

The problem is that we believe we are our physical body and mind. We fill them up with toxic food and thoughts. We believe that our outer world is more real than our inner world. It is because we spend nearly all of our time in our outer world and precious little on the inner. We are mismanaging our lives based on our past. It is almost impossible to change our world from this outer perspective.

Because we live in this false, old world reality, we spend much of our life energy in working, obtaining, selling, using and it wears us out. It is time to change. It is time to get in touch with who we really are. One of the most powerful ways is to meditate.

When we meditate we find the true center of our being. A center that has no limitations has no time, no space and is the most powerful place to be. In this place, we quiet the conscious mind and discover the ability to reduce the stress of planetary living.

Meditation leads to mindfulness. Mindfulness is the basic human ability to be fully present, aware of where we are and what we're doing, and not overly reactive or overwhelmed by what's going on around us. A simple technique is focusing on your breath. Inhale through your nose and fill your belly and chest with oxygen to a comfortable count of

3. Exhale through your mouth, releasing the air slowly filling your stomach contract to a count of 5 or 6. Modify it so it works best for you.

This is a way to accelerate our ability to create what we truly desire: love, peace, joy, caring, compassion and prosperity. When we live from here, we are totally abundant. Life will become a treasure and a pleasure. From my abundant heart to yours, Thomas

Make time today to breathe and go within – do the breathing exercise mentioned here as often as you need – feel true abundance overflowing!

July 23   Hot hands circle...sponsored by Kleenex!

Lou Ann and I are traveling in the Washington D.C. area. We are staying in a home in the woods in northern Virginia, which is an Airbnb vacation rental. Our dear friend Norris Orndorff invited us to a spiritual service last Sunday in Winchester Virginia. There is a large building that houses The Lord's Chapel – The Light Center.

About fifty folks gathered there and sat in circular fashion. The spiritual leader, a gracious woman, facilitated the event. Our time together was filled with song and many shared their spiritual experiences. At a certain point we were invited to form two circles. The inner circle was those who desired to receive a healing or some loving energy. The outer circle was those who wanted to give their love and energy to those in the inner circle.

I chose to be in the inner circle. I closed my eyes and several folks came up behind me and placed their hands on my heart and shoulders and head. So many of their hands were very warm, almost hot! It felt so good to be given so much love from all the caring beings gathered there.

The leader then spoke with us about our personality. We are not our personality, our personality has limitations. It feels like it has to protect us. In truth, it desires protection for itself. Our authentic nature is our original limitless self. It needs no protection. It has nothing to fear. When we live from the place of our authentic self, life flows more easily. It is then when we are in alignment with our soul's purpose. Then our hands are hot with love and healing and caring! From my authentic heart to yours, Thomas.

When you pass any mirror today, wink at yourself and take a deep breath! All is well!

July 24   Peace on Earth

The planet Mars will appear to be much larger than a few months ago. In Astrology, the planet Mars has a powerful energy. Although Mars is always seen as responsible for war, hurt, destruction, and fights, Mars is simply an unconscious animalistic nature we don't give enough freedom to. Restrictions in our expression of energy will lead to inhibitions of all sorts and accumulation of anger and frustration below our surface, beyond the face we show to the world.

Mars represents our basic energy, our first chakra, and speaks of fears that tend to control our lives. If we are brave enough to live up to our full potential on planet Earth, Mars is the one to help us find our grounding, resolve any material and existential issues, and provide us with the energy we need to follow any of our plans and reach any goal we wish to.

We are in a time of a lot of Mars energy on our planet. Millions of people have drawn lines in the sands of their lives. We are in a time of opposition and adversity. This is the time for those of us that realize the more subtle energies present in life to be the peaceful center. We can balance the Mars energy with the Venus and Jupiter energy that is present on our planet. Venus can bring us love and Jupiter will inspire us!

Let us do our best to be not "against" others. Let us find a way to be "for" what we believe. When we create a scenario of right and wrong, we all lose. We lose our gentility, compassion, caring and civility for each other.

I encourage us to find a quiet place and tune into the Oneness of everyone and everything. When we hold each other high and celebrate our divinity we can move through this challenging Martian time. From my peaceful heart to yours, Thomas

Find your grounding in Mars, your loving nature in Venus and inspiration through Jupiter as you go 'for' it in your life today!

July 25   Oneness chooses everything

Choices are just choices, events are just events. We often find ourselves stating "we need something", needing implies there is something missing, we lack something. There is nothing we need; there is only what we choose. The word need has baggage, the word choice is cleaner. We don't need anything. We choose everything.

This is how we create our lives. We make them seem so real that we totally buy into the events. If we did not, we would realize that this is not real and we probably wouldn't be here very long. Once we see that Oz is behind the curtain we may as well return to Kansas.

As players in the finite game of life, it is the things that could go wrong, that keep us interested. In sports, it is the possibility of non-success that keeps us interested. Think about it; if your team made every shot, scored every goal and won every game; you would soon lose interest. It's the miss, the error, the strike out, that keeps us coming back for more. It is the same with our lives. It is the mystery that keeps us in our skins time after time.

It is the unrequited love, the failed business venture, death of the body, a miscarriage of justice that has us hooked. If everything in your life experience was always juicy, you would soon lose your excitement for life. And so it is. We intentionally limit ourselves in every conceivable way to make the game more entertaining.

We all have the ability to have our lives abundant, joyful, loving and free. When we realize our divine nature and tune into our amazing power, then life becomes what our soul intended. From my divine heart to yours, Thomas

Be in the Oneness and choose from this place!

July 26   Longer Healthier Life

This morning at the Veg Fest I went to a presentation by two doctors. It was given by Dean & Ayesha Sherzai. They co-authored the book The Alzheimer's Solution. It is a breakthrough program to prevent and reverse the symptoms of cognitive decline at every age. Also, go to teamsherzai.com and take your own assessment quiz to determine your risk of suffering cognitive failure.

Alzheimer's disease is devastating and increasingly widespread. More than forty-seven million people are living with Alzheimer's worldwide. Ten percent of adults over the age of sixty-five will develop some form of dementia, and doctors predict more than half of adults will be diagnosed with the disease by age eighty-five. Despite the terrifying statistics, the truth is ninety percent of Alzheimer's cases are preventable through lifestyle factors.

It is clear that if you eat a whole food plant based diet that you can not only reduce your risk; you can increase your health tremendously. I will be sharing with you as much as I can to help all of us to live the longest, healthiest life possible. In addition, the doctors have a comprehensive lifestyle program that will help create total body and mind health.

Let us all do all we can do to live long healthy, loving, prosperous lives. From my healthy heart to yours, Thomas

Life the healthies life possible for as long as you are able!

July 27   Science of the Heart

The next two paragraphs are taken from the Heartmath.com website

Most of us have been taught in school that the heart is constantly responding to "orders" sent by the brain in the form of neural signals. However, it is not as commonly known that the heart actually sends more signals to the brain than the brain sends to the heart! Moreover, these heart signals have a significant effect on brain function – influencing emotional processing as well as higher cognitive faculties such as attention, perception, memory, and problem-solving. In other words, not only does the heart respond to the brain, but the brain continuously responds to the heart.

In the new field of neuro-cardiology, for example, scientists have discovered that the heart possesses its own intrinsic nervous system—a network of nerves so functionally sophisticated as to earn the description

of a "heart brain." Containing over 40,000 neurons, this "little brain" gives the heart the ability to independently sense, process information, make decisions, and even to demonstrate a type of learning and memory. In essence, it appears that the heart is truly an intelligent system.

In my life, it became clear to me that when I listened to my brain, there were limitations in my life experience. However, when I felt what my heart was saying, a whole new universe seemed to open up to me. We have been "educated" to use our mind and of course we could not be human without it. The challenge is that our brain has parts that are limited in scope as to how they perform. Now we are learning that the heart has intelligence. We can make decisions straight from the heart!

I love this! I have been telling folks "to follow their heart" most of my life. It just felt natural to do so. Now science is confirming that this is a powerful way to live life. I am encouraging all of you to get Dr. Joe Dispenza's book "Becoming Supernatural"; from my "intelligent" heart to yours, Thomas

Follow the intelligence of your heart today! Woohoo!

July 28   The Earth is on Fire!

There are probably a few ways our title could be understood. Our planet seems to continue to have record temperatures year after year. Due to drastic climate change around the globe, there are actual fires erupting! There are devastating drought conditions in many places. So the forests are drying up and become a giant tinder box. A most tragic statistic is that eighty four per cent of forest fires are human caused.

When we are unconscious about life we are often unaware of our actions. So the majority of fires would not have happened if we were more awake about what we do. Our flora and fauna suffer greatly because of our less than loving actions. It is time to wake up and become people of action! PLEASE, PLEASE, PLEASE make every effort to stop climate change. Go to cooleffect.org and read and share the information. Their theme is carbon is the problem, action is our solution.

I know I have shared this before and I suppose I will keep on doing it! It follows that the vegan diet, by eliminating meat and dairy, would reduce emissions the most, as confirmed by a subsequent study. Adopting a plant-based diet is, therefore, one of the most powerful choices an individual can make in mitigating environmental degradation and depletion of Earth's natural resources.

"Beyond contributing significantly to greenhouse gases that cause rising temperatures and sea levels, here's what eating meat also does to our world: While almost 800 million people suffer from chronic undernourishment and insecure food supplies, 35% of grains worldwide are fed to livestock.

So, what keeps us from following a plant-based diet? It requires overcoming our habits and our tastes, learning new ways to cook, planning during travel, and navigating the social aspects of eating and meal sharing. However, when seen through the lens of the fate of Earth's climate and resources, don't these challenges all of a sudden seem minuscule?

It is rare that a single choice of ours can have a broad and decisive impact on the climate crisis. We have a moral imperative to choose and advocate for plant-based diets for the health of our planet and the well-being and survival of generations to come." The above three paragraphs were written by George C. Wang in a CNN Op Ed titled Go Vegan, Save the Planet.

Right now there are so many fires burning out of control and our brave firefighters are dying. It is time to save our planet and put out the fires! From my hopeful heart to yours, Thomas

Eat a meatless meal today and help heal our planet!

July 29 Best Friends

In 1997, Lou Ann and I and our film crew went to an animal sanctuary in Kanab Utah. It is called Best Friends. We filmed some segments around the sanctuary. At the time, they had rescued some 1500 animals of many different species.

It was one of our favorite segments for our television show we were creating back then. Best Friends Sanctuary is still thriving today! On Facebook today, I saw a wonderful story about a man who created another animal sanctuary named Barn Sanctuary. Here is a description:

"Barn Sanctuary provides shelter to horses, cows, pigs, chickens, turkeys, ducks, sheep, goats, and rabbits that have been rescued from cases of abuse, abandonment, and natural disasters.

We are a place where visitors can come face to face with the animals they may only know as dinner and learn about the devastating effects of modern-day farm factories on the animals, the environment and human health. Here you can play with goats in a large open field, sit down with a pig who wants nothing more than a belly rub, cuddle with chickens who seek out your attention or get nuzzled by some very friendly sheep!

We're a hands-on animal sanctuary dedicated to rescuing, rehabilitating and caring for animal refugees. We educate the general public about the horrific treatment of animals raised for food, and the positive impact that a plant-based diet can have on the environment and our health."

A lot of us have had pets that we could consider our best friends. So many of them are so loving and respond to our love and care. Lou Ann and I are watching a movie tonight about someone who inherits an African animal sanctuary. I have an uncomfortable feeling about most zoos. However, I love the idea of gathering animals on a reserve so that they can be free and safe to live in harmony with nature.

We plan to include new inspiring animal programs on our newest version of our TV show. If you want to be involved, let us know. I encourage everyone to do all we can to make our planet safe and loving for all of its creatures. From my animal loving heart to yours, Thomas

July 30   Kindness is forever

Lou Ann and I were watching another romantic Hallmark Christmas movie just now. Yes, they even have them in July, which I absolutely love! The story line is about a young woman doctor who is very successful in a hospital in Los Angeles. She is depicted like most physicians in this series; overworked and little time for any other kind of life experience.

She finally gets a short Christmas vacation and heads home to be with her family. Her dad is a family physician who has had a practice in their small town for decades. At one point in the film, she shares with her dad why she chose the medical profession. She had a boyfriend whose mother was dying. The mother was naturally scared about her life. Her father, the doctor, told the woman that he would be right there with her, all the way through her illness. She told her father how kind he was to that woman. She decided she wanted a life where she could provide that kind of care.

There is another scene in the movie where an elderly lady shares her philosophy of life. She said being kind can be a wonderful moment. She said being kind can make someone's day. Being kind can make someone's life.

Kindness can look like this: A kind word, a smile, opening a door, or helping carry a heavy load can all be acts of kindness.
Celebrating someone you love, giving honest compliments, sending an email thanking someone, telling someone how s/he is special to you, helping an elderly neighbor with yard work or food, taking a photo of someone and sending it to the person, sharing homemade food, refusing to gossip and donating old clothing and things you don't need are all ideas about how to practice kindness.

I am blessed to be living with one of the kindest persons that I have ever met. Lou Ann lives from her heart, the place where kindness dwells. Let us all make an even greater commitment to be as kind as we can be. Our world will never be the same if we do so! From my kind heart to yours, Thomas

Find ways today to be kind – reread the suggestions – do at least one!

July 31   Going to miss it!

The other morning I was sitting in the sun meditating and moved into a space of deep joy. I realized I am joy. The times in my life when it appeared like I am not expressing joy, are simply me getting in the way.

One day I was traveling down the Kawaihae highway on the Big Island of Hawaii, gazing at the deep blue pacific, turning my 1990 Mazda Miata through the twists and turns of the Mauka road. I was overwhelmed with deep feelings.

Cruising along I can see several small boats out on the water dancing through the waves. I am reminded of the movie "Michael". John Travolta plays an outrageous angel who over eats sugar and is irresistible to women. In one scene he is talking with a Jack Russell Terrier named Sparky. He exclaims how wonderful life on planet Earth is and that he is really going to miss it when he leaves.

I too think about all of the other sensuous things I will miss. Lou Ann's touch and beautiful smile. My children's faces and the memories of them when we grew up together. The taste of peanut butter and watermelon and hot buttered popcorn, beyond burgers and fries, tacos and more. The smells of fresh brewed coffee, plumeria blossoms.

The sight of geese flying south for the winter. The changing leaves in the fall, the zest of another football season. Disneyland, Mount Rushmore. Sunrises and sunsets. Sitting in the dark in a big movie theater holding Lou Ann's hand and watching a romantic movie. Huge thunderstorms with window shaking lightning and the smell of the air after the storm has passed.

Chirping red Cardinals that have escorted me all over this country. Hearing John Denver sing. Being on the edge of my seat as my team played in championship games. My many friends around the world who have shared a meal, a tear, a laugh, a smile, a hug, a birth, a death, an aha!

The dozens of times we were together being so close and bonded perhaps forever. What an adventure I have been on. I don't really know what is next. I have had many recollections of past incarnation and if it isn't just my imagination then I would have to say "I'll be back".

We live in an amazing Universe! Follow your dream and watch the magic happen!

August 1   "Terrible Twos"

Most parents know what our title means, especially if they had boys! Lou Ann and I went to a movie tonight at the Mary D Fisher Theater here in Sedona. The movie title is "Dolphin Man" It is a story about a deep diver named Jacques Mayol. When he was 49 he dived down to 100 meters without any diving gear whatsoever. He is legendary among free deep divers.

The movie was also about dolphins that Mayol loved. In 1994 Lou Ann and I went to the Dolphin Research Center on the Grassy Key in Florida. We had the honor to swim with two female dolphins named Aleta and Rainbow. While in the water we got to hold on to their dorsal fin and they took us for an amazing ride! After our experience we felt their energy and love for hours.

Lou Ann and I have had a morning ritual of me tossing 2 stuffed toy dolphins we named Rainbow and Aleta and Lou Ann catching them. We bless them as Lou Ann places them on our bed pillows in the morning.

When we were in Hawaii, we went on a dolphin excursion off the Kona coast of the Big Island, where we lived for four years. I am not a good swimmer. The boat went far enough from shore that we were in ocean waters that were 12,000 feet deep. We came upon a school of Dolphins and almost everyone immediately jumped in the water to experience them. I tentatively lied down on a float and cautiously drifted from the boat. I was scared and tense. Then a large dolphin and a baby dolphin appeared below me with another adult dolphin. They floated right below me for several minutes. I finally began to relax and was aware that they sensed my fear. They did not leave me until I decided to paddle back to the boat.

After the movie tonight we were treated to a presentation by three dolphin experts. A lady named Linda Shay has written a book titled Dolphin Love...From Sea to Land. One of the other presenters said that the dolphin species are thirty million years old. He said the dolphins understand that the human race is still in its infancy, like being in our "terrible twos". Well that explains a lot!

Linda Shay has a CD called Opening to Dolphin Energy. She says the dolphins wish to love, support and nurture us along our path of healing – and opening – our hearts. They wish for all of humanity, a life of freedom, harmony, love, joy, peace...and PLAY! From my dolphin heart to yours, Thomas

Let your inner dolphin energy come out today and play!

August 2 The Positive Place……

Is the bridge between your heart and your mind. There is a place inside of you that knows the truth. It is that place that sets you free to be all you can be.

The Positive Place was founded in Sedona Arizona by us in 1995. The mission of the Positive Place is creating a space where people can access their divine nature and create both happiness and abundance.

Most of us have made childhood decisions that do not support our magnificence. Our home environment, early education and peer influence often gave us feedback that we were not quite okay. We felt that there was something wrong with us. We then spend much of our lives either validating our opinion or attempting to overcome it.

Often some trauma like divorce or job dissatisfaction or a loss prompts us to ask some basic questions like: Why am I here? Where am I going? What should I do with my life? Is this all there is? There seems to be something missing. We want more joy and abundance and personal satisfaction.

When we arrive at this place, it is important to assess our choices and see what can be done to create what we really want in life. Our creation priorities are often in reverse order. We think if I have this job or this mate or this home or this physique I will be happy. Or if I get this much education or exercise this much or save this much or eat this little, then I will have the results I desire.

We believe if I do things or have things then I will be happy. Happiness is not a result, it is a choice. When we choose happiness, then what we achieve or create has much more value.

The Positive Place is the eighteen inch journey from our mind to our heart where we can discover who we are. The process involves surrendering to that place of goodness that resides in all of us. We are so much more magnificent then we believe.

Come and discover how you can be happy and live a wonderful abundant life. We invite you to your own Positive Place, enjoy the journey! From my positive heart to yours, Thomas

Let happiness within create opportunities for a new job or mate or home or....all the endless possibilities we desire!

August 3   Forgiveness

On Earth, we play the limitation game. Here on our planet, we make choices from a narrow understanding. Even though we are part of Oneness, we humans are limited in our perception. We make decisions that affect each other and sometimes it feels less than loving. When that occurs we may judge the other person and make more choices that do not support each other.

At this point, we may often blame and find fault with another person. We then set up an energy that separates us. Then our mutual energies are stuck. We often withdraw and withhold.

When this occurs, it is helpful to forgive. It really doesn't matter if someone is at fault. What matters is that two eternal loving beings of light have hidden their brightness from one another.

When we choose to forgive we become vulnerable. Being vulnerable is one of the most powerful expressions of our humanity. When we allow ourselves to be seen as someone who is okay with themselves, it creates a transcendent moment.

We no longer care whether we are correct or not. We no longer care about what others think of us. We have discovered a place of peace that creates open hearts and unconditional love.

Let us find a way of forgiving or forgetting and free up the energy between us so that we shine so bright that all we feel is love! From my forgiving heart to yours, Thomas

If any situation has been unhealthy or doesn't allow your light to shine in your life, choose again a brighter direction!

August 4th Universal principle #15: Non-attachment and Freedom

"Our perceived need to hold on to anything or anyone demonstrates our belief in shortage and personal incompleteness. Holding on to anything— people or possessions—block the flow of love through us thereby reducing the joy of our experience with the person or object. Holding onto what we have also inhibits new people and new things, along with the new experiences they bring, from coming into our lives. As we open our hearts, feel our state of Oneness and expand our trust in the natural abundance of the Universe, we give ourselves and everyone else the gift of freedom."

Right now you may want to create something special in your life. Here is my advice. Make an agreement with Universe. Universe has all knowledge. We have limited knowledge. Tell Universe in your limited knowledge that you are going to take a particular action. If Universe does not want you to take that action; it is its responsibility to create another alternative action or path to follow. Universe is always on purpose and you are a Divine spark of Eternal Oneness.

Surrendering to Oneness or Universe is one of the most powerful actions you can take. We do not know all the answers and when we open up to Limitlessness our lives can shine! From my heart to yours, Thomas

Open your heart to the natural abundance of the Universe and give yourself the gift of freedom!

August 5   To Love and be loved

The essence of life in human form is simple. We all want to love and be loved. This simple desire outplays in about seven billion different ways. When we are born we are generally surrounded by those who love us. We can feel their caring. As we move through life we often lose this tender feeling. Sometimes the most innocent of events is interpreted by our minds as not being loved. Somehow we feel like we need to earn that tender feeling we felt at birth.

The magnificent Persian poet Hafiz said: Admit something: "Everyone you see, you say to them, "love me!" Of course, we do not say this out loud otherwise someone would call the cops. Still, though, think about this, this great pull in us, to connect."

Sometimes we block our ability to love others and for them to love us. Many times we are "Looking for love in all the wrong places." Many times, our loss of love of ourselves, allows us to do less than loving things.

However, I encourage all of us to never give up on love. It is who we are. It is the eternal breath of life in Universe. It truly does make a sad heart sing and the birds take wing. It all begins with us knowing at our core that we all want the same thing: to love and be loved! From my loved and loving heart to yours, Thomas

If inner and outer love is being blocked, take action from your divine heart and BE who you truly are! Begin by loving YOU unconditionally and then others. Breathe this in today whenever you think of it!

August 6   Beautiful friends

We met two wonderful people from Prescott Arizona while we were working on the Illuminate Film Festival team this year. They came and visited us this weekend. They live in Prescott and are deeply spiritual folks who like to laugh and play.

Our new lady friend is Cynthia Daddona. She has been in a few films and is an upbeat powerful woman, so fun to be around. Her husband Jim used to be a dentist and he is now blossoming as he discovers his beautiful essence. He has a kind heart and gentle manner that I love.

We made awesome vegan food together and told stories of our lives. We have found two more dear people to travel on the path together. Life is such a joy and treasure. We never know what is just around the corner. A chance meeting and then a deep friendship can develop. When we are like minded, there is such an immediate heart centered connection.

Another wonderful meeting is with a young couple who are moving their Tiny Home RV onto our property. They will be with us for six months or more. She is a body worker and they do organic farming. We have been hoping to connect with someone who could assist us in permaculturing our land.

Tomorrow we meet with a couple of filmmakers who will brainstorm with us about our television show we want to create. I believe all of this activity comes out of surrendering to Spirit. We can just give our heart to Oneness and let the miracles happen! I wish for all of you a life full of dear friends and magical experiences! From my deeply grateful heart to yours, Thomas

When we come from a deep loving place within ourselves, we create like-minded people in our lives – watch the miracles happen!

August 7   Christopher Robin

Lou Ann and I went to the movies, here in Sedona, to see the latest adaptation of the Winnie the Pooh adventures. The plot is a lot like life, for many of us. If we are fortunate, some of us get to spend a childhood filled with fantasies and characters that entertain our imagination. We also develop a hopeful spot in our hearts.

Then most of us "grow up", or at least become adults in age, if not in decorum or success. We create careers that are often filled with so much work and pressure. It wears us out! We continue obtaining and using more than we need. We lose the magic and hope that filled our childhood.

This was the theme of this recent Disney creation. Then something wonderful happens, when Christopher Robin gets lost in the illusion of a successful career. His best friend Pooh comes and finds him and asks him questions that penetrate Christopher's misconceptions. You will have to see the movie to find out how it all turned out!

This seems to be the story for many of us. We believe it is important to be successful and we often spend way too much time doing so. Then we arrive at a place in our life when we need rescuing. We need our "inner Pooh" to come find us!

Oscar Wilde said "To live is the rarest thing in the world, most people exist, that is all". Winnie the Pooh said "I used to believe in forever, now I believe forever is too short!" And Pooh said "don't underestimate the power of doing nothing!"

I wish for all the beings on Earth to rediscover the magic of their best childhood days. Days that are filled with play, adventure and delight! May we create the balance of achieving our dreams and living in the moments of joy and love and just doing nothing! From my fanciful heart to yours, Thomas

Re-read Winnie the Pooh's sayings mentioned above and live from that place of newness and wonder!

August 8 The soul of a Fairy, the hide of a Rhinoceros

We were speaking to Dev Ross and John Reynolds, a couple of wonderful beings of light about writing and performing for our upcoming television show. They have decades of experience in the entertainment field. Dev shared, that in this business, it is helpful to have the soul of a fairy and the hide of a rhinoceros.

I wonder if that applies to all of life. We live in troubled times, where there is so much polarization of folks. I see people who I have known always as gentle and caring; come unglued about certain events taking place right now.

And I can hardly blame them. I mostly look at things from the perspective of the fairies' heart. It feels like so many of us have developed the rhino hide. This is not to find fault or blame about either position. Simply to find the place that serves the highest good of all living creatures.

Perhaps a balance of the two is what could help? I love thinking the best about life and all of its amazing creatures. I believe it serves us well. Maybe having a hide of a rhino is not only protective but it can help heal a situation.

The hide of a rhino is nearly in-penetrable. It may not even feel things cast towards it – like arrows (physical or non-physical)! When this occurs, we can keep our gentle loving countenance. When we don't feel threatened, we can continue to come from our heart and bring healing to the situation.

It might be helpful, if we heed the suggestion of this wonderful woman and keep a fairy heart, while our rhino hide keeps us in a safe loving place where all of us will thrive! From my fairy heart to yours, Thomas

If you feel out of balance on the fairy and rhino front, allow yourself more of whichever is lacking!

August 9   Take a risk

Risking is an inherent part of life. We risk every time we drive our car or fly in a plane or jump in a swimming pool. Most of us do not have lives of high risk and yet each of us takes interpersonal risks when we interact with one another. We risk rejection in love relationships, or when we apply for a job.

All of life's decisions involve the element of success and failure. Some are scary and some benign. Our choices create our ultimate destiny. For those willing to take more risks there seems to be more reward. It is easier not to risk, however not doing so, keeps us trapped in a comfort zone that could imprison us.

When we retreat to a safe place it is like keeping a ship in a harbor and never to sail the seas. We are here to experience change, growth and discovery. We do this by taking chances and opening ourselves to the unlimited possibilities of life. We may look like a fool and fall on our face, but risk takers made this World.

All creative people take risks by giving their personal energy to their art or passion. When we step out into life even though we may be in fear and have the courage to go for our dreams, we make the world a richer and more beautiful place.

What risk are you willing to take today that will have you leaping out of bed every morning? Find something you love and give it all of your energy because it is better to have risked and failed than to have never tried at all.

If you go for it and do not achieve your goals think how much further you are. Then you too can say as the author, Dawna Markova exclaimed: "I will not die an unlived life!" From my passionate heart to yours, Thomas

Give your personal energy to your art or passion it can strengthen you!

August 10   Let's develop our Negatives…and bring forth beautiful pictures of Life

Sometimes our inner language keeps us stuck. We have a monologue with ourselves that things are not going to work out. We may have had past experiences that lead us to believe the same results will occur.

I have seen so many people who overcome numerous setbacks. They have some quality that keeps them going, no matter what. I call it the "Lou Ann" method. Even when it appears that you won't succeed at what you are creating. Even when others may try to discourage you because they don't want to see you fail. You give it one more try!

That is what seems to be happening with our renewal of the television show we tried to create twenty three years ago.

I was out on my walk this morning and noticed a new home being built near us and made a connection with one of the new owners. Her name is Joanne and she has been a television reporter for twenty years and is moving here from Colorado. I invited her to join our team on the Positive Place TV show.

Then Lou Ann and I went to one of our favorite Mexican restaurants in Sedona; Javelina Cantina. We were checking out and stopped by the hosting stand. We met Debbie whose family owns and operates the Clear Creek Vineyard and winery in Camp Verde Arizona. She shared that the wine is organic. We agreed to meet her at their winery and see if they desired to be a sponsor of our television show.

We still do not know for sure if our dream will become a reality. However, we have pulled out our old negatives and it is time to have them developed into the beautiful, colorful pictures that have lain dormant in our mind and our soul.

I encourage you to leave your house and follow your heart on what you desire to do. There are so many opportunities for all of us when we just head in the direction of our feelings. It is time for all of us to recreate the pictures of our lives! From my colorful heart to yours, Thomas

When the thoughts in your mind, say you can't, tell them who is in charge – the inner Divine Self that observes those thoughts!

August 11   There is Hope!

Lou Ann and I were watching Bill Maher tonight. He had a guest named Steven Pinker who has written a landmark book. Bill Gates said: "It is now my all-time favorite book!" The title is Enlightenment Now, The Case for Reason, Science, Humanism and Progress.

His book scientifically shows that life expectancy is the longest ever. Ninety per cent of the world's population under 25 can read and write. 200 years ago ninety per cent of people lived in extreme poverty, now it is ten per cent. There are 137,000 people a day escaping extreme poverty; rates of death from wars are one quarter of what it was as recently as the 1980's. In general, we are ninety five per cent safer than we were a century ago.

Of course, this doesn't mean we can rest on our laurels. We have a long way to go before all of the planet will live in prosperity. I am encouraged by the premise of the book. It gives me hope that those of us who are accentuating the positive, are in alignment with scientific statistics.

I think back to 2004, when the then unknown, Barack Obama shared his vision of hope for America. He said "I'm talking about something more substantial. It's the hope of slaves sitting around a fire singing freedom songs; the hope of immigrants setting out for distant shores; the hope of a young naval lieutenant bravely patrolling the Mekong Delta; the hope of a mill worker's son who dares to defy the odds; the hope of a skinny kid with a funny name who believes that America has a place for him, too. Hope in the face of difficulty. Hope in the face of uncertainty. The audacity of hope!"

I encourage all of us to take hope with this extremely important book for us. Then go out and make planet Earth an even safer, more prosperous, more loving, more caring, healthier and more inclusive place. From my hopeful heart to yours, Thomas

When we look at the bigger picture, there is indeed hope for us all!

August 12   Say Yes to Life!

Life is all about choices. Millions of times we get to choose. Often, we just react to circumstances, as they occur without much forethought.

When we are in fear, we often say no to life.   When we say no to life, we get stuck. Our energy is low and we withdraw. We want to be alone. We make choices that don't empower ourselves. We say no to life when we worry. We say no to life when we use up our time being busy and not really connecting with our true selves.

If things have not been flowing for you lately, take a moment and look at your choices. Maybe you have unconsciously been saying no to life.

When we say 'yes' to life:

We breathe deeply

We laugh a lot

We hug each other

We exercise regularly

We share our deepest feelings

We eat healthy food

We think healthy thoughts

We notice the beauty of everyone and everything

We contribute without thought of reward

We are confident

We listen intently

We ask for what we want

We say no when it doesn't serve us or other person(s)

We encourage others

We feel powerful

We get aching muscles from smiling a lot

We create circumstances that fulfill our dreams

We surrender and let go

Try saying yes more and see how your life flows. Say yes to being alive. Yes to life. Yes to your own life. Yes to each year, each day. Yes to each minute.

Imagine that life is whispering yes. Yes to all beings, and yes to you. Everything you've said yes to is saying yes to you. Even the things you've said no to are saying yes to you! Each breath, each heartbeat, and each surge across a synapse: each one says yes, yes, all yes, all saying yes. Universe is rooting for you to say yes! From my yes heart to yours, Thomas

Say 'yes' to life by picking of few of these choices today and notice the difference in your life! Breathe deeply and you have already begun!

August 13   Choices of Love!

When I was out on another magical walk around the hills of the Village of Oak Creek, I began thinking about love. How do we love? Thousands of ways, I would guess. Some may not be as obvious.

Lou Ann and I, attempt to escort out every bug or insect that enters our home. She leaves the big spiders to me!

When we make life choices, we often come from love or fear or some rendition of both those feelings. When we became vegans, it was largely because we didn't want to have another animal killed for our food consumption. It felt loving to do that.

When we are out on a walk, we are burning calories. We are reducing our weight and increasing the healthiness of our cardiovascular system. This is both self-loving and a loving thing to do for those who love us personally and globally.

This is to say, when we begin to wake up to our responsibility to give back to our planet and all of its inhabitants, it is important to live longer and healthier. Quality of life reduces the load on our overtaxed medical system. Health of life, can allow us to make more powerful choices for ourselves, our family, our community and our world.

When we remember to recycle, the Earth and all its environs and systems and sentient beings are benefited.

When we open a door, say thank you, let someone merge in traffic; ask someone who serves us, their name, we are making loving choices. When we wave at a stranger, pet a lonely dog, take home a stray...it's endless of how much we can love.

Yes, we have limitless choices in our lives. Let us see how many can be loving ones. From my loving heart to yours, Thomas

We choose the 'ability to respond differently' when we get the meaning of love and responsibility!

August 14   You Belong!

Lou Ann and I were watching a movie named "The Town without Christmas" about folks who felt lonely and separated from their environment. There was a man who was adopted as a young boy and felt like he didn't fit in. At eight years old he runs away from home around Christmas time. He ends up stranded out in the snowy woods and is about to freeze to death when a lumberjack finds him and takes him back home.

Through it all, there is this mysterious quirky character that shows up at the most appropriate times and creates miracles in the life of the man and a little girl whose parents are fighting. Finally, the man meets the love of his life and the girl's parents reunite. Then at the end, our mysterious stranger tells the man "You belong! They were two words that felt so profound to me. I got goosebumps when I heard them.

I think for many of us, there are times when we feel like we don't belong in our life. Perhaps our career has soured. Our marriage has faded. Our finances are challenging. We are not doing what we love to do. There are so many ways we can feel on the outside of life.

The truth is, life is a journey of discovery. Our soul wants us to realize who we really are. Magnificent, magical, creative, loving spirits, remembering our Divinity! And along the way Spirit often sends angelic messengers to help us discover our eternal beauty. It could be a bird or a person or a song or a rainbow!

We are here for each other. We are all connected. We are not alone. We are one! If you are feeling out of sorts sometimes, just look in a mirror and say "You belong!" From my joyfully quirky heart to yours, Thomas

You belong; your soul wants you to know this here and now!

August 15   The Yin and the Yang

Yesterday, I was feeling pretty vulnerable about my personal creations. I value that part of myself that is willing to feel exactly where and how I am at the moment. I have often said that being vulnerable is one of the greatest gifts we can give to each other.

When we connect with our own sadness and tenderness and express it; it gives others permission to do the same. More than that, we all know that feeling and we immediately identify and move toward the injured one. This Yin part of us, bonds us in a way that the Yang part of us does not do!

Recently, I participated in a tennis tournament down in the Phoenix area. I played with and against better players than I. Most of the time, when I play against higher ranked players who have greater skill levels, I play much better. So I asked myself, "if you can play that way at those times, why not play at that level all of the time?" Today I did that. It was such a joy to do something well; far more important than the score. So the yang part of Thomas showed up today!

The truth is for me, one is not more important than the other. They are equal parts of me. However, in my lifetime, I more identify with the Yin. After all, I do have a pussy hat for the women's marches that I am honored to attend. If you are struggling, whether male or female with the choices you have made there is almost always a solution. Make a more powerful choice from your heart and have it in alignment with your soul!

Thanks for taking this Yin and Yang journey with me. I unconditionally love and support you, just the way you are, in all your magnificence! From my Yin/Yang heart to yours, Thomas

Sit with your frustrations for a bit and let them be okay. Making peace with what is can bring clarity and even joy into our lives!

August 16   Thank you Universe

Note to the Universe from the Universe: Thank you, Thank you, thank you, thank you, thank you, thank you, thank you! No matter how many times we could say thank you, it could never be enough. We are so blessed to be here right now, in this time, in this place, with this body, mind and spirit.

Yes, we could look around our planet and see all of the challenges we have before us. And we created them in some way. We could judge a lot of what we see. We could blame ourselves or others for what is occurring here. When we do this, it will continue to lock up the energy around our situation. It will prevent us from finding the way back to our Divine selves.

Instead, let us simply say, thank you to Oneness, or God, or Spirit or Universe or Mother, Father God. It doesn't matter the name we give to Universal love. It only matters that we acknowledge that this energy is who we are. And that we feel the gratitude deep in our heart of hearts. It makes everything worthwhile. From my very thankful heart to yours, Thomas

Thank you Universe for our being in the here and now, reading this and finding our way back to our divine selves!

August 17   One Source

One of the challenges for souls that incarnate on planet Earth is remembering who they are. When we take on a body and a brain, we feel separate. We see each other and think that we are not One. We intentionally forget that we are all parts of the same essence. It is a game of discovery and reconnecting with the One Source, which is who we are.

In our human condition we make so many choices. These choices lead us on our journey of expressing our divinity in our own unique way. It is easy to get lost along the way. There is a split in our knowingness. One part totally believes in what it is seeing and experiencing. There is another part that is not encumbered by the senses. It is the observer. It is leading us home.

The beauty of the Earthly dance is the ongoing revelation of the twin parts of our soul's adventure. There comes a time when there may be a discontent. Something about life is not working. There is a place within that feels sort of empty and needs to be filled. This leads us through all kinds of adventures to a kind of coming home. One of our powerful choices sets up a chain of circumstances that lets us know that there is more to life than our humanness. We find our true self.

Welcome home! You have created every moment of your life to find yourself. When this occurs, sometimes all hell breaks loose. Our limited part is almost scared to death! It may take many excursions to find our way back, and it is worth it. When you are going through your days and you feel like things are not going well; it is time to go within. Whether through meditation or study or just being grateful, you can find yourself.

Lou Ann and I were having dinner today and we stopped to remember five things for which we are grateful. Mine were being alive, being with Lou Ann, being aware of being grateful, eating delicious healthy food in a gorgeous place and being happy as we were served by such loving folks at the restaurant.

I invite you to take time along your journey of inner remembrance to find five things for which you are most grateful. It is an awesome exercise. You will think of many more as well. And like us, you may feel such a deep sense of connectedness with the One Source. From my grateful heart to yours, Thomas

Throughout your day today, stop and find five things for which you are most grateful!

August 18   A New Earth

For decades, I have attended dozens of seminars and workshops. Some have been very intense and allowed me to have breakthroughs. If I hadn't continued on and adapted these ideas and actions into my life, the trainings would have failed.

I have experienced so many wonderful, inspiring, knowledgeable, well-meaning teachers at exciting programs. The problem is, that most people who attend these functions, go back to their daily lives. The concepts they learned, soon are forgotten. Then they return to the way of life that they had before they attended.

One of our goals at Enriching Life Forever is to create television programs that will inspire, uplift and have people take action. Then we plan to organize supports groups all around the world that take the lessons and messages from our programming and build a force for good.

It is wonderful to be entertained and inspired. It is more vital to take action and do whatever it takes to make our planet a better place. Our support groups will be the engine that drives like-minded, caring people to build a new world.

We would love for any of you who want to join our team to come on board. We will need all the love, energy and support we can receive to accomplish this wonderful mission.

Michelle Alia shared this on her Facebook page. Happiness is the new rich. Inner peace is the new success. Health is the new wealth. Kindness is the new cool. These are wonderful concepts for our community of like-minded loving beings.

Let us begin a new paradigm and build a New Earth together. From my inspired heart to yours, Thomas

Choose happiness, inner peace, health and kindness!

August 19   Fly Your Freak Flag!

There was a wonderful scene in the movie "The Family Stone." One of the characters in the movie tells an uptight person that what they need to do is let their freak flag fly.

It is time for us to let our freak flag fly! Here is the definition: "a characteristic, mannerism, or appearance of a person, either subtle or overt, which implies unique, eccentric, creative, adventurous or unconventional thinking."

In simplest terms, a freak flag is something that sets you apart from everyone else. We all have one. We are all unique and when we express that divine spark that only we can do and no one else can; we light up the world!

Let us become so comfortable with our divine, eccentric, creative, adventurous, unconventional, unique nature; that we fly our freak flag for all to see and celebrate! From my positive, freak flag heart to yours, Thomas

Find your freak flag and let it fly! Be who you are!!

August 20   Stop Trying So Hard

There was a short post on Facebook where someone asked "Sometimes I wonder what would happen if I just stopped trying?" I replied "Sometimes when we stop trying and just surrender to our innate goodness, then life leads us exactly where we desire to be. It may not look like what we have been trying to achieve. It may be something entirely new that will lift our spirit, fill our heart and satisfy our soul!"

We have said often, that we act like human doings rather than human beings. Our Spirit is the part of us that is being. When we arrive on Earth and don our amazing space suits, we start doing. And there is nothing wrong in that. However, sometimes along the way we lose the connection with our Spirit.

When we get weary, it is time to stop and count our blessings. It helps to find a quiet place and recall all of the amazing and wonderful things we have done. Then take stock of our current blessings, our health, our family, our friends and our home.

Success in life can be as simple as remembering who we are, why we are here, who we love and just being thankful! Then life will take care of all the rest. Relax and enjoy the journey that you are creating every moment of your life! From my surrendered heart to yours, Thomas

Surrender to your innate goodness today and let it lead you to exactly what you desire filling your heart and satisfying your soul!

August 21 Leave Nothing Undone

Having quit a lot of things in my life, I have made choices that made others sad. I have not done things I wish I had. Life is short. Sometimes we only get one chance to do something or say something that can have a profound loving effect on someone.

If there are people in your life that you love, call them up and tell them so. This time, don't text it, let them hear the love in your voice. If there are folks that for some reason, you chose to do something that hurt them in some way, let them know they are loved.

We all want to be loved. We all want to know we matter. We could always use more encouragement, support, honesty and care. Most of us love to be touched. Find someone to hug. Find someone to walk with while holding their hand.

If you owe a personal debt to someone, find a way to repay it. If you have left anything undone, that feels like it could be completed, find a way. Find strangers to smile at. Find folks to wave to. Tip your postal delivery person. Leave a bigger tip at your restaurant than ever before.

On a personal level, find ways to love yourself. It might be reading a book. It might be refusing desert. It might be seeking medical assistance. It might be calling your kids, having dinner with friends or taking a walk in the moonlight.

It is when we give, that we feel most alive, whether to others or ourselves. Take time in your life to leave nothing undone that matters to you. Then your life will feel fulfilled. Please do it now, because we always think we have another day. From my tender heart to yours, Thomas

Give love to yourself and others today – feel how it feels to overflow with caring and kindness!

August 22 Take a Walk!

On my hour and a half walk around our neighborhood, which I do two or three times per week, are pine tree covered mesas that tower about five hundred feet above the homes and golf courses. Most of the streets have well-manicured desert landscaping. I have never seen a front lawn of grass around any of the new homes.

I was strolling along and I became aware of being present in the moment. I noticed each breath, each time I swallowed, the beat of my heart, the sun on my skin. I felt at one with everything, I was grateful for the realization.

It is the little things in life that I so appreciate, a bright yellow desert flower on a prickly pear cactus, a towering Sycamore tree swaying in the breeze. The gathering of huge white cumulonimbus clouds on the horizon. Soon they will bunch together and turn a dark grey. Then the breeze will pick up. Soon another monsoon storm will brew and give life to the sometimes parched land. It feels magical, like creation!

As I climbed a hill at the top of the neighborhood, I looked out and saw the magnificent red rocks. Huge stands of a multicolored backdrop of giant rocks that stand like guardian sentinels. They have been there for more than a billion years. What stories they could tell! About all of the folks who climbed them through the years; each climber drenched in sweat and huffing and puffing to reach the top.

Long ago, we may have been donned with feathers or covered in leather. Most likely though, we stopped and looked out across this part of the Verde Valley. We probably gave a silent prayer of thanks for being connected to this part of the Universe.

Now I could smell the scent of chaparral as the drops of rain began their dance. It was time to head home and enjoy the thunder and lightning from our front deck. We are all so blessed to be alive and feel with all of our senses.

I encourage everyone who can, to go take a walk and experience nature and the grandeur of creation. It is a reflection of all the love in the universe dressed up in a rainbow of colors for us to enjoy. Happy walking! From my ever grateful heart to yours, Thomas

On your walk today, be aware of all your senses – smell, taste, touch, sight, hearing and beyond these to feel the Oneness with all that is!

August 23 We've come far and have a long way to go!

Last night I went to see the movie Green Book by myself. I grew up in Hollywood and I had a very eclectic young life experience. There were so many cultures, religions and beliefs that were available for discovery. However, Tinsel town was mostly white folks.

I will repeat a dramatic event that I have shared with you before that bears repeating in light of the movie I saw last night. When I enrolled in the Air Force I traveled by bus from Los Angeles to San Antonio. On the way we stopped at a small town somewhere in west Texas.

I disembarked the diesel smelling blue monster and headed over to a building to get some food and perhaps a drink of water. As I approached the building, there were two water fountains. One had a sign over it that said colored only. Wow, I thought they have colored water in Texas, how cool. I wondered what flavor it might be.

In a couple of moments my brain froze and my heart stopped. I noticed that only people with dark skin were drinking the colored water. I felt sick to my stomach as my mind wrapped itself around the idea that there was a fountain for colored folks and one for white. I knew intuitively that something was wrong. Why was this so?

Growing up in my neighborhood I had not learned of or experienced a bias about other humans, either of race, color, nationality or anything else I knew at that time. I couldn't quite wrap my mind around the concept that one color of people hated another race only because of their color!

While I watched Green Book and saw how people treated each other I think we have made a lot of improvements and still have a long way to go. The voting rights act in the sixties and the acceptance of same sex marriage, legalizing Marijuana and the recent influx of female power in the recent election.

And so once again it is up to all of us who care. Whether you fight for animal or human rights, work on poor eyesight or mental illness, challenge the government for wrongs local or global, seek to lessen the burden on the poor, or battle to bring water, health care, and education to those who need it, you are a change maker, part of the warp and weft of social change. We can bury the Green Book and all that it stood for. From my hopeful heart to yours, Thomas

Visualize the world changing in the next few years to support all regardless of race, age, gender or social class – let's fill the world with as much loving kindness as we can!

August 24   Self-Talk

Found this on a Facebook post. " Speak to your children as if they are the wisest, kindest, most beautiful and magical humans on Earth, for what they believe, are what they will become!" I couldn't agree more.

However, I thought, you know, all of us have within us our inner child. It is the part of us that still has wonder and still believes in magic. Here is the definition of the inner child. "Each of us has a child residing deep inside us, one that is a direct descendant of the child we once were. This inner child is with us at all times and shows up here and there when we least expect it."

When we are feeling tired and defeated and worn out, it is time to access our inner child. Somewhat like the ho'o pono pono prayer we can remind our self: "I love you, I thank you, I forgive you, I am sorry." Somehow, our grownup self, got so deep in the daily illusion of life that a spark went out. That light inside that was so bright when we were children doesn't ever go out.

The inner child is the eternal connection with all that is wonderful about life. Please take time to speak with it. Then take it and your older self on adventures of the body, mind and soul. Your inner and outer light will shine brighter than ever!

Remember each of you are the wisest, kindest, most beautiful and magical humans on Earth! From my childlike heart to yours, Thomas

Speak to your innermost being with care, love and respect! Let your self-talk know of your magic and wonder for being alive!

August 25   Find a Coach

Everyone could use a coach. The most successful entertainers, sports professionals, Olympic athletes all have coaches. Even though they have reached the pinnacle of success they still get coached.

Most of us do not perform at such a high degree of excellence. Many work hard and create much life success. However, there are issues in our lives that often overshadow what we have achieved. They show up in our life and often sabotage our intended results.

The challenge is that we are mostly unaware that these life issues even exist. We often feel a discontentment, like something is missing. Or these unconscious issues create negative life experiences like divorce, bankruptcy, addictions, obesity, and even criminal activity. I have experienced most of these!

As young children we created a pattern of choosing that has served us in many ways. Now as adults, it is time to look at those choices and perhaps choose a more powerful way of creating our desired results. Coaching can help us look at things differently.

Coaching can help create powerful results and lasting happiness. Don't go through life alone. Your coach should be unconditionally loving and supportive. They should know your life history and how you arrive at the decisions you make. Find a coach and live a wonderful, fulfilling, abundant, joyful life.

I fortunately have a wonderful coach, who not only gives me wonderful ideas and she also lets me know when I am not in alignment with my heart's desires. She is also my best friend and wife, Lou Ann. From my coachable heart to yours, Thomas

Find a life coach you can trust to share and release many of the unnecessary things you hold onto, so you can be your best self!

August 26   Blue Dragonflies

Over the past several years, I have had this wonderful connection with blue dragonflies. In 1985 my oldest brother Bud, passed away at the tender age of 54. I was asked to officiate at his memorial service.

I was sitting on a lounge chair by our pool at our home in Scottsdale Arizona, gathering my thoughts of what to say to my family and friends about life and death. Here is what came to me.

Life is like the dragonfly family. Dragonflies gather as larvae at the bottom of pools of water. Every once in a while they noticed that some of their members had disappeared. This was so mysterious to them! They made an agreement that the next time one of them had left that they send back the news of their new location.

Soon, one of the larvae had actually gained the strength to climb a green stalk and go up to the top of the pool and lie down on a lily pad. Something was happening to her physically. She was magically changing. She was growing wings and a body and legs and she could see. As she laid there resting, she noticed her surroundings had drastically changed. There was a blue sky above and mountains and trees and a gorgeous yellow ball of light that seemed to warm her body.

Then suddenly a strong wisp of wind lifted her up and she instinctively flapped her wings and soared high in the air. As she floated around she noticed a small body of water and new that was her former home. She recalled the agreement she had made with all of the other blue larvae to report back about her new life.

She realized that it would be impossible. Her family in the pond would never be able to understand the magnificence and majesty of this whole new world of mountains and rivers and endless vistas. Alas, she kept on her journey and knew in her heart that they would join her there and they too would know the beauty of the next life!

At the very second I was finishing writing this memoriam an actual blue dragon fly landed on my foot and stayed there for several seconds. I got goosebumps all over!

Two decades later I was looking for a rental property for Lou Ann and I in Sedona. I went into the house which was locked tight and discovered a blue dragon fly, very much alive on a window sill. How did it get in and more how was it still alive? I set it free.

In 1998 I was playing tennis in Sedona with my friend David and was telling him this story about blue dragonflies and once again another one landed on the tennis ball holder that he was using and it did not leave for several minutes!

Now I see these wonderful creatures as messengers from spirit telling me about the wonder of life on our sacred blue planet and perhaps life hereafter in another realm. From my dragonfly heart to yours, Thomas

What messengers have you seen or heard or felt? There is so much more in this realm of reality than what meets the eye!

August 27 Universal principle # 16 Means and ends are the same.

"The action and outcome are one. To achieve peace, we feel and express inner peacefulness. To enjoy a life that works perfectly, we see and feel the perfection of everything and everyone, including our Selves. To experience the natural abundance of the Universe, we feel and express gratitude for the abundance we already have".

There is so much turmoil on our planet right now! So many folks are diametrically opposed to each other. Both sides believe that the actions they are taking justify their beliefs. The spirit in which we create is the ultimate factor. How we hold our heart and how we act with others is the means to an end that will serve us and our fragile society in this day and time.

It is time for us to focus on the big picture of life. We are all in this together. Even though we appear to be far apart; at our spiritual core we are one. Now would be a great time to consider not only what we do and how we do it. It is time to be in touch with why we do what we desire. To find that place of love and caring to all of the Earth's inhabitants and then we will create peace on Earth. From my meaningful heart to yours, Thomas

Creating peace on earth begins inside of us caring about self and others and expressing it outwardly with love and kindness!

August 28   Being Human

This weekend I watched the finals of the boys Little League World Baseball championship. The teams that played each other were South Korea and Honolulu Hawaii. Before the big championship game the Hawaii coach, Gerald Oda, got his team together and said to his players: "You are going to have the greatest joy, the greatest moment, the most fun. Whatever happens today, just love each other and hug each other today. Have a great game!" He never mentioned winning or even playing their best. He only spoke about the feelings he wanted them to experience and share!

Then his team won the championship! He gathered them together and said: "Okay guys be humble, remember, humble, go and greet the Korean team's fans." Then his team went and hugged the other team. Usually teams shake hands. I have never seen a team hug another like that. Then they went over to the third base side of the playing field and waved and acknowledged their opponent's families and fans. I have never seen this before. I was amazed. Wow, if those children could grow up and bring that sense of loving and humility to life, the world would have a better chance.

While we are here in physical form it is a basic human experience to express our likes and dislikes. When we do, it is somewhat limiting in either case. It is almost labeling. However, it is human to do so.

Let's choose to continue to compliment, tell others they are great, acknowledge their divinity and let them know they are loved. I encourage us to choose to lift people up and encourage them to fulfill their greatness.

I encourage us to speak up when we experience things that are not loving and supportive. I encourage us to take a stand when others are being treated unfairly. While we are in the body, let us be in the body with all of our heart, mind and spirit. From my human heart to yours, Thomas

Let your heart know that you are having the greatest joy, the greatest moments and the most fun in this lifetime!

August 29   The Dream

The other night I had this dream in which I was encouraged to sing. When I began, an enormous amount of energy was available. A stream of powerful light flowed through me and I was able to sing as loud, as clear, as long as I chose, without taking a breath. It felt like it could go on forever. I was amazed as were others around me who heard me singing. It was so exhilarating!

I awakened and was so excited! Then these thoughts came to me: life has always been about love. The music that flowed through me in the dream wasn't about me. It was about our limitless energy we all possess. Let us all be for all of us. We are the human race; we are not in a race. Slow down, be present! We are limitless beings. We are one.

Focus on the love we feel in our hearts. Bring all of your love to everything you do. Stay present without judging. Now is the time–this is the time we have all agreed to come together and shine our light. There is no darkness that is not self-created, everything is light and love…that is all there is.

All infinite beings throughout creation are invited to join us now in bringing forth the truth of our unlimited love, prosperity and joy. We are *here to serve in any way we can.* Thank you for being here and sharing this journey. From my awakened heart to yours, Thomas

In this dream we call life, focus on the love in our hearts so we can serve in the best way we can!

August 30   Heroic Living

Most people have heroes of some kind in their life. In recent years there have been a lot of Hollywood blockbuster movies about old comic book heroes. On Facebook every day there are dozens of real life heroes showing up in amazing ways that have a profound affect in our world.

I would like to speak about the most important heroes in our own lives. It is us. Yes, we are all heroes. The dictionary definition of hero is: a person who is admired or idealized for courage, outstanding achievements, or noble qualities.

For some of us it is an effort to get out of bed and go to work. We may have physical, emotional, mental or monetary challenges. And somehow, we drag ourselves to be where we are expected. We may be in a lot of pain and we still show up. I call that heroic.

We make thousands of choices in life. Most are made without being conscious of doing so. Some are vital life choices, where we choose between whatever we think we should do and what our heart desires of us. It could be our daily tasks or our wildest dreams!

There are probably people all around us who are making heroic choices. We don't know what is inside each other's hearts and souls. Let us acknowledge that each of us is a hero in some way, in our own life. Let us look at each other and take a moment and give each other a hug, handshake, smile or a nod. And know that we are each the star of this song - When a Hero comes Along by Mariah Carey which you can find on YouTube at:
https://www.youtube.com/watch?v=Mb0tMUStkW0

The song says it all. We don't have to look any farther than the nearest mirror to find our hero! From my heroic heart to yours, Thomas

We are each heroes in our own ways – acknowledge yourself for it!

August 31   Take Time to Vote

It's been said "to vote your political party," I have heard it said "to vote your pocketbook." I am initiating a new voting phrase;" vote your children and grandchildren." Our planet is in trouble and the past several generations have done much of the destruction.

We have created two major problems in the past hundred years. One is pollution of our sacred Earth. The other is that many of us have mostly thought of our own prosperity. We have left billions in poverty. This abject poverty has probably been the major factor in so many wars and so many deaths by violence and disease.

We have shared on this post many times about simple things that all of us can do to delay climate change. Here is another list:

1. Improve Your Home's Energy Efficiency. ...
2. Buy Local. ...
3. Compost. ...
4. Conserve Water. ...
5. Choose Eco-Friendly Producers. ...
6. Drive Less. ...
7. Learn from the Experts. ...
8. Recycle, Reuse, Re-purpose.

The second part of saving our planet is creating prosperity for all. When folks have enough food, water and shelter, they find more room for expressing their love. Right now there are some alarming statistics about the amount of abundance owned by a small percentage of us. The richest one per cent own more than the bottom ninety nine per cent. I am not here to denigrate wealth in any way. I desire for all beings to live in luxury, if they so choose. Here in the United States and other democracies, we the people (ninety nine per cent) can create the society we desire. One that educates, nurtures, feeds, and inspires. We have the votes to do so.

Once again, this is not us against them. We are all in this together. This is the one hundred per cent agreeing, that all may live in abundance, peace and happiness, regardless of our political party. Please vote for candidates that will enact policies which create a vibrant loving Earth for our children and grandchildren and their children.

We are the only ones who can do it! More than one hundred million eligible voters do not vote in the U.S. I know that politics doesn't seem pleasant, and is sometimes downright awful! However, if our children were going to somehow be injured, would we do everything possible to protect them? I believe most of us would say a resounding YES!

The pundits say that this upcoming election may be the most important ever. This is mostly because we have created a polarized society and the stakes seem very high! I believe it is the most important election because the one per cent and the ninety nine per cent can cast ballots to save the planet, feed the hungry, educate our children, nurture the lost, love the lonely and care for the elderly.

PLEASE get involved and at the very least, vote to create the world we desire in our hearts. From my voting heart to yours, Thomas

It's up to each of us to teach our children to be caring and loving adults – even the inner child in us!

September 1   What Love Feels Like

When I play tennis, a lot of the guys and gals exchange good natured barbs. It is a form of sarcasm. Most of it seems to be light hearted and not meant to hurt. I can tell when we cross over the line however. There is an energy present that feels like an old hurt still attached to someone's damaged heart!

After all, when you come right down to it, sarcasm is a subtle form of bullying and most bullies are angry, insecure, people who have a lot of personal pain. Alternatively, when a person stops voicing negative comments, especially sarcastic and critical ones, he or she soon starts to feel happier and more self-confident.

If you want to be happier and improve your relationships, cut out sarcasm since it is actually hostility disguised as humor. Despite smiling outwardly, most people who receive sarcastic comments, can feel put down and think the sarcastic person is unkind.

I also thought about teasing. This can feel good natured as well and yet, once again for me, there feels like a hidden message of personal hurt. To tease someone means to laugh at them or make jokes about them in order to embarrass, annoy, or upset them.(Webster definition).

Lou Ann and I don't tease each other or speak with sarcasm. We had enough of that kind of banter growing up and it didn't feel good. We go out of the way to have the other person feel loved and nurtured and supported. We find ways to compliment and encourage. We look for the value in what the other person does while giving some alternative suggestions that might improve their effort.

There seems to be a movement to discourage political correctness. It is pictured as a weakness. I believe that when we stay centered in our joy and compassion for all life, it is okay to say things that love and support, rather than to denigrate and criticize.

It is also a choice for love to stand up and defend humanity, against those that are intent on creating chaos and mayhem and destroying our planet by their insecure and unloving choices. For me, when we come from our heart and not our bias or unhealed pain it feels more like love. From my loving heart to yours, Thomas

Sarcasm and teasing are counter-productive and generally don't feel good! Find ways today to compliment encourage and be kind!

September 2   RE-birth of a Nation

We live in an unusual time. I am a very liberal person. I disagreed with John McCain about many things. We have in common, among other things, love of country and honor of commitment, we both served in the Armed Services. I was fortunate to not be captured by the enemy. If I had been, I am not sure I would have done what John did. He could have returned home from Viet Nam because of his family's military heritage. He did not. He stayed behind with his comrades and he suffered deeply for it. I don't know many human beings who would have done that.

I mention this because our nation is being challenged in a way that has not occurred in a long time, if ever. There is an energy being expressed that is not loving and supportive. There are decisions being made that are harmful to the planet and all of its inhabitants. I may need your help here.

Our goal in sharing this book has been centered on a principle. I have mostly attempted to be for things and not against them. I think it was Mother Theresa that put it so aptly. When asked if she would march against war; she declined and added "when there is a march for peace, count me in!"

So it is challenging sometimes, for me to keep always moving in a forward direction. There are times when I am deeply frustrated by what is happening to our society and I want to stand and shout ENOUGH! I do get to do it, when I am honored to participate in the several Women's marches we have had.

Today, for me, was a significant celebration. The remembrance of John McCain and all the kind words that were shared today gives me hope. Even though many of the speakers at his memorial were diametrically opposed politically, they were in harmony in their humanity.

The current administration in 2018 is moving in a direction that is so destructive to our Earth in so many ways. Of course, there are those of us who oppose their policies. We find ourselves on the brink of a constitutional crisis. It is time for all of us to find the courage to heal our differences and create a loving nation that is for all people. It is time for a rebirth of a nation, dedicated to the freedom, fulfillment, equality and happiness for its entire people. Thank you John McCain for who you were and for what you taught us. From my reborn heart to yours, Thomas

When you can today, be FOR something rather than against!

September 3 Our Mission…Should we choose to take it!

While walking today these thoughts came to me; right now our world would thrive when we create these scenarios.

Heal veterans and their PTSD and save at least the 22 lives per day that are destroyed, as these honorable servants commit suicide.

A world where all people of all color, live as equals in opportunity, freedom, safety, and abundance.

A world where folks of all loving expressions, share their love, whether LGBTQ or any other loving way of being and have the freedom to do so.

A world where young black men and women get the opportunity to live in safety, and learn life skills, that propel them to the greatness they all have inside.

A world where all people, both women and men receive equal pay for doing equal work. A world where there is no glass ceiling or any other ceiling that presents any of us from achieving our magnificence.

A world where all people of the Earth receive a "living wage" that meets their basic needs for shelter, food, water and comfort. Then our fellow humans can flourish without the pressure of "making ends meet". This will help us eliminate poverty and then there will be less violence and wars. Then peace on Earth will begin to flourish!

A nation (U.S.) that creates the way for all people to vote, including a legal holiday to do so. A country where fairness in elections is created and honored, including no gerrymandering.

A world where teachers are paid for what they are worth to society.

A nation (U.S.) where a college education is free for everyone who chooses to go or trade schools as well.

A nation (U.S.) where prisons for profit are eliminated. Where criminals are rehabilitated and educated and healed to return to society.

If we choose this mission and realize it is possible, and achieve it, we will have left a lasting legacy for generations to come, to live in prosperity, love and magnificence! From my mission possible heart to yours, Thomas

Visualize these events happening with gratitude in your heart!

September 4   Being Present

We have all been blessed in so many ways. Sometimes we go through our days in an unconscious way. It may be Friday and we say what happened to Monday through Thursday? It is easy to do. Here is something that Ram Dass said: "much more of the time, when I am 'here,' this is it, I am here, and when I'm not here, I'm not here.

It's interesting how when you give another human being, your family, or your business, the fullness of your being at any moment, a little is enough; while when you give them half of it, because you're time binding with your mind, there's never enough. You begin to hear the secret, that being fully in the present moment is the greatest gift you can give to each situation."

I remember a talk given at Income Builders International many years ago. The presenter was Barry Spilchuk. He was having some challenges with his presentations and he asked Jack Canfield for some advice. Jack told him: "When you're in the room, be in the room!" It was the first time Barry had ever heard this concept and he was so funny trying to figure it out. At that point in his life, he couldn't wrap his mind around the notion of Jack's advice. As far as Barry understood if he was in the room he had to be in the room. It was hilarious at the time! The advice simply means be fully present to life!

Life is such a gift and it seems to go by in a blink of an eye. When we take the time to be present, life becomes immortal in that moment. There are no clocks ticking, no schedules to be kept, no check list to do. That is why one of the Buddhist admonitions is to chop wood and carry water. When we do this, there is nothing lacking, nothing else we need.

Meditation and practices like it help us to focus so intently, that we can slow down life and be present. I encourage everyone to ease up, take a deep breath and be present. Please give yourself this gift as often as possible. From my present heart to yours, Thomas

Breathe in and out in the present moment as it is a gift to you and others!

September 5   Pay it Backward

Remember the wonderful movie, Pay It Forward, where the young actor Haley Joel Osment began the wonderful act of doing loving things for others and only asking in return, that the recipient pay it forward.

In 2000, Catherine Ryan Hyde's novel, Pay It Forward was published and adapted into a film of the same name. In Ryan Hyde's book and movie it is described as an obligation to do three good deeds for others, in response to a good deed that one receives.

Such good deeds should accomplish things that the other person cannot accomplish on their own. In this way, the practice of helping one another can spread geometrically through society, at a ratio of three to one, creating a social movement with an impact of making the world a better place.

I thought of this today when a friend of mine purchased something for me as a gift, for something I had done for him. I thought maybe our "loving" paying can work in reverse as well.

Let us take some time and perhaps write down a list of people that did thoughtful things for us in the past. Then go take an action that would do a loving thing for them as well. It could be a random act of kindness, or it could be a chance for us to let them know how our lives were brightened, by their gift to us. Then they could make a list as well and all of our Pay It Backward angels could help create more love and compassion and joy on our planet. If we all shared at least three of these gifts, it would exponentially accelerate the love energy around the Earth. From my totally gifted heart to yours, Thomas

Pay it backward or forward 3 times today and feel it bring more love, compassion and joy to our planet!

September 6   Spend Time in Love

Let us think of the times in our life when we felt love and caring from others. Let us also think of the times when we were in such a loving place that we easily gave our love to others. Remember when you were held by someone who cared. Remember that teacher who praised your efforts. Remember that warm tongue of your puppy on your nose. Remember your first time you held someone's hand in a romantic way. Remember the smile on your friends face when you wished them happy birthday. Remember the time you risked doing something you feared and you succeeded! Remember your first kiss! Remember your last kiss!

We could go on and on about recalling all the times we felt love. Now let us do it one more time. Go look in a mirror and tell your reflection how much you love yourself. Yes, challenges in life may continue to arrive. When we are full of love, we can meet them and welcome them. They just give us another reason to remember we are love, From my loving heart to yours, Thomas.

Choose leaning toward love today – look in the mirror and tell yourself how much you are loved by you!

September 7   What One Man Can Do

Buckminster Fuller was a futurist with a comprehensive understanding about Universal energy. What you might not know is that Fuller designed a lot of other things, cars, houses, cities, even maps. His goal, always, was to promote something he called "ephemeralization." This is the idea of doing more with less so all of humanity could thrive on a planet with limited resources, a world he dubbed 'Spaceship Earth'. He also invented the Geodesic dome. Bucky once said: "Now there is one outstandingly important fact regarding Spaceship Earth, and that is that no instruction book came with it." And therein lies the rub!

Randolph Craft (Randy) was a good friend who recently died. He lived on the Big Island, and was an expert in the teachings of Buckminster Fuller. Many years ago he was giving a "Bucky" presentation at a large business conference in Los Angeles. I was sitting in the audience and Randy spoke about Bucky's close relationship with John Denver and that John had written a song about Bucky. Spontaneously I raised my hand and said I knew the song. Randy invited me up front and I sang "What One Man Can do" Here are the lyrics on YouTube with a beautiful memorial to John: https://www.youtube.com/watch?v=t36Cs28dFCI

What stands out for me in this song are the lines:

It's hard to tell the truth when no one wants to listen, when no one really cares what's going on.
And it's hard to stand alone when you need someone beside you, your spirit and your faith must be strong.

This is a time on planet Earth when so many of us need to tell the truth about what is going on particularly here in the United States. There were people in our previous administration who did not speak the truth; in fact they lied most of the time.

We get to stand and say what is true for all of us.

We get to care what's going on.

We are not standing alone!

We get to choose how we live our lives on Spaceship Earth.

This is not what one man can do.

This is what a group of committed caring people can do.

Our faith and our spirit is strong!

Please join, attend, and lead any organization whose purpose is inclusive and loving. Let us get involved now like never before. This is our time to save planet Earth. This may be the reason we incarnated at this time. To make a difference that will serve our children and their children. We have seen what Bucky can do and what John Denver can do. Now let's see what one people can do! From my heart to yours, Thomas

Get involved in an organization that is loving and inclusive! Let your faith and spirit be strong, like Buckminster Fuller and John Denver!

September 8 Land of the free and the home of the brave?

When Francis Scott Key penned those words, he ended the sentence with a question-mark, not a period or an exclamation! I love this amazing country, which is now, some 245 years into a grand experiment of a nation that is of, for and by the people. It may have been unique in all the history of the Earth; up until that time on a hot summer's day in the City of brotherly love. These framers of the Declaration of Independence, risked life, limb and property to stand as one against tyranny. They literally pledged their lives, their fortunes and their sacred honor!

We live in a day when many of us do not have to go that far to live in a country where we have the claim to life, liberty and the pursuit of happiness. We can create that on our own, each and every day. However there are some of us that this is not the case. We have people in our country who are hated because of the color of their skin. We have others who are looked down upon, because of their choice to love whom they choose. We have folks who believe in God and some who do not and others whose God is something that might be judged.

There is a new Nike company sports equipment ad that focuses not on what product to buy but on the idea that any person, who chooses to express their inalienable right, can do so. In this case, a professional football player decided to kneel when the National Anthem was played, instead of standing. He was objecting to the state of affairs of the people of his race who were being arrested, tortured and murdered without cause because of the hate of the perpetrators. He has the right to do that! He was given that right, over two hundred years ago.

When Key wrote those lyrics on the horrific night on September 13, 1814 when the British were destroying Fort McHenry in Baltimore Maryland. Perhaps he ended it with a question mark because he was against the war when it began in 1812? It may be that he thought there would not be a country anymore?

Freedom is precious. It is not given by any government. It is the nature of life! It is sometimes taken away by others by force or other measures. However, it can never be taken from our hearts. The reason our country, with all of its faults is great, is because of its heart. One reason we celebrate bravery is because it comes from our heart. Our mind would not commit to action, if it were not for our heart!

I am encouraging us all to find the heart and the courage to stand up for the freedom for everyone and everything. Then perhaps our country and perhaps the Earth will be the world of the free and the home of the brave! And it will not be a question any more. It will be an exclamation! From my free and brave heart to yours, Thomas

Let's allow all people the chance to be in the world of the free and the home of the brave!

September 9   Makers

Violet Palmer became the first woman referee in the National Basketball Association in 1997. She was told to "go back in the kitchen!" She didn't! She was ridiculed by those whose minds are from another time in our country. She went on to referee 919 games in the most prestigious and powerful basketball league in the world! She became the first female to officiate in an All Star game, in any major U.S. sport. She became the first openly gay person to officiate a professional sport! She has gone on to be a referee manager for the NBA.

I grew up in a time in our land when women, minorities of all colors, races, nationalities and those who loved the same sex were insulted and degraded. When I heard some people talk, it puzzled me that they would speak harshly about someone they didn't even know. I know that friends of mine when we were young boys would denigrate another boy who didn't play well. We would say "You throw just like a girl!" There were unkind words for immigrants who came from all over the world. It seemed natural for folks to speak that way at the time.

We still have millions of people who may still speak and feel that way. This past two years has shown us a dark side of our country. Sports are one of the places that have become a meritocracy. The definition of meritocracy is: Meritocracy (*merit*, from Latin *mereō*, and *cracy*, from ancient Greek, *kratos* "strength, power") is a political philosophy which holds that certain things, such as economic goods or power should be vested in individuals on the basis of talent, effort, and achievement, rather than factors such as sexuality, race, gender, or wealth. In athletics, if you have the skills, attitude and perseverance to compete you will be respected and accepted. Violet Palmer has that.

MAKERS is a feminist media brand for newsmaker's, history MAKERS, and troublemakers'. They tell the stories of today's trailblazing women to inspire the change MAKERS of tomorrow. If you want to join the movement and raise your voice, go to makers.com. Right now, forty per cent of Democrats running for office in the U.S. House are women! Let us all support these new world makers! It is time for the amazing, powerful, inclusive, feminine energy to be leading the way for our Earth to discover its magnificence! From my feminine heart to yours, Thomas

Be a trailblazer and inspire others to do the same with love and peace in their hearts!

September 10   Success

A measure of a person's success is not what they accumulate. It may be who they get to share it with! That was the theme of my favorite movie; it's A Wonderful Life! For me, the things that have been the greatest gifts are the smiles on my families and loved ones faces. The hugs we all gave each other. The kind words we shared together. The silent moments we spent together. Those are the successes I would love us to celebrate!

Rob Siltanen the advertising genius said this: "Here's to the crazy ones, the misfits, the rebels, the troublemakers. The round pegs in the square holes, the ones who see things differently. They're not fond of rules. And they have no respect for the status quo. You can quote them, disagree with them, glorify or vilify them. About the only thing you can't do is ignore them, because they change things. They push the human race forward. And while some may see them as the crazy ones, we see genius. Because the people, who are crazy enough to think they can change the world, are the ones who do."

Let us be the crazy ones. Let us be outrageous and push the human race forward. Let us celebrate each day by doing all we can to change the world in a better way. Let us have a sign on our cars that says she/he who cared, gave, loved, included, shared and hugged the most, won! From my successful heart to yours, Thomas

Celebrate being the change the world needs with your love and caring nature!

September 11   Magnificent Monday!

As I am sitting here on Monday evening at the computer, with a blank stare, I always want to be an inspiration to others. I want you to know how wonderful you are. I want you to know there is so much more to life than appears. I want to say to all, that this moment right now is unique. It has never occurred before. You are unique; there has never been anyone like you ever! Take a deep breath and let that sink in. Your thoughts have never been before. Your special way that you see life has never occurred before.

On my way home driving in my car, I looked to the night sky in the South and saw the gorgeous Milky Way galaxy. I had a lump in my throat as I contemplated the extent of creation! And I thought of each soul on Earth that gets to connect with another part of Oneness.

If you are feeling like you are stuck or in a rut, stop. There are no ruts, only unique paths that only you can create. There is no limit to the paths you can take to remember who you are and why you are here! Today is Monday and a workday for many; instead of it stressing us out; let us look at it in our own wonderful way and declare "this is the day I realize my greatness of heart and passion of soul". This is my moment to shine. Let us declare a new term: Thank God it is Magnificent Monday. From my magnificent heart to yours, Thomas

Let this magnificent day help us realize our greatness of heart and passion of soul!

September 12 Perhaps Love

Lou Ann and I went to see a movie at the theater here in Sedona, titled "Great Voices Sing John Denver." It was an excellent documentary. The creative team put together a film in which fifteen opera singers sang Denver's music. We wept for an hour and a half. My tears were of the beauty of the words, the orchestrations and the transcendent voices.

John would have loved it. We discovered, in an audience question and answer session, a couple of not well known things, about John. He was very disappointed that he did not get invited to sing with the people who made "We Are the World". Secondly, he was the number two most popular performer in history, next to Elvis Presley, for RCA records and he wasn't recognized for it.

John Denver's words and melodies have had the most profound effect on me than any other performer or music. There was something innocent about this music. It came straight from his heart.

John's lyrics were for me, deeply spiritual. Several of his tunes are among the richest and heart felt songs that I memorized and sing often. He also wrote and sang many love songs. One of my favorites is the title of this page. Here are the lyrics on YouTube: https://www.youtube.com/watch?v=Ikb8qX-kyts

Perhaps love is these things and more for many of us. I wish for everyone to feel the love from John Denver's lyrics. May they become a reality in our lives! From my loved heart to yours, Thomas

There are so many facets of love spoken of in this song, let love in your heart today and allow it to bring you comfort and warmth and joy!

September 13   The Gift You Are

It has been clear to me for most of my life, that the giver gets the greater gift! I think most of us love to receive gifts for ourselves. It is a joy to be gifted by someone else, particularly when it is a surprise. However, it is sooooo much fun to give to others and see their excited eyes, their whoops of joy and tears, of being honored with a gift.

There is another John Denver song that I adore! It is titled "The Gift You Are". Here are the beautiful lyrics that you will find on YouTube: https://www.youtube.com/watch?v=RG31OE6tKRY

The Universe is a giant brightly wrapped colorful gift box with all of us in it! It is a huge Hallmark Christmas movie with all of us hanging from the evergreen branches, waiting to be opened! Please remember that you are the one unique gift that is not the same as any other.

Your spirit, your heart and your soul is the gift you bring to life each incarnation. We can relax and know that we are here to make someone's moment, day, week, year, perhaps lifetime. And it may be that we are our gift to ourselves as well. You are a priceless treasure. May you always feel that way! From my priceless heart to yours, Thomas

Feel the priceless treasure that you are in this divine now moment! And the next….!.

September 14   Bragging

It seems to me that not many people like a braggart. When someone tells us how much money they make, or how cool they are, or good looking they are, it can be a turnoff. Right now, we are watching a lot of bragging going on in Washington.

I began to think why do we brag? It feels like when we have to tell everyone how good we are, we probably don't believe it. Behind all the self-boasting, lies a small wounded child that somehow feels they are not good enough. And the louder we brag, is probably equal measure, to how little regard we have for ourselves.

When we are emotionally and mentally healthy, we feel good about ourselves. It is vital to have high self-regard, if we are to live a happy and successful life. There have been times in my life when I have shared somethings about myself with others that didn't quite feel good! Later, I cringe when I recall what I said and wish I hadn't been so candid about my accomplishments or whatever I shared. I think we can brag all we want to ourselves.

It appears that we are often our worst critic and judge. However, it is so important to balance our self-criticism with our self-approval. I believe it is healthy to know the truth about ourselves. When we hold ourselves in love and caring even through our flaws, we are powerful, capable human beings.

The other side of this kind of behavior is self-effacement. When we are humble and self-deprecating we are often more attractive. It feels like when we are being humble, we are saying we are like everyone else. It feels more inclusive. When we brag, we are saying we are better than others and that feels exclusive. All of this is the realm of our egos. At our core, we are all the equal, limitless, talented, creative children of the Universe. From my humble heart to yours, Thomas

Know that you are an equal, limitless, talented, creative child of the Universe!

September 15   I'll Always Fall In Love Again

Remember the old song from Dionne Warwick "I'll never Fall In Love again?" It was a tune from the musical "Promises Promises" in 1969 written by Hal David and Burt Bacharach.

I wrote different lyrics to it. They are:

What do you get when you fall in love?

A lover with a heart to keep forever.

That's what you get for all your fervor.

I'll always fall in love again.

What do you get when you kiss your puppy?

Lot's of wet noses to keep you happy.

A friend to hold while you take your nappy

I'll always fall in love again!

Don't tell me what it's all about.

Cause I've been there and I want to shout!

An awesome feeling that keeps me grinning!

I know with my love, we'll just keep winning!

I'll always fall in love again.

That is why I'm here to remind you

What do you get when you fall in love?

A life that's filled with joyful living

One that's filled with lots of giving

I'll always fall in love again!

There can be quite a bit of pain when we risk our hearts and open them to another person. Many of us get into a fear space because we have had our hearts broken. I encourage us to always keep finding and expressing as much love as humanly possible! For me, it is always worth it. I'll always fall in love again! From my heart full of love to yours, Thomas

Even puppies and kitties give us so much love – send it back to them as well!

September 16 What Shall We Tell Our Grandchildren?

What will we tell our grandchildren when they ask...why did you let this happen? How come there are so many people starving, Why are there millions of children hungry? Why do 200 species become extinct every day? Why have you let our planet become polluted? Why have you killed three to five billion trees each year? Why are the sea levels going to rise some six or seven feet by the end of this century? Why are the polar ice caps melting at astonishing rates? Who killed all the wild animals? Why are so many people killing each other? What will I tell my children? Here is this magnificent John Denver song you will find on YouTube: https://www.youtube.com/watch?v=yUNQfvihsLI

Will we tell them that we got involved? That we recycled? That we demanded that our governments become conscious? Did we vote in the people who cared about all the beings and flora and fauna of the Earth? Did we march for peace? Did we make a difference?

We still have a chance to slow down climate change. We still have time to feed the poor, clothe the naked, nurture the homeless. It is true that many things that are damaging our planet are beyond our ability to fix. However, we are the spiritual beings who came here to experience the fullness of life in human form.

We are the ones who can make a difference. We are amazing, intelligent, talented, resourceful, resilient, tenacious and persevering. This is our home and only we can save it; then perhaps, when our grandchildren thank us for leaving them a beautiful, healthy loving planet. We can say I was thinking of you while I got involved and helped create heaven on Earth. From my environmental heart to yours, Thomas

As the Native American does when he makes choices about the future, s/he considers how it will effect several generations in the future!

September 17   Rumpled or Smooth

Let us picture Oneness as a gigantic cloth. We are all threads that make up this wonderful cloth. Each thread supports every other thread and keeps it intact and looking beautiful. When one of the threads gets torn or raveled or snagged, it affects the rest of the fabric. It is easy to become unraveled! We experience losses of jobs and loves and loved ones and homes and dreams. Then the whole cloth begins to look rumpled. It is no longer smooth and whole.

Each thread in life is connected to every other thread, in an infinite amount of ways. We are indivisible in spirit, in mind, in soul, and love, so it seems. When we do things that do not support our own life experience, it affects our mates, our children, our neighbors, everyone across the globe, in some way. Simple things, like if a person smokes a cigarette and it affects their health, it affects the cloth. If someone says an unkind remark, it spoils the fabric. It I choose to eat unhealthy food, it hurts the team. If I hurt anyone or anything in any way, it damages the cloth.

We are infinitely, eternally tied to each other! We are our sister and brother's keepers. We are so intricately bound to each other that when one of us is injured in any way, we are all injured. The giant hurricane happening now on the east coast of the United States is happening to our family's cloth.

Let us take some time to appreciate our uniqueness and our Oneness. Let us take a deep breath and connect with all the other threads of life. They are animal, mineral, vegetable, human, and every subatomic particle of Creation.

Let us be very conscious of our thoughts and words and deeds and know that they make up the fabric of life. May we love each other to wholeness and become the smooth cloth of Life! From my heart threads to yours, Thomas

Honor the tapestry that we each are part of, breathe and feel the interconnection of all that are touched by the single thread and the whole cloth!

September 18   Rich Beyond Measure

Sometimes we get stuck and we look around at our lives and we question our status. Perhaps we don't have the love relationship we have always desired. Maybe we don't have the career, and the house and the car and the travel and the perks we feel we could have. We look in the mirror and maybe our physique isn't quite what we had pictured it would be. At times like these, it is only natural to have some feelings of regret and sadness.

Then there is another way we might see ourselves. All of us are the same at our core. We are amazing, brilliant, magnificent bubbles of light! From this perspective, there is nothing we need to do, to make us better than we are. We are already enough! We don't need more classes, intelligence, experience, money or heart. To step into the fullness of who we are is to be content with ourselves.

Let us be grateful for all that we are! All of our human warts, limitations, annoyances and fears are not who we are! Let us stop regretting and let us start expecting. Expect a miracle to happen for you and your family or friends and all humanity. When we are thankful for this moment in our life, it opens doors to places we have never been. Gratitude allows us to open our hearts and minds to creating a whole new life expression.

We are literally treasures. There is nothing we lack. Now is the time to remember our Divinity! Now is the time to see the incredible, limitlessness of our being. Then we can know that we lack nothing of true value. We are rich beyond measure. From my grateful heart to yours, Thomas

As often as you can today, be grateful for and contented with who you are right now!

September 19   How are you?

What is going on in your life? Is everything good or is there room for improvement? What would you do differently that would make your life flow? What kind of people are in your life? Are they loving and supportive? What kind of a friend are you? Are you following a plan? How is your health, physical, mental, emotional? Are you working too hard? How are your days unfolding? Too much work, not enough play?

Are you doing things that will create your innermost desires? Are you eating food that enhances your health? Are you doing things that support the planet and its inhabitants? Are you making decisions that will support your children and grandchildren's future? Are you exercising regularly? Have you called mom, dad, daughter, son, sister, brother, friend to cheer them up?

These are questions that I often ask myself. It sounds like a lot of mind chatter. However, it is easy for me to get lost in daily activities and forget why I am here. It starts with being okay with me even if I don't answer the above questions very well.

We are here together and it would be wonderful if we take time to look at how we might make the world a better place. And one way, is to ask some of these questions and allow the answers to lead you to perhaps a more fulfilling life that is connected to everything. "Just asking" from my questioning heart to yours, Thomas

Allow the above questions to lead you to answers that will bring more fulfillment and enjoyment to your life!

September 20 There is nowhere else I would rather be

In truth, the past is a mind recording of events that either have gone or are happening as we speak. Either way when we give our energy to what did happen or what might happen, we are not happening? When I worry about what took place, part of me goes there and when I give it more thought and energy more of me goes there.

When I worry about what might take place in the future, that part of me leaves as well. When those parts of me are running my life, I have little left for you or me! We are both robbed of the totality of this moment in time.

Ellie Cooper reminded me the other day that dogs are always in the present. Children are almost always in the now. Mature adults are almost always somewhere else, so much for growing up. We don't know how long we get for a lifetime; even thinking of it takes us out of the moment.

In every moment we find ourselves at the cross roads of life. We often get lost. By this I mean we lose the ability to see all of the possibilities of our lives. The conscious mind does not, cannot know the infinite array of opportunity present in any given moment.

To allow ourselves to be truly in touch with where we are, we will want to pause and allow the present experience to sink in. What does it look, taste, smell, feel or sound like? We get so caught up in our history and our desire to escape some of it that we lose the magic of the only moment there is.

In Buddhism we are taught mindfulness as opposed to mindlessness. Most of the time we are not aware of who we are and what we are truly creating. We are asleep. In order to wake up we get to focus on the present.

One way is through meditation by slowing down and noticing. Another way is to be present with whatever we are doing and bring all of our awareness to the activity and the Universe will take care of the details. From my present heart to yours, Thomas

Here is a helpful affirmation to bring us back to this moment: I open myself to all the wondrous and bountiful gifts the Universe has to offer me and I allow it to flow through me now!

September 21   Stardust

Every atom in your body is billions of years old. Hydrogen, the most common element in the universe and a major feature of your body, was produced in the big bang 13.7 billion years ago. Heavier atoms such as carbon and oxygen were forged in stars between 7 billion and 12 billion years ago, and blasted across space when the stars exploded. Some of these explosions were so powerful that they also produced the elements heavier than iron, which stars can't construct. This means that the components of your body are truly ancient: you are stardust.

It is wonderful to consider the physical nature of our being, as well as the spiritual. We are ancient. No wonder most of us have such a love affair with the stars in the sky. It is home and who we are. Gazing at the Milky Way Galaxy on a dark night gives me shivers. It makes me feel what E.T. felt when he was left behind. We are recent inhabitants of our wonderful blue space craft Earth. However, atoms that are a part of us are part of our gorgeous planet as well. I believe we feel that connection too. That is why it is so important for us to care for this sacred place. It is us!

When we realize who we are and what we are, we begin to glow inside. And when we all turn on our heart lights, we may even light up like E.T.! Remember....phone home! From my ancient heart to yours, Thomas

Several times today, let yourself BE stardust and feel the Oneness of all that is!

September 22   Rhyming

Here I am typing in beautiful Sedona. Thinking about what we can all do to make a difference every day. Perhaps we'll find a way.

Find a way to love ourselves. Find a way to pay our bills. Find a way to cure our ills. Find a way to get love chills. Find a way to heal our Earth. Find a way to reduce our girth. Find a way to our own self-worth. Find a way to feed the poor. Find a way to live without more. Find a way to love our chore. Find a way to our inner core. Find a way to stay in love. Find a way to save a dove. Find a way to heal our hearts. Find a way to make cherry tarts. Find a way to make words rhyme. Find a way to get more time. Find a way for auld lang syne.

Find a way to live with passion. Find a way to live without dashing. Find a way to slow down our life. Find a way to reduce our strife. Find a way to love your wife. Find a way to get more hugs. Find a way to not sweep under the rug. Find a way to give our heart a tug. Find a way for free health care. Find a way to love and share. Find a way to work together. Find a way to change our weather. Find a way to get folks to vote. Find a way to give homeless a coat. Find a way for a vegan float!

When we find a way to stay in our hearts, we will find the ways to create the world we desire. There are infinite amounts of ways we can work together. Let's do this. There is no one that can stop us, but us. Let's find a way! From my rhyming heart to yours, Thomas

Slow it all down for a few minutes each day and allow your passion to ignite you with love and laughter!

September 23   Moon in Aries

The full moon is just a day away, blossoming in her radiance on Sept. 24th. Light is shining on karmic shadows and long-standing wounds in us and in our relationships. What will carry the relationships through is our commitment to the bigger picture and trusting that Divine order is at play.

This moon in Aries forms a conjunction with Chiron — the "wounded healer" ruler of fear, insecurity, and vulnerability, bringing up deep seated insecurities and vulnerabilities. Your deepest spiritual wounds may be coming to the surface, as well as those in your relationships. This recipe offers a mix of the lunar feminine energies with warring masculine energies revealing shadow and truth.

The T square with karmic Saturn brings in an aspect of setting boundaries and bringing discipline. This spells a recipe for drama in personal, planetary and possibly extra-planetary affairs, as that which has been stuffed under the carpet, is now revealed.

The important thing to remember is that you can re-write your story, in a more loving way. If the story you are telling yourself makes you stark-raving mad, ask yourself if it is true. If you expand your vision to take in more information, you may be able to rearrange the elements to tell a kinder and more empowering story. This information is courtesy of Astrologer Elizabeth Wilcock. You can access her at elizabethwilcock.com.

This seems apropos to what is occurring right now in the United States Senate Confirmation Committee. It is time to shine the light on our darkness and bring to light the divine nature of who we are. Many men are stuck in an old patriarchal paradigm. They have a lot of fear about losing all the power that has been in their hands for thousands of years.

It is time for the rise of Venus energy, where both men and women connect with their feminine nurturing energy. Once again, let us all come from a place of love and not judgment. Let us suspend, at least for the moment, our political leanings and truly ask for Divine intervention to help guide us through this maze. From my Aries moon heart to yours, Thomas

Sit down and rewrite your story so that it has a loving and magical component to it! Let the Divine You shine through!

September 24   Fahrenheit 11/9

Lou Ann and I just saw this movie. It was a huge movie about vital issues that concern us all. Michael Moore, the creator of the film, is a brilliant, thorough documentary movie maker. He goes to great lengths to develop a story that must be seen by everyone who cares about the United States.

Moore doesn't pull any punches in his narrative about the state of our country, before and since Donald Trump became president. He is also not soft on President Obama and Hillary Clinton. I encourage everyone to see this movie. Whether you are politically knowledgeable or active, it can still enlighten you as to what Americans might do to take back their country.

I have avoided sharing politics with you as much as possible. I have wanted to keep the essence about heart and soul issues. I still want to keep the spirit of our message centered in Oneness. Now I feel I must take a stand for all the Earth's people and animals and beings that have no voice.

We inhabitants of planet Earth are standing on the brink of potential tragedies, for a majority of its citizens. Climate change, poverty, war, hunger and a myriad of other challenges face us. It is time for the extraordinary, ordinary people of the world to stand up and be counted.

The powers that be, have mostly sold out to money and power. We need to encourage heart centered fellow Americans, just like us, to run for office. Then, we get to do all we can, to get them elected. It may not be easy, but it will be worth the effort.

Right now, more than a hundred candidates for office are women. This is fantastic! Hopefully there will be more. When we get more than fifty per cent women holding office, we can move forward to a brighter tomorrow and change the world.

I encourage everyone to get involved in some way, so that Michael Moore makes movies about how wonderful everything is! From my engaged heart to yours, Thomas

Look at the bigger picture of Planet Earth and shower peace and gratitude all around it everywhere!

September 25   Make a Difference

Lou Ann and I are having fun creating entertainment segments for our television show. We are focusing on themes like climate change and sustainability and kindness, animals and healing others. We have an unlimited supply of different kinds of shows we might do. We want to have the program entertaining and trans-formative.

It is not enough for us to just entertain. Our goal is to inform in a way that has people take action. We want to have audience participation in each show and then encourage the attendees to get involved. This world is a mess and we all need to pitch in to make it work.

Each of us in every town can get involved by doing just a little. A lot of "littles" add up to a lot. There is a local Kindness group here that makes kindness charms and many other kind gestures.

The Kindness Charm Story

A group of women in Sedona have been focused on a special approach to kindness for many years. The women have been making "Kindness" charms out of broken, recycled and surplus donated jewelry and dispersing them, not only around Sedona, but across the nation and worldwide.

Each Charm had a tag that says "Take me home and spread kindness". To date the women have distributed over 6,000 charms to every state in the US and over three dozen countries, in the hope that they are found by someone that needs to be reminded that they are loved.

This effort is carried out anonymously. Charms appear laying under a bench, hanging from a branch, draped over a rock or on some other object where they will eventually be found. The goal is simply to encourage acts of kindness, large and small, both in Sedona and around the world.

This amazing group of dedicated, hardworking, committed women is called SedonaKind. If you want to join this wonderful life changing organization contact them at Sedonakind.org. From my grateful heart to yours, Thomas

There are a myriad of kind actions we can take today. Which one or ones will you share?

September 26   Like an Eagle

Our blog title is the name of a song we sang in the Sedona Canyon Singers for many years. We learned it from Larry Reid who died prematurely and we sang it at his memorial celebration! When I sing the words, I cry. I remember Larry and his wonderful wife Sandy who is still directing music back in Iowa. The words are so rich with feeling, written by Carl Strommen. It is available on YouTube.com Sung by a young person's choir; here is this glorious song:
https://www.youtube.com/watch?v=MlSzZHmLMhc

We are all eagles! Some have decided to stay in our nests. Some have decided to spread our wings and fly to places unknown. Life goes by in a flash and we may look back and wonder how we got to our current place. Then perhaps reminisce about how our lives might have been if we had taken more chances to soar above the clouds and discovered the magnificence of flying like an eagle.

We don't know how much life we have left to experience. I encourage all of us to fly like eagles and go beyond our wildest dreams!   From my soaring heart to yours, Thomas

After you listen to the song, let yourself hum it throughout your day and feel it uplifting you into your wildest dreams!

September 27   A Loving Act

Sarah Nathan, a good friend of ours sent us an article from Daily Good News, that Inspires. It tells the story of a teacher who does a wonderful loving thing that she has been doing since the Columbine massacre.

Every Friday afternoon, she asks her students to take out a piece of paper and write down the names of four children with whom they'd like to sit the following week. The children know that these requests may or may not be honored. She also asks the students to nominate one student who they believe has been an exceptional classroom citizen that week. All ballots are privately submitted to her.

And every single Friday afternoon, after the students go home, she takes out those slips of paper, places them in front of her, and studies them. She looks for patterns.

Who is not getting requested by anyone else?

Who can't think of anyone to request?

Who never gets noticed enough to be nominated?

Who had a million friends last week and none this week?

You see, Chase's teacher is not looking for a new seating chart or "exceptional citizens." Chase's teacher is looking for lonely children. She's looking for children who are struggling to connect with other children. She's identifying the little ones who are falling through the cracks of the class's social life. She is discovering whose gifts are going unnoticed by their peers. And she's pinning down—right away—who's being bullied and who is doing the bullying.

As a teacher, parent, and lover of all children, I think this is the most brilliant Love Ninja strategy I have ever encountered. It's like taking an X-ray of a classroom to see beneath the surface of things and into the hearts of students.

It is like mining for gold—the gold being those children who need a little help, who need adults to step in and teach them how to make friends, how to ask others to play, how to join a group, or how to share their gifts. And it's a bully deterrent because every teacher knows that bullying usually happens outside her eye-shot and that often kids being bullied are too intimidated to share. But, as she said, the truth comes out on those safe, private, little sheets of paper.

This brilliant woman watched Columbine knowing that all violence begins with disconnection. All outward violence begins as inner loneliness. Who are our next shooters and how do we stop them? She watched that tragedy knowing that children who aren't being noticed may eventually resort to being noticed by any means necessary.

And so she decided to start fighting violence early and often in the world within her reach. What Chase's teacher is doing when she sits in her empty classroom studying those lists written with shaky 11-year-old hands is saving lives. I am convinced of it. This story was authored by

Glennon Doyle-Melton who wrote "Carry on, Warrior: Thoughts of Life Unarmed."

All that I have to offer is this. Why don't all the rest of us find ways of connecting with each other, so no one feels left out? We could call it The Love Connection! Find someone today that is feeling less than, ostracized, neglected or estranged for any reason and let them know that they are loved! From my loved heart to yours, Thomas

What a brilliant way to help children who feel disconnected! Use your inner radar today and find someone who may need some extra attention and let them know in some magical way that they are loved!

September 28   Integrity

Being a vegan and still overweight, I decided to reduce my consumption of grains and carbs. I have been doing it for three days and lost a couple of pounds. Today I got home after three sets of tennis and it was 93 degrees and I was hot and thirsty. I could have just had more ice water but wanted something with some flavor in it. There was an unopened bottle of grapefruit juice left over from one of our guests. It had 32 grams of sugar.

I thought, well I've exercised a lot and have already lost some weight so I will pour the juice into my drink container and mix it with the little bit of vitamin drink I had left. I picked up the container which has a screw top and most of the juice went splashing all over the kitchen floor. Thank you, Universe from keeping me from myself and staying in integrity!

I believe we have integrity when we line up our mind and heart with our soul. Perhaps we had a plan before we arrived? Maybe our soul wanted us to create something special for us and for humanity. Maybe we wanted to find a soulmate and live with our best friend. Maybe we wanted to invent something that would be the cure for one of our major diseases. I feel integrity is often about being inclusive. Athletes often do this. They give credit to others when they could have been the one that got the reward. When we do what we say we are going to do, more often than not, we are living in integrity. We apologize to others when perhaps they could have, but didn't. We give others the benefit of the doubt when circumstances were unclear.

Doesn't it feel good to do something so others will feel good about themselves? It doesn't take much to live in integrity. It mostly takes a little time to think what others desire and take an action that makes the world a better place. From my hopeful heart to yours, Thomas

Let integrity be your guiding light today. If you falter, let that be okay too!

September 29   Love Yourself

In 1979 when Terry Cole-Whitaker wrote "What You Think of Me is none of my Business?" It was such a landmark book at the time. In 1982 Lou Ann and I created a Healing Conference in Scottsdale Arizona and Terry was our keynote speaker. She was fabulous!

We are often our own worst critics; we don't need someone else to help us out! I have shared before that I still think thoughts and then sometimes take actions solely based upon what others think.

Why do we suck in our gut when we are around others? Why do we wear lots of make up? Why do we get plastic surgery to improve our looks? There is nothing wrong with dressing well, or having a beautiful home or car or whatever. However, when our self-worth is tied up in these things, it can keep us from our real value.

Most of us have old patterns of not loving ourselves enough. They were learned in our homes and schools and local environments. They just are not true! We are all beautiful and capable of the most important things. That is, being the best me I can!

So if your personal self-regard suffers sometimes like mine, just remember that you are always doing the best you can. When we pause and realize that, then we can relax and let ourselves be okay with all that we have done. Let us unconditionally love and support each other in all of our magnificence! From my lovable heart to yours, Thomas

Pause, relax and realize how beautiful and capable you are!

September 30   Your Significance

You may think that you are completely insignificant in this world.

But someone drinks coffee every morning from their favorite cup that you gave them.

Someone heard a song on the radio that reminded them of you.

Someone read the book you recommended, and plunged headfirst into it.

Someone remembered your joke and smiled, returning home from work

in the evening.

Someone loves themselves a little more, because you gave them a compliment.

Never think that you have no influence whatsoever. Your trace, which you leave behind with even a few good deeds, cannot be erased.

By Christina Makeyevka

"Life is so simple and pure at its core. We often make it so complicated. Let us dedicate ourselves to do the smallest, kindest things for each other. It will perhaps change the world, like no other thing has." From my significant heart to yours, Thomas

Choose doing even the smallest and kindest thing for another today!

October 1   The Gift of Life!

Here I am on Sunday night, wrapping up another week of sharing this blog with you folks. Lou Ann and I are so blessed to be living in our home, atop a hill just south of a wide expanse of ancient red rocks. We call it the Million Dollar View! Actually, it is priceless. We are so thankful that the Universe has gifted us with this place, this life and this love!

I thank you for reading and responding and sharing our blog, when you desire. We've been doing it for 471 days in a row. When I started, I had no idea that this would occur. I have things inside my heart that I want the world to know. They may not be profound. They may be just my perspective. They may not ring true with others. I feel like I have to share them. Not as an obligation, but as a passion and a responsibility.

It is an honor, to be read by another light being. We are both part of the same Oneness. We have something to say to each other that might make a difference, in a positive way. We live in a world where many folks are yelling and screaming. And many are in such pain, that it makes sense that they do yell out! We can hold one another when we suffer and help us each to feel loved. We can listen to each other without thinking what we might say next. It is one of the greatest gifts in life, to be heard by another's heart and soul.

I believe that everything is on purpose. It is not an accident that I write and you read and respond. It is part of some great grand plan of consciousness that we get to live it out together! We are the gift of life! From my very thankful heart to yours, Thomas

Share from your heart with someone today – connection is one of our greatest gifts here!

October 2   Every Step We Take

When I was out on my walk, which I have done hundreds of times, today, it was a difficult journey. I was more fatigued than usual, going up one of the hills.

Two days ago, I felt like I could run up the hill! Perhaps my *Biorhythms* are off? These are the supposed cycles that your mind/body/spirit complex experiences as a result of an abundance or lack of universal energy within the self. Physical, emotional, intellectual and spiritual aspects of a person are affected. Science has largely negated this. However, I know there are days that I have higher and lower energy, mentally, physically and emotionally.

So today, I was trudging up the hill instead of gliding. What I did become aware of is, that I was going to continue no matter how I felt. I also remembered a little mantra that I sometimes say, which is: One more step I take, is one more step I take.

Let me explain. It is clear that the better physical shape we are in will most likely lead to a longer, healthier life. Is it guaranteed? No! The odds are with us though. I believe it is important to believe that this may be the only life we get to live. It will encourage us to live better, love better, eat better, think better, laugh more, be healthier, be present and live in the moment.

I returned back home from my four mile walk and I was not as tired, as half way through the walk. I realize that I am blessed to be able to exercise like this. I am healthy enough to do it and I have the time.

I am encouraging all of you to take one more step. One more emotional, spiritual, physical step will earn you many more perhaps. Then your journey may be longer, healthier and happier and richly blessed! From my healthy heart to yours, Thomas

Know that this life is the only one we are conscious of at this moment, so take one more emotional, spiritual, physical step and enJOY the journey!

October 3 'Why' is not a Useful Question

This was a song that a good friend of ours used to sing, named Rudi Harst. He is the leader of the Celebration Circle in San Antonio Texas. A better question might be, what am I going to do with what I have just created? You see, when we ask why, it keeps us separate from our creation. It often implies that someone, something, outside of ourselves, did something to us. It allows us to avoid responsibility for our creations.

Our wonderful mentor, Arnold Patent, taught us a powerful way to move through self-created obstacles. Instead of asking why did this happen to me? Inferring we didn't have anything to do with it. Patent said, don't get stuck trying to analyze your way out of your predicament.

Simply, visualize what you have created and get in touch with the feeling you are experiencing around it. Once in touch with how you feel, let go. Then immediately allow yourself to feel how you truly want to feel. Once you have accessed that new feeling; stay with it and allow it to be what you are experiencing. Not the old feeling of being a victim!

It can be a challenging thing to move away from always asking why is this happening to me? We have been trained to look outside of ourselves for someone else to blame.

It is a powerful thing to take responsibility for everything in our life. This is not to blame ourselves; it is to find solution by going inside and creating what we desire, on the feeling level. Once we do this, then we begin to live powerful lives! From my inquiring heart to yours, Thomas

Instead of 'why' which avoids responsibility, feel your feelings, then let go of it. When you're ready feel how you truly want to feel.

October 4 A Life that's Full of Wonder!

Lou Ann and I went to see the wonderful young person's movie, "Small Foot." However, I was enthralled by the fabulous music. I was overwhelmed by the script and the story. This is a movie for everyone from 2 to 92. This is a movie for your eyes to sparkle, your cheeks to flush, your face to hurt from smiling so much and your sides to ache from laughing out loud! The message is all about what goes on in life, since we beings had a brain. The story tells us that when we give up our beliefs that no longer serve us, we will create the planet we all desire!

Seldom has a movie moved me this much! Please go see it if you are able and take the whole family and live a life full of wonder! Here is the song" Wonderful Life" from YouTube:
https://www.youtube.com/watch?v=ow9_519_xVQ

From my overjoyed heart to yours, Thomas

If you get a chance watch the YouTube video of this wondrous song! Better yet, watch the movie 'Small Foot'!

October 5   Use Your Heart While It is beating

This is a line from another song from the wonderful movie "Small Foot". Get involved! Don't go through life and not show up for yourself and for others. Life is so precious. We each get to constantly choose how we spend each moment.

There are so many possibilities in life, that sometimes it can be overwhelming. What is the best path for us to take? The road less traveled? No one can decide for us. We often get advice from well-meaning folks who want us to succeed. They love us and sometimes feel they know what is best for us. The deciding factor for me is to follow my heart.

I am reminded of the sixth chapter of Matthew in the Bible, where Jesus says among other things: "for where your treasure is, there will your heart be also!" I believe he was encouraging us to not put our treasure in finite things, but in things that are eternal.

The things in life to treasure are love, joy, happiness, friendship, family, loved ones, doing what we love, holding hands, getting hugs, encouraging each other, serving each other. The list could go on and on. Watch this wonderful video by Niall Horan called "Finally Free" from the film. Here is the URL for YouTube https://www.youtube.com/watch?v=OWs7CRvV9Bg.

Yes, it is fun to have a career and have a beautiful home, excellent car, fine clothes, travel, and retire with wealth. They pale in comparison, to love as you are loved. To have a friend who is with you forever. Having a loving partner to share all our moments. Having children, and loving, guiding and nurturing them, as they move through life. Finding a cause to believe in. One that will help humanity, the environment and all the beings of the Earth.

Let us, step in to the unknown of heroic living. We see that kind of living on Facebook, everyday; like the little girl who is dining in a restaurant and sees a homeless man outside. She then takes her uneaten meal out and gives it to the man. When we live from our heart we find the way to transcend the limitations of modern living. From my beating heart to yours, Thomas

Find what cause you passionately believe in with your whole heart! Share it with us all!

October 6   Another March

A few of us men and a whole lot of passionate women, will be marching again in Sedona Arizona, tomorrow at 10 am. Regardless of the political choices you normally make, please get involved for the support of women, who have been violated by men.

There should be no sides in this action. Every human being on Earth must be treated with love, respect and safety. It is not funny to get drunk and do stupid things. It is time for all people to stand up and create a planet that is totally safe for all of its beings.

It is true, that those of us, who act out on others in inappropriate ways, have damaged places within. For those of us who have been hurt and have never healed, it is time to find a way to inner peace. Even though we men do not like it said of us, we are responsible for most of the violence in this world.

I urge all men to get the courage to find a way to heal the pain inside of us; that creates all this mayhem. We were not trained well and we carry so much unexpressed sorrow and pain that women and children and all the other creatures of our Earth suffer for it.

Not only is it time to march, it is time to vote. It is time to vote in as many women and men with open and healed hearts as possible. We are standing on the brink of a huge shift in consciousness. It is time to heal the hurt and stand together as one. If you are in Sedona or some other place in our country, please join us! From my marching heart to yours, Thomas

Reread Eckhart Tolle's book A New Earth about our pain bodies – heal and forgive!

October 7 The Magnificent Seven

Lou Ann and I went to a rally today in Sedona. It was to take a stand against the possibility of enrolling a Supreme Court Justice who has questionable credentials at best. Only seven of us showed up, compared to the 1500 that showed up here in January of 2017. The numbers were not that important. We were taking a stand against tyranny!

Like the 1960 movie The Magnificent Seven, we were few against many. We didn't care. We displayed our signs and placards. We waved at the passing vehicles. At a certain point, I felt like we were making some headway, when some of the folks were becoming halfway peaceful. That is, they waved back with at least a half of a peace sign!

Yes, there were those that opposed us and let us know how they felt. However there were many more that beeped horns and gave us thumbs up! We didn't expect to make a difference in the foregone vote that would happen today. We showed up anyway, because the world needs us seven, plus many more millions to take a stand for decency, honor, love and respect.

Yes, we are angry. We have watched our democracy being torn apart by others. We are standing for all oppressed people and in particular women, who have been violated and not believed. It is time for the Magnificent Seven to ride into town again; this time, not for revenge, not to do harm to another, but to band together in the principles of love and freedom for all. To encourage others to find their voice, their hearts, their courage to say "enough is enough!"

Please join those of us who will not back down, who will not go away, and who will rally other like-minded folks, to take action and vote! A new day is coming for America. A day in which America will be kind again! From my magnificent heart to yours, Thomas

Begin kindness in your own life today to yourself and others!

October 8   It's Sunday Night

Another week finished, another on its way. We have been through a lot, all of us. We are feeling a lot of emotions about the world we have created. We can look at all the events and take sides about what is right and what is not. I don't believe that serves us. Without trying to change the other person, which we cannot, we get to make some powerful choices.

A nation divided will not stand. At least it will not stand, as a beacon for others to see and emulate. From each side of the issues, it is easy to see how we are right and they are wrong. If we remain in this position, the gridlock will literally kill us.

As we begin the next thirty days together, let us take a different tack. We can still do the same things we planned to do. We can volunteer, canvass, make phone calls and help others to get involved to vote, march on the Capitol, make passionate speeches. This time let us realize that there is only one race, human, deeply flawed, and currently not serving planet Earth.

However, we are the only ones who can break this stalemate. Let us pause, perhaps pray, maybe visualize, that what will occur in our world, will be the power of love, healing hearts that are broken and minds that are poisoned. So that we will all stand together one day and hold hands around the world. From my hopeful heart to yours, Thomas

Visualize what the power of love can do for healing hearts that are broken and minds that are poisoned.

October 9 Two Wolves

There are two wolves that are always fighting, one named Darkness and Despair the other named Light and Hope. Which one wins? The one that you feed!

A good friend of mine once shared: Means and ends are the same. The action and outcome are one. To achieve peace, we feel and express inner peacefulness.

The polarization of our country and perhaps the world is at a critical point. It will not serve our planet for us to continue to insult and attack each other. It is important for those of us who desire to create peace on Earth, to understand this. Means and ends are identical. The way we go about achieving our desired outcome is exactly what we will receive.

It does not matter what others may say or do, it only matters how we respond. We get to be clear; we get to focus on the divine principles of love and support, forgiveness and empathy, compassion and caring. We get to come from that deep part of our heart and soul connection that transcends our human frailty.

Let us all become the reason for hope. Let us be capable of having the audacity to hope. In the end, it is what we feed the world that will determine our mutual destiny! From my hopeful light heart to yours, Thomas

Feed your inner wolf of light and hope – express peace and be it!

October 10 Light Beings

Lou Ann and I were watching a Hallmark movie. The heroine in the film loses her memory in an auto accident somewhere in Vermont. The male lead is a local doctor who is taking care of her. They decide to give her the name Elizabeth. While we are watching the movie I got a message of an Airbnb guest who wants to book a room in November. Her name is Elizabeth. Love those simple kinds of synchronizations.

Life is a magical adventure that we sometimes take for granted. We work hard, have families, and explore all of our life choices. We can get lost in all the activities and not remember who we are; spiritual beings having a human experience. We came here to express our beauty and our magnificence. We intentionally forget about our Divinity. Then we begin to wake up and to live in the moment, in the midst of this beautiful Universe.

Then as we move through life, we get the opportunity to discover that eternal loving nature of our soul. Now is the time to re-focus on our reason for being here. It is the reconnecting to a purpose for living. Let us renew the dance with our heart. Let us treasure our experience and our mission. To be fully expressed human beings, who love our families, our creatures, our friends, and our planet!

A new climate report just came out yesterday about how we are doing; we only have until 2040 to turn ourselves around. The clock is ticking, louder than ever before. Let us return to the wonder we felt as children and the belief we could do anything. We can do this, if we all pull together. We are the light beings that the world has been waiting for. Now is our time to shine! From my serendipitous heart to yours, Thomas

There are so many creative possibilities to turn around our world. One small suggestion is refill your glass water bottle rather than use plastic bottles. This can help landfills and the ocean!

October 11   When Your Heart is Free!

Adshanti said "Until you give the whole world its freedom, you'll never have your own freedom!"

Mooji said: "When you don't want to be interesting, then you are free!"

Tolle said: "When you become aware of silence, immediately there is that state of inner stillness. You are present. You have stepped out of thousands of years of collective human conditioning!"

Nisargadatta Maharaj shared: "When you don't require anything from the world and nothing from God, when you don't desire anything, when you don't strive for anything, don't expect anything, the divine will enter you, unasked and unexpected."

Pema Chodron said: "The truth you believe and cling to makes you unavailable to hear anything new!"

I share these wise words tonight from folks just like you and me. They have the same physiology, the same kind of brain, mind and heart. The major difference is that they took the time to listen.

They became quiet long enough to achieve a level of self-realization. They are not better than we are, they are not smarter than we are, and they are not more spiritual than we are. They allowed themselves to open up to the possibility of who they are.

We can do the same thing. Perhaps we won't be able to meditate as much and as long as they did. Perhaps we will get to spend most of our time doing, rather than being.

However, if for a few moments each day, we become quiet enough to stop thinking, we too can connect to the beautiful Divine nature of our being. Then we can feel free and perhaps give the world its freedom! From my free heart to yours, Thomas

Choose one of the quotes above and follow it for the day! Be the Divine Being you truly are!

October 12   He Filled Up Our Senses!

Twenty one years ago, John Denver left us, on Wings That Fly! Literally! There are many celebrities that enter our lives and entertain us. There are few who have had the transcendent, spiritual effect of John Denver. He wrote songs that touched our hearts in very deep places. Here is one of his most deeply touching songs that many may not have heard: Here is the URL for the whole song – On the Wings of a Dream, please enjoy every second of it: https://www.youtube.com/watch?v=xrovGPLw9SQ

It is so true; life goes by so quickly while we are here on Earth. John was only with us for almost fifty four years. Way too short for many of us. And yet, if you are like me, he changed my life forever with his words and his voice and his heart.
We have mutual sadness about not having John with us in person anymore. However you and I can listen to his gifts and his genius as long as we are able. From my dream filled heart to yours, Thomas

Take time to listen to 'On the Wings of a Dream' – it will touch your heart as it did ours!

October 13 Rhymes and Reasons

It was fifty years ago that John Denver released his album Rhymes and Reasons. It seems like yesterday in many ways. I was having many sad days about my love relationship. His words were like he had read my mind when he wrote this song a half century ago. Here are the amazing lyrics on YouTube: https://www.youtube.com/watch?v=BN4AZtep4wQ

Now here we are, Lou Ann and I, amongst the flowers of our garden, and it feels like a returning to a more innocent time like 1969. What are the rhymes and reasons of our life? Ours right now is to be digging the dirt and nurturing the plants and flowers that are our sisters and our brothers. It is a delight to be in the soil and feel connected to our beautiful planet. May we all feel a deep relationship to this fragile spaceship and find our rhyme and reason. From my nurtured heart to yours, Thomas

Create your garden of flowers, veggies or even a symbolic one!

October 14 Notes in an Octave

Lou Ann and I went to see A Star is born tonight. The movie is raw, visceral, emotional, exciting and brilliantly directed and acted. I would guess that Bradley Cooper, who directed, produced and starred, and Lady Gaga and Sam Elliot who starred, will get Academy Award nominations. If you like highly entertaining, well-made movies don't miss it!

I was going to title this blog tonight A Star is Born before I went to the movie. There is a scene in it where Elliot's character shares with Lady Gaga about something that Cooper's character said. He said there are 12 notes in an octave and that musicians get to play with that. That is all they get. And that she (Lady Gaga) did those notes in a special way.

I thought about all of us. We are all given life, and breath and brains and minds and hearts. We all get to play our songs, our music, sing our words. Cooper's character tells Gaga's character earlier in the movie, (my recollection) to sing her words, not to sell herself short, to sing what she believed.

I am encouraging all of us tonight, to sing our songs. We may not be musicians; we may not even be good at singing. We all have something inside of us that longs to be shared. We have gifts that no one else has. We have a way of expressing that is totally unique to us!

Please find your voice; whether it is a whisper in your lover's ear, or encouragement to your children, or shouting to the full moon. Say it loud and say it with the knowledge, that it comes from a deep place inside of you that is sacred to the Universe. And say it till the day you die! You came here with a purpose to let your light so shine, that all of the rest of us are illuminated forever! From my 12 note heart to yours, Thomas

Let the dream in your soul that is filled with your love and light express itself!

October 15 Givers

This afternoon a 2011 dark blue Prius parked in our driveway. It is the identical color and model and year of our dark blue Prius. The one in the driveway is owned by Hank and Sharon Yuloff of Yuloff Creative Marketing Solutions. They arrived at our home to give us a gift. At the last Sedona Chamber of Commerce meeting we were fortunate to have won a drawing for the amazing gift of two hours with this brilliant couple.

They have a slogan on one of their marketing kits that says "If Everything Happens for a Reason, BE THE REASON THINGS HAPPEN" Lou Ann and I have a lot of abilities and Internet and Social Media marketing are not among them. For two hours they gave us answers, asked the right questions and shared their deep experience in the new marketing world.

Lou Ann wrote notes continuously and we amassed a wonderful marketing plan which we will be working on in the months and years to come. I was so impressed with the knowledge, experience and the spirit in which they shared their gift with us. We felt like we had met another portion of our family and boy are we glad to have met them.

They gave us new insights about producing and marketing our TV show. They shared many ways to increase our visibility of the show and about the release and marketing of our first book. For a sneak peek about the show, go to Enriching Life Forever on You Tube. Here's the URL: https://www.youtube.com/channel/UColxOBAIudg5IKwY384eoZg

And if you are inspired, please subscribe for us. All you need is a Gmail account and hit the bell.

This may seem like promotional material for Yuloff Creative Marketing Solutions and it is. However, never during our time together did they try to sell us on anything for their own benefit. They were here to give and they did it wholeheartedly and warmly. We felt so supported in our vision and it will be accelerated by these two wonderful givers.

Everything happens for a reason and once again the Universe did not fail us. I wish for all of you, continued success in your deepest dreams and your heart's desires. And, you be the reason it all comes true! From my receiving and giving heart to yours, Thomas

Be a heartfelt giver and receive it back tenfold or more!

October 16   What Will They Say When You Die

Lou Ann and I have taken many personal trainings in our time together. They were focused on creating the best life possible, from a variety of perspectives. One of the events we attended had a session in it, where we were to imagine our last day on Earth.

We were lying in a bed. Who was there for you? Was there anyone? What were those who gathered at the foot of your bed, thinking or feeling? Were they sad? Were they just being polite? It was a profound experience for me. As I went through the session I cried and cried, almost inconsolably. The sadness was more about what I felt I had not been, for those gathered at my final day.

I read a tribute to a person on Facebook today given by Cathy Gazda to her beloved friend, Kevin. I just want all of us to have someone write words like this about us on our final day. Here is what she said today.

I wish each of you could have known Kevin, even if you only met him briefly, you'd remember him forever. Like many others, I will miss his brilliant mind, astute observations and profound insights. Which is what brought us together 50 years ago – but, even more so, about life...and what it is to love and be loved. Kevin was kind, funny, witty, generous, considerate, charming, possibly the most eloquent person I've ever known.

Along with these many qualities, Kevin had an extraordinary gift for living in the present moment. He was an active listener...reflecting on what had been said, and what hadn't been said...and offering a thoughtful response. Even with enormous trials over the last 3 years since his diagnosis with a rare form of cancer, he maintained a keen sense of humor and unwavering focus on living each day to its fullest.

You always led by example, Kevin...forever a trailblazer. And, though we will no longer see you in your physical form...like stars in the sky, the radiant light you brought to the world will continue to shine, more boundlessly than ever. Thank you, for being my friend.

I wish this for all of us. Even more wonderful, to hear these words of praise while we are alive and can look in each other's eyes and feel each other's souls.

Cathy was able to share the words she posted today with Kevin, before he died. May we all live our lives so that these words might be said to us! Not to live this way to earn praise, but to live this way because it is who we are and how we showed up! From my thankful heart to yours, Thomas

We each can be our own unique selves just like Kevin!

October 17   Thankful and Forgiving

Be thankful for every breath,

Every swallow   Every grin

Every smile

Every tear

Every frown

Every pound

Every friend

Every daughter

Every word

Every kiss

Every hug

Every romance

Every movie

Every walk

Every bed

Every birthday

Every touch

Every Universe

Every challenge

Everything!

Every son

Every ex-wife

Every thought

Every doubt

Every aha

Every house

Every victory

Every sunrise

Every sunset

Every desert

Every rain

Every song

Every cloud

Every sky

Every planet

Every star

Ask forgiveness for

Every harsh word

Everything I don't recall right now

Every lie

When writing this list, it occurred to me that the forgiveness list could also be on the thankful list. In truth I am thankful for every moment, every thought, every action I have experienced. They are all my life experience.

I encourage you folks to write down a list for yourself and see how rich life is. It doesn't have much to do with things and accomplishments. It has everything to do with being human and blessed. From my thankful and forgiving heart to yours, Thomas

Write your own gratitude/forgiveness list and see how rich your life is!

October 18   They also serve….

They also serve who only stand and wait, was originally the last line in a poem by Milton. It was also a slogan used when I was growing up, during World War II. It signified that those not in the actual battles of the war, were also supporting the efforts of the military, by doing other things to help the cause, like recycling.

I had a dream last night, in which I was giving advice to a young armed forces officer. He was perturbed about not being chosen for a higher rank. I shared with him that being an officer in the armed forces was not about personal gain, it was about service.

I wanted him to know that as an officer he would someday lead a platoon or a squad or a division. There may be thousands of fellow service personnel following him. His job was to serve them. Yes, he would be their leader. Their very lives would be in his hands. His leadership would be healthiest, if it came from a place of caring. When he cared for his troops, he would make better decisions on their behalf. If he used his heart as well as his head then he would eventually rise to the top.

I awoke and thought about service, for all the rest of us. When gentle-men serve their partners, they create all the love they would ever desire to receive. When gentle ladies serve their partners, it is in line with the nature of who they are.

Right now, in our life together, Lou Ann is working a couple of days per week as a pharmacist, about an hour north of here. When she comes home, I always have a hot home cooked meal for her. We serve each other. As I think of it, this has been a major strength of our relationship, serving each other.

We have shared time in our careers, homemaking, cooking, yard work, laundry and almost any task that we were physically able to do. We are one in service. It is a delightful way to partner.

Let us think about the ways we all can serve others, not what is in it for ourselves. It may be a wonderful way to create a whole new Earth that we all want. From my serving heart to yours, Thomas

Serve with all the love in your heart and create a whole new Earth!

October 19 Dreamers

Dreamers are the ones who make the world the magnificent place that it is. It is when we give up dreaming, that our hope fades and our hearts are saddened. Here is something I read on Facebook:

"There's nothing as practical as a dream, well-formed. Every invention, discovery, creative masterpiece, and impossible accomplishment started as an idea then blossomed from there. But dreams are also small business start-ups, college degrees, and marrying the right person. They are common miracles.

Many years ago, a teenage friend and I passed a freshly boarded up gas station that had gone out of business. It was just a defunct gas station to me. Her misty eyes perceived otherwise.

"How sad, that was somebody's *life dream*." Her parents had just lost their own family business. They were moving out of town so they could find other work and begin again.

Dreams aren't just about sleep. They very much inhabit our waking worlds. Whatever your dreams are, I hope you are diligently working towards them to make them reality."

Years ago, Lou Ann and I were involved in Income Builders International (IBI). It was a company that put on seminars about teaching people how to take their dreams to market.

On one weekend, I went to Huntsville Alabama with the director of IBI. He took us to a hill to look at a Saturn V rocket in all of its stages as it lay along the ground. It is over 360 feet long! He brought us there to see what the scientists had built and had taken us to the moon. He went on to say that one of the greatest values of the space program is the inspiration it creates. It allows humanity to keep on dreaming about our origins and to keep moving into the future.

We were watching the movie Tomorrowland again; a wonderful adventure fantasy about our Earth and the possibilities for it. As the movie moves toward its conclusion, we discover that the way to rebuild our Earth in a healthy and natural way is to wake up the dreamers. Once we begin to connect into a powerful reason for living, we get to live amazing and exciting lives. I encourage everyone to keep on dreaming, to paraphrase, "we are our only hope, Obi Wan!" From my hopeful heart to yours, Thomas

Keep on dreaming to bring your light into the world!

October 20 Blogging

We have been doing this together now almost five hundred days in a row. It has been challenging for me to sit at my computer, often late at night and come up with something to say that will be of value. I have an aversion to saying the same thing twice. I don't mind writing about the same subject. For me, it feels like I always want it to be fresh. So, thanks for reading, responding, liking, loving, sharing and commenting.

Today, Facebook gets a lot of criticism. Perhaps a lot of it deserved. However, you and I would not get to have these evening chats unless we Skyped or Zoomed or other computer connections. Lou Ann and I have been discussing making this a podcast. I am not sure if that will be of more value. I am willing to test it out. Please give me your feedback as to whether that would add value or not. Thanks.

We live in a critical time for our planet. The energies present are perhaps as negative as I can remember. Here in the United States, we are so divided. Both sides think they are right. There appears to be little room for compromise.

It might be time to speak from our hearts and not our emotions. The heart is a place where we can all be one. It is the center of our spiritual being. It is easy to know when we come from our heart. It is a place of forgiveness, caring compassion and love. When we are in the space of those feelings, we can overcome any hurt, anger, transgression or event.

Let us take the time to go to a quiet place and inquire of our heart. Let us ask it, what would you like me to do? I believe it has all the wisdom of the Universe and it will lead the way if we take the time to listen.

Once again, thanks for being here for Lou Ann and me. We wish you the best life experience in all that you do. From my thankful blogging heart to yours, Thomas

When you can today take time to go inward to a quiet place, slow down your breathing and ask your heart what it wants from you.

October 21   Pumpkin Bread

This may seem like a fall recipe blog. The bread is what Lou Ann baked tonight (vegan and gluten-free). By the way, they are fabulous! Lou Ann loves to bake and we both love to cook. It is a pun to say that our relationship is delicious! We have been together thirty-eight years. We have learned so much about being partners. It is as if I don't know where I end and she begins. We are so blessed!

What has made our life so sweet is the communication of our hearts. We have learned to ask for what we want. We have learned to find our own space. We have learned how to honor another soul. It hasn't always been peaches and cream! There I did it again!

We took much personal training over the years so that we could be the best friend and lover for the other. We survived three bankruptcies and losing everything we owned. Those financial tragedies only made us closer and stronger. I share all this not to brag. I want everyone to have the best life possible.

Experience has taught me that there is a lot of work to make that happen. It is worth everything to make an effort to be in love with ourselves and with another kindred soul. We don't have to be married or even in a committed relationship. What works is to care so much for someone else that their happiness is even more vital to us than our own. When we love from that place we create a magical treasure of love!

I wish for all of you to have this kind of partnership or friendship with another. If you do not, then let go of what you have been doing that doesn't serve you. Find another person who wants to be in love with life, as you do. Then give it all your intention and energy. When you do that and surrender to the possibility of living from a place of joy, you too will be using the sweetest puns possible! From my sweet heart to yours (I know, I did it again!} Thomas

One of the secrets of a deep, loving relationship is light heartedness!

October 22   Fail Till You are Great at It!

While teaching someone how to hit a tennis ball one day, they were having some difficulty doing it. I shared with them, "how many times do you think Roger Federer, the greatest tennis player of all time, has hit a tennis ball?" They replied "thousands!" I said "millions!" Then I shared if you did something over and over a million times do you think you would develop excellence in doing it?" They said, "of course!"

We often want the easy way to success. There is a joke in Hollywood about Academy Award winners being an overnight success. It only took them twenty years!

Being successful at doing most things will require a lot of repetition and a lot of failures. Even in the area of our personal lives. If we want to have happy lives, it will require practicing being happy from the inside. If we want to have good friends it will require us being a good friend as well.

When we smile at others, it often creates smiles back at us. When we are angry, it is most likely we will receive the same response. I believe if we develop some patience with ourselves and just keep applying our efforts, we will create the desired results. However, it will most likely require lots of failures.

Take a mental inventory of your life right now. Are there things that you have not given enough of your time and energy to create your desired results? I encourage you to find that treasure within you by digging a little deeper. From my never quitting heart to yours, Thomas

Be happy starting from the inside out! Make mistakes and start again! That's how we do it!

October 23   Inner Sustainability

We know that our planet is in trouble and we know who did it! Back in the 1960's comic strip character Pogo famously said about the Vietnam war, "We have met the enemy and he is us!"

Humanity is destroying our precious Earth at an alarming rate. These are ten ways we humans are destroying our sacred home. 1. Overpopulation, 2. Pollution, 3. Global Warming, 4. Climate Change, 5. Genetic Modification, 6. Ocean Acidification, 7. Water Pollution, 8. Deforestation, 9. Acid Rain, 10. Ozone Depletion. These are all major systems that are in vital danger of drastically harming all of the planet's inhabitants. And to repeat, it is being caused by homo-sapiens.

That is the bad news. The possible good news is, we caused it and only we can fix it. The challenge is, will we?

We have made the choices that have created our current environment. We made many of these choices in ignorance. Now we know what we must do to turn this epidemic around. When we didn't know, we had an excuse. This is no longer the issue. However, knowing what to do, or even how to do it, may not be enough.

In order to become sustainable around the globe, we must become sustainable within our hearts and minds. You and I may start to see that our lives are interconnected with the lives of all living entities on earth, from microorganisms to all people to the ecosystem of the planet as a whole.

We may gain a humble awareness that the small choices we make, day by day — what to consume how to handle our garbage and waste, how to conduct our work, and how to spend our time — do indeed have effects on the larger systems around us. We may also start to recognize that our ability to care about others — people on far-flung continents, people in unfortunate circumstances, people caught in disasters, or people anywhere in the chain of life — makes a difference.

One path to creating our inner sustainability is to do the inner work like meditation and prayer. It would be helpful to learn mindfulness through the practice of Yoga. This will connect us with our inner wisdom and we will make healthy choices for our fragile spacecraft.

A wonderful local organization, Inspiration of Sedona, is making this their predominant purpose right now. When we create our inner sustainability we will then do the outer sustainability. Eventually, we want to become THRIVEABLE! From my sustainable heart to yours, Thomas

Begin our outer sustainability by thriving on the inside!

October 24   One Human Family

Every evening before I write my blog I go on Facebook. It is exciting to see all of the things that are going on in this world. There are so many people giving of their time and talent and resources. It is easy to get depressed if you live in the United States. However, around the globe and yes even in the U.S. folks are sharing their love in so many ways. I get to see blogs and posts and videos of miraculous events.

So many children are also doing wondrous acts of service. And often, the animals steal the show. Children and animals get millions of views. W.C. Fields once was to have said: "never work with children or animals, they will always upstage you!" He was right!!

There are a lot of criticisms of Facebook. However, it is a wonderful place to explore and find out what others are doing about our current crises on planet Earth. I share a lot of these on my Facebook page. I hope you will not only look at them and like them but also follow the folks who share these inspiring posts.

We need each other more than ever. This is the time for us to recreate hope. Remember the lyrics of "Cockeyed Optimist? Here are the lyrics from YouTube: https://www.youtube.com/watch?v=Ao4gKsFpqys

Let us be one human race that has a heart so big that nothing will break it. From my unbreakable heart to yours, Thomas

We are One human family. Find out about all the good stuff that is happening, even create some of the helpful stuff yourself!

October 25   Breaking out in Song!

Here I am sitting in the Village of Oak Creek

It's about seven o'clock at night

Writing words on my personal computer

And everything feels right.

Life is such a busy place nowadays

It can sometimes steal our heart

If we choose to stop and listen

It will keep us from falling apart

I wish you knew how much I love you

How my life is so full of joy

The caring things that you always do

Make it easy for this wondering boy

We got hope for the planet

We got hope for ourselves

We got hope for the little things

that live inside their shells

We got hope for the Universe

Shining down on planet Earth

We got hope in our loving hearts

Won't you join us in our rebirth?

It's about joy, it's about love

It's about working on peace together

It's about caring it's about sharing

It's about opening our hearts forever

It's about giving our souls a treasure

From my rhyming heart to yours, Thomas

Let your heart rhyme and soar and play and most of all love!!

October 26   Who Can I Help Smile Today?

There is a man on Facebook named Jason Schneidman who is a celebrity barber who is cutting the hair of the homeless! He said "what I find is when their appearance changes, their attitude changes. Other people begin looking at them differently.

There is another guy named Jason who drives a mobile shower called "Hope thru Soap". Some people Jason visits haven't showered for weeks or even months! His slogan is to make someone's day better than the day before. Every Friday he loads up his van with 125 gallons of water and food. He feeds them; they get showers and haircuts and get to dance.

A girl named Sofi got the money from her very first paycheck and bought a boy at school named Jaheim some shoes. He was overwhelmed with joy!

Phil Seidler posted:

You may think that you don't matter in this world, but because of you, someone has a favorite mug to drink their tea out of that cup you bought them. Someone hears a song on the radio and it reminds them of you! Someone has read a book that you recommended and got lost in the pages! Someone has remembered a joke that you told them and smiled to themselves on the bus! Never think you don't have an impact. Your fingerprints can never be wiped away from the little marks of kindness that you've left behind!

Rumi said, "in a night full of pain and darkness, be a candle spreading light until dawn!" From my smiling heart to yours, Thomas

Such genuinely kind examples are listed of giving. Create one in your life too!

October 27 It's that time of the year!

Yes, I know it is still two months till Christmas. However, in this house, the season begins when the Hallmark Channel begins showing Christmas movies. From now until the end of December, we will be watching many of the same movies over again.

Tonight we had hot cider while we watched. For me Christmas has always been a feeling of hope. It can be a time when we are nicer to each other. We take time to reconnect with friends and family for no other reason than to celebrate!

I know the season gets a lot of bad raps from folks complaining about the commercialization of it all. And there is truth to that. However, I choose to celebrate it in a different way.

In my childhood, it was perhaps the only time I found any joy in our home. It was almost magical. So I have affection for it all. For the next, sixty days or so, Lou Ann and I will be reminded of the true spirit of giving. Each evening, we will sit huddled together and hug and laugh and sometimes cry. Our lives will be richer for it.

I hope all of you have a chance to be reminded of love and charity and compassion and hope each and every day of your lives. In truth, it is always that time of the year! From my Christmas season heart to yours, Thomas

From an inner deep source of love within you, be inspired to enjoy your life to the fullest and let it overflow to others around you!

October 28 Just the Way We Are

Lou Ann and I went to a jazz concert in Page Springs Arizona, about twenty minutes from our home. The star performer was Neamen Lyles, an incredible saxophonist. He had a five-person group that played wonderful jazzy pieces. I contacted Neamen and asked him if he would be interested in being the ensemble for our television show and he was honored that I asked. We will get together in the near future.

At one point, a guest singer sang a song called Just the Way You Are. It reminded me that we are perfect, just the way we are. Oh yes, there are things we have done, that could have been better. There are things we said, that might have been clearer. There are choices we made, that may have been wiser. They all were exactly what we were supposed to experience.

We get to create everything in our lives. Sometimes it seems like we are not in charge. Sometimes it seems like things are out of our control. Sometimes it appears that no one is in charge, that life is chaotic and happenstance and we have little choice.

Right now on planet Earth, there is so much pain and suffering. Tragic events are happening here in the United States and around the world, there are millions starving every day. It is not an easy time to be alive, here on this fragile planet. However, we are all part of the One mind, One heart, One spirit. We have agreed to play our parts in the great dance of life.

Our souls know the truth. That this painful existence that we are now part of is an illusion. We are not our actions, our thoughts, our words, our deeds. We are at our core, limitless beings of light and love, who have surrendered our divine nature, to take our place in this finite manifestation.

It doesn't lessen the personal pain, or anguish or utter despair, while we are in the human condition. The soul lets us know that this is temporary and this too shall pass. We get to keep holding the space for all beings to discover their Divinity.

When we gather our hearts together and continue to love unconditionally, in spite of events, we will create peace and love, just the way we are! From my hopeful heart to yours, Thomas

Brighten your corner of the world with your inner light!

October 29   The Colors of My Walk

When I went for an hour and a half walk today, I stopped several times to take pictures of the beautiful flora. We have a unique collection of plants here in the upper desert in Arizona. I passed by a giant blue Spruce, some bright red Pyracantha, purple butterfly bushes, olive green cactus, and Agave plants. I also noticed red and yellow roses, massive Cottonwood trees blossoming sunlight yellow. The usual autumn red and gold Sycamore and Maple trees were showing their colors as well!

I also noticed places along the way where weeds were still flourishing. I wondered why some plants are weeds and some are flowers. Who made that decision? I felt like we favor one over the other, why? Who decided that one is more worthy?

Then I began to think about what we humans do with these judgments. We decide to pull up and discard the ones we call weeds and to keep and nurture the ones we call flowers.

Maybe we do that with people as well. Maybe some people are not nurtured enough. Not given enough care. Those folks feel neglected. That neglect can turn to antisocial behavior.

In the desert, so many plants have thorns to protect themselves. Maybe we folks grow emotional thorns to protect ourselves. When we feel so ostracized we can act out in dangerous ways.

Maybe the Tentacula in Harry Potter books was once a plant that got treated badly. Then its last resort was to attack and try to harm others.

Maybe weeds don't like to be treated with products like Roundup! Maybe humans don't like to be treated with toxic environments either. Like plants, we come in all kinds of colors and sizes and shapes. Organically there is nothing wrong with any of us when we enter this planet.

Almost our entire neighborhood is filled with properties that are manicured to perfection. The tiniest weed is "rounded up", (intentional pun!) and removed. Our own acre lot is mostly the same as it was millions of years ago with the exception of our house and all that goes with it. I love that we are not removing the weeds. We are going to add to it by permaculturing the land the way it grows in nature. All of our plants and so-called weeds will be welcome!

Let us take time to see all of us as valuable. Let us nurture all of our baby humans and have them grow into wonderful beings! Let us help heal our damaged mature humans with love and caring. All of the colors of our lives are worth saving! From my colorful heart to yours, Thomas

Nurture and care for the people in your life to the best of your ability! Let them know they are loved!

October 30 Sedona, the Conscious Film Capital of the World

Our programming team met for two hours today to begin finding amazing movies for our festival in June. Some of the most recent films that inspired most of us were *Heal*, *City of Joy*, *Walk with Me* with Thich Nhat Hahn and narrated by Benedict Cumberbatch, *The Golden Age*, and *Becoming Supernatural* with Joe Dispenza, *All the Rage*, *What the Health* and *Rumble*. See if you can find these movies, you won't be disappointed.

Lou Ann and I are so excited about being part of this team of dedicated people who want to make a difference. I know that movies have had a huge impact on me throughout my life. Of course, you folks know as well after all my ramblings about how I love films. Our teams may look at five hundred films to find twenty-five for the Illuminate film festival in June.

There will be about thirty of us choosing and reviewing films over the next few months. If any of you want to join this team just let us know; we would love to have you. You might have to look at two films per week and then send in your evaluation. If you are a film lover, come and join. From my "wonderful life" heart to yours, Thomas

Watch conscious films and let them change your life!

October 31   I Believe

I believe in the goodness of the human heart.

I believe that love can overcome any situation.

I believe in the miracle of life.

I believe in the magic of believing.

I believe that we can save our planet.

I believe that we will find a way.

I believe that we are Divine.

I believe we are responsible for what we do.

I believe in being nice to everyone.

I believe in being kind.

I believe in standing up for what we believe.

I believe that everything is on purpose.

I believe that love is stronger than hate.

I believe that it is powerful to be vulnerable.

I believe that happiness is a choice.

I believe that we are all one.

I believe that surrendering will lead you home.

I believe we are eternal.

I believe we are light beings.

I believe we are limitless.

I believe in equality.

I believe in being passionate.

I believe that we need to be touched more.

I believe each of us is unique.

I believe that love is the energy of life.

I believe in kissing my wife every time we leave and when we return.

I believe in heart to heart hugging.

I believe the more I learn the less I know.

I believe that we choose everything in life.

I believe we are responsible for our own happiness.

I believe a smile is a treasure.

I believe in you.

I believe in me.

From my believing heart to yours, Thomas

Choose a few of these 'believe' ideas today and share them in your life through your heartfelt actions!

November 1 It's the time of year when the world falls in love

Lou Ann and I grew up in families where Christmas was a special time of the year. For me, it was practically the only time of the year when there was happiness in my home. My dad, who was mostly unemployed would buy several gifts for my mom and write secret messages on them. We carry on that tradition of putting secret messages on gifts. Now it takes a couple of hours to unwrap gifts, because we do it one gift at a time and everyone tries to guess the gift.

Christmas was huge in my personal family and we would buy our four children lots of gifts that would fill up the living room. We have always purchased a live tree and decorated it around Thanksgiving and took it down on New Year's Day.

Many years ago, when we were doing Spirit Church we used to have large gatherings in our home in Sedona where food and gifts were shared with those who might not have so much. The church members were so giving, it was a lovely experience!

Now, Lou Ann and I continue the tradition of getting that fresh tree and then spending the day decorating and listening to holiday music. We would also love to be Secret Santa's to folks around our community that do not have enough in this holiday season and throughout the year. In a later post I will share one of our favorite movies and how it has opened our hearts even more!

This is what Lou Ann and I aspire to do. Create enough abundance and resources to become Christmas Angels for those who could use some help. This to me is the deepest meaning of the holiday. The holiday season is short and for us goes by too soon. My wish is for many of us to extend the season of being Angels all year through. Then the whole year through will be "The time of year when the world falls in love"! From my Secret Santa heart to yours, Thomas

Find out what brings joy to your soul and others in the holiday season and do that!

November 2 Our Planet

Lou Ann and I went to the Inspiration of Sedona meeting tonight. It was wonderful, nearly a hundred people showed up! They showed the movie 'Planetary'. It is a very important film that everyone would benefit from watching. It is about our planetary connection to everyone and everything.

It begins with the lift-off of a Saturn V rocket going out into space. It seems that almost every astronaut that gets the opportunity to see our planet from that perspective is changed forever. They are shifted by the immense size of the Universe. They get to look out at the Milky Way from an expanded view. They can see the enormity of the heavens and the tiny spec of creation that is the Earth.

When we see our Earth from space, there are no borders, no walls, no races, and no artificial divisions. There is a gorgeous blue-green planet teeming with life. Most of us will never have this experience. However, it would be helpful if we could see the oneness of all living things on Earth. We are not separate from anything. Each species, each minute subatomic particle is connected to every other one. On a human level, each of us is connected to each other.

We are once again, standing on a threshold of the possibility of creating a peaceful loving world or destroying it. There are factions present who are in so much fear and pain that they are creating an energy that is truly harmful. Those who are not in such a fearful place, have the opportunity of holding a space for unconditional love. At the same time, we get to take action that will create the loving world so many desire. I believe it is vital for us to do both; come from love and take action that will heal our Earth.

Let us find ways to nurture each other and all the living things on our planet. Let's not wait for others to do it! Let's get involved right now. For, after all, it is our only home! From my active heart to yours, Thomas

What is it that you love to do that nurtures planet earth? Do that!

November 3   Our Life Depends On It!

It is a tough time for me right now in writing this blog. I am committed to finding the good in everything. Now, we in the United States are facing an event which will be among the most important in our history. I know that sometimes I get excited and am given to hyperbole. However, it is difficult to understate the depth of the challenge, which faces all caring people.

We are in the fight of our lives. We are confronting a menace of our own making. Only we can create a solution. On next Tuesday, more people will go to their voting booths or have already voted, in what may be the largest mid-term election ever.

We literally have no choice. We the people chose two years ago, what we thought was the lesser of two evils and look what we created! We were so brainwashed by others or uninformed and chose horribly, or perhaps we didn't even choose to vote! Whatever the reason, we did this to ourselves!

On November 6th, we can choose another course. We can decide that we love each other and our planet so much, that we will vote for candidates that support those values. We have a planet that is being threatened more than ever by this administration in Washington. In their ignorance, they have chosen a path that will harm their loved ones. They are still asleep. We are semi-awake. We are the ones who can stand up for all the beings on the Earth. We can make choices for all those who have no voice.

I often say life is simple. It may be challenging and difficult and ever-changing, but it is easy on Tuesday next week. VOTE! Whatever you have to do to get there or vote early, or mail it in. Please do it! Next, take someone with you or call someone or encourage someone to vote. We cannot have any excuses this time. We cannot say we did not know. Our choices have never been clearer. We are choosing light over darkness!

If you stand for love, caring, compassion and inclusion, find a way to make your voice heard by voting. Our lives depend on it! From my concerned and committed heart to yours, Thomas

Stay in a place of unconditional love as much as you can!

November 4   In Nature

A few years ago when Lou Ann and I decided to become vegan, we also desired to reduce our carbon footprint. We discovered permaculture.

Permaculture is a system of agricultural and social design principles centered on simulating or directly utilizing the patterns and features observed in natural ecosystems. We have an acre of ground surrounding our house. It is all natural desert land, no landscaping. It is red dirt and it is covered with over a hundred pine trees. We discovered a few garden plots that had been left unattended for years. They were overgrown with lots of different kinds of local vegetation. In the desert, many plants grow thorns to protect themselves from being eaten by thirsty predators.

A couple of days ago, a young woman named Ashley, posted on Facebook that she is a farmer and wanted to get involved with local folks. We connected and she and her husband Austin came over to our home and we worked those old garden plots. We discovered a lot of rich brown soil beneath the shrubbery. It was exciting to be digging and raking and building mulch piles. It felt like home to me.

I grew up in Hollywood California. It was a delightful Mediterranean climate that had warm sunny days throughout the year. I hardly ever got cold. I spent most of my childhood out there in the flora and fauna of Southern California. We boys would play a lot of outdoor games of chasing each other. When we got hungry or thirsty, we would stop at a tree or bush and eat the produce. There were ample amounts of citrus, plums, peaches, apples, figs, nuts, and berries to consume to our tummies delight! It was our Garden of Eden. It felt so safe and nurturing to be in nature for all those years!

Now some seven decades later, I was again out on the land; this time with Lou Ann and our new friends, preparing the soil for our new Garden of Eden. It feels like I have returned home to that wonderful childhood feeling of connecting with nature and feeling complete! I wish for all of you to return to your roots of pleasure and connection with goodness. From my natural heart to yours, Thomas

Be out in nature; plant a garden even if it's an herb garden or flowers on a window sill!

November 5   Our Choices

It is still always about choosing love over fear, and hope over despair. It is easy to get caught up in the energy present here in the United States these days. It is a challenge to stay centered when we are feeling attacked. It is a challenge to stay peaceful when people are being killed. It is only natural to feel anger and want to strike back perhaps.

In history, those that have had the greatest positive impact upon life were people of peace. They were people who turned the other cheek, like Jesus and Buddha and Gandhi and Mother Teresa and Martin Luther King. They were folks who marched into Hell for a Heavenly cause. As soon as I wrote this, I recalled the words of The Man from La Mancha. Remember these? Here it is on YouTube: https://www.youtube.com/watch?v=oo7VlD66ISM

These are noble lyrics about a fictional character. The words still inspire those of us who dream the seemingly impossible dream of peace on Earth. While I don't advocate physically fighting a foe, I do advocate taking a stand for love and joy and compassion and inclusion. In the end, they are the qualities that will create our souls' desire.

May we continue to follow our star, no matter how hopeless, no matter how far! From my indefatigable heart to yours, Thomas

Communicate non-violently with yourself and others! Here is where peace begins with you and me!

November 6 Back Home Again

Each time I return to California it brings up for me a strong feeling of being home even though I have spent most of my life in several other states. I had the feeling growing up in Hollywood that something special was going on. The people here always seemed upbeat and that they were going to make their mark in society.

As I look back on my life I think maybe many people feel this way. Do you think that you are supposed to do something special? I don't mean to imply that if you feel this way that it makes you better than anyone else who doesn't have that feeling. It is a feeling that we are here for a purpose; that all of this is not just random; that we are connected to a force that is greater than us; and this force is a divine, all inclusive, kind of energy.

I don't believe that if you don't do something "special" your life has less value. I think that if you live with a conscious connection to the Force, that life somehow has more meaning; and things like helping the world be a better place is important.

When we go through life and desire good things for all Earth's inhabitants, life takes on a different meaning. So that when you get up each morning it is not just another day. It is a day with all the potential of creating something wonderful and amazing and transcendent.

So here we are not far from the Magic Kingdom and Tinsel town and all kinds of possibilities for the child within us all. I am home, somewhere over the rainbow, wanting to click my heels together! I get to once again dream of the possibilities that life here on this fragile spacecraft is something special. I can hardly wait to get started! May all of us rediscover that childlike wonder without limits, and soar to new heights of creativity that will bring us HOME! From my nomadic heart to yours, Thomas

Be yourself. You are enough. From here you can be connected and creative!

November 7   La La Land

We are watching La La Land tonight. I grew up there. It was unique in many ways. In my early childhood, many movie stars lived in Hollywood as well as Beverly Hills. I remember seeing famous actors at the local hardware store and they would be buying something for a home project. No paparazzi, no cameras, no fans screaming out loud in hysterics; Just Henry Fonda picking up some nails. I knew who they were and that they were famous and they were also neighbors. It didn't feel unusual for this to occur.

My older brother Bob and I would go to the movies and it was ten cents for an all day Saturday ticket. We had five cents for a box of popcorn to share and two cents for candy, which was a pocket full. When we ate the popcorn, we would chew one piece at a time, being careful to bite each kernel carefully to make it last.

I watch films in an unusual way and I don't remember when it started. When I watch a movie, I don't just watch the characters in the scene or focus totally on the dialogue. My mind wanders and thinks things like, why did they film the scene that way. Why did the director plan it that way? I would have done it a different way.

I attended Hollywood High School and went to drama class. In my class were several students who went on to fame as actors for many years. I was so shy, my instructor gave me a C for trying.

When Lou Ann and I watch a film like La La Land, we both get the urge to perform again. I told her we should take tap lessons and just break into dance when we go shopping or whatever.

For me, there is something magical about performing live. There is a memorized script and scenes set with places for actors to be. However each performance is different because it is live. Sometime when I act, I lose myself in the role and it is powerful. And there have been times when I leave my body and watch myself perform. It is truly magical to do that!

I invite everyone to see life as a script that you have written, and you are the director and producer. You are the star of your life movie. Everyone else is an extra and we signed on to help you create the best life ever. So get your tap shoes, banjo, guitar and kazoo and live the best life ever. Fill it up with passion, risk, and the best ending ever filmed! See you in your movie! From my dancing heart to yours, Thomas

We are each starring in our own movie right now! Choose happy and magical as much as you can!

November 8   Loving

Lou Ann and I have been kissing each other for some thirty eight years. We mostly always kiss whenever we leave each other and when we return, even if it's just a few moments or so. It is wonderful to be with someone who is so like yourself and to receive so much love.

I have often said that people who truly love themselves hardly ever commit crimes or break laws. When you feel loved and know that you are okay, there is no desire to act out in a negative way.

Our society is in trouble. Mostly because there are too many of us who don't feel loved by others and mostly don't feel loved by themselves. If we are to ever create wide scale peace on Earth; it will be when we discover how to love and be loved.

Most of us like to be touched and cared for. I don't think we get held enough. When we were newborns, we got so much touch and nurturing. As we grow and become our own special selves we often miss out on the vital essence of being touched and told how much we are loved.

The most simple and easiest way to accomplish this is by loving ourselves and loving all others in the same way. From my loving heart to yours, Thomas

Look in the mirror today and tell your reflection 'I love you' and really mean it. From this place it's easier to love others.

November 9   No One Is Above the Law

The Woman's March was at it again! A hundred of us gathered in Sedona in the cold wind and stood tall against tyranny! Eighty percent were women. We listened to a few speakers encourage us to not give up! We said chants together and sang We Shall Overcome! Once again, I was thrilled to be a part of a group of people who care! They care about all of us! Some of the rhetoric was us against them. Some were inclusive, and even mentioned the apparent huge hole in Donald Trump's emotional heart.

We were told that there were some nine thousand rallies going on today about the current events here in the United States! As soon as I wrote that, I thought: "It doesn't feel so united, does it?" Well, even in the best of democracies there will be times of struggle. We sure are at a major impasse! It is so important that we continue to send love to everyone and at the same time stand up for everyone as well!

There are those in our country family, which are in such pain that they are attempting to disenfranchise others. Then we see another mass shooting in California. It is often a challenge to not react to the killing of innocent sisters and brothers. Not only must cooler heads prevail; warmer hearts must prevail as well!

Once again, we get to speak out and tell how we feel about these crimes against defenseless people. We also get to speak out about political parties trying to manipulate the voting maps and laws for their personal gain.

In the meantime, let us take time to pray or meditate and find our spiritual center. Then perhaps, our collective energy will move us all in the direction of love and caring. It is worth it! From my marching woman's heart to yours, Thomas

Tune into your own inner peace and loving nature, which allows more kindness to flow!

November 10   Green Book Take Two

This time I went with Lou Ann to see the movie Green Book which I saw by myself three weeks ago. Once again, I wept at certain scenes, with more tears streaming down my face at the end.

Based on a true story set in the 1960's, Green Book is a road movie that captures New York bouncer Tony Vallelonga (Viggo Mortensen) and African-American pianist Dr. Don Shirley's (Mahershala Ali) unlikely friendship. The film follows the two as they embark on a journey of a lifetime that confronts racism, intolerance, loneliness and understanding in an era of segregation in the United States.

Peter Farrelly's delightful little film is all heart and a sure shot Oscar contender. It uses humor to touch upon an issue as unsettling as racism and leaves you moist eyed with its observation and understanding of human behavior. Uplifting and heartbreaking at the same time, the story has the ability to change your life and how you look at people. (This was a review from the Times of India).

Every once in a while, a film comes along and steals our hearts. This movie has been out almost six weeks and today we sat in a full theater. It was packed because we filmgoers love to share the beauty of intimate and transformative filmmaking.

I am encouraging us all to go see this movie. It will remind you about the trials of being human. It will fill your heart and your eyes with tenderness about people discovering love behind the veil of our broken hearts. From my encouraged heart to yours, Thomas

Take the message home and share from your heart with all human beings! Notice that even a smile can make a difference!

November 11   More Loving Kindness

Lou Ann and I were fortunate to meet with the board of the Sedona Kind organization. They were open, friendly and of course, kind! They are also so dedicated to their wonderful mission! There were six passionate women who give so much of their time and energy to make the world a kinder place! We met with them to exchange some ideas on how we could include their loving work in our television show program. Please go to sedonakind.org and get involved!

In the afternoon, we went to see the latest rendition of "How the Grinch Stole Christmas." It is a delightful animated version that will keep you laughing and sometimes crying. When I watched it this time I was impressed by the message. I have seen it so many times in different ways.

The Grinch, of course, hates Christmas. The reason we are given is his heart is two sizes too small. We eventually find out that he is lonely. He takes out his anger on those who he sees are not lonely but connected. He ends up stealing all of their presents and decorations.

What he does not steal, is their hearts. He discovers that after his theft, they still sing "Fah Who Foraze, Dah Who Doraze, welcome all who's, far and near" and they are still joyful! Once again, we are thrilled to see Cindy Lou Who, connect with the Grinch and love him unconditionally!

Just like the folks at Sedona Kind, it is Cindy Who's kindness that allows the Grinch to grow a heart several times larger. May we all follow the lesson of this timeless story! It is our kindness and love with each other that makes all the difference. Then perhaps there will be less of us lonely. Then we will all be one great Who! From my expanded heart to yours, Thomas

Find ways to bring kindness to your town. It catches like wildfire!

November 12 Declaring Peace

Tonight, Lou Ann and I had the privilege of being in a sold-out Mary D. Fisher theater experience. We attended a concert by William Florian who was one of the members of The New Christy Minstrels back in the seventies. The concert was titled The John Denver Story. He sang several of Denver's most popular songs. He invited the audience to sing along with him. It was so much fun!

At the end of the evening, he introduced us to a song he wrote called "I Declare Peace!" Here are the lyrics: *If war was the answer, then we'd be at peace. And the battles in the distance would've all finally ceased. We still have a choice to live and be free. So let's all raise our voice and become a planet of peace. The chorus goes: I'm declaring peace, I'm declaring peace, deep within myself, I'm declaring peace, I'm declaring peace!*

In the middle of the concert, he sang a wonderful Christy Minstrels song called: Today, here is the YouTube link: https://www.youtube.com/watch?v=9KCbJnAaaB4

We only have today. Tomorrow is not promised. Yesterday is just a memory. Today is our moment to create peace by being peaceful. Today is our story of creating peace on Earth. Today, I am declaring peace within myself, won't you join me? From my peaceful heart to yours, Thomas

Declare peace within yourself and spread it around as you unfold your own wings to others!

November 13 Universal principle #17 Harmony in Relationships

"Our primary relationship is with God. How we see and feel about God determines the quality of all our relationships. Knowing that God loves and supports us unconditionally, allows each of us to feel unconditional love and support for our Selves. We are then able to feel and express unconditional love and support for everyone. Aligning with this sequence allows you to see your Self and others as who you really are: the Power and Presence of God eager to surrender to all possibility. When you hold this Truth in your consciousness that is what is reflected to you."

Since we are all parts of God, then all relationships are with the Oneness. We can have amazing relationships with others when we do some simple things.

On our thirtieth anniversary, eight years ago; I realized we had been married for more than ten thousand days. I then began to think of all the things we had done over those three decades. Lou Ann and I are very affectionate with each other. We probably kiss ten times per day and we touch each other ten times per day and we tell each other we love each other ten times per day. We are so blessed!

They are simple gestures of love and when someone gives you that much feedback about how much you are loved, the relationship has a good chance to work. I wish for everyone to discover how much you are loved and how much love you have to share!

Another thing that Lou Ann taught me is being thankful. In the very beginning of our marriage she thanked me for the smallest things like handing her something or following up on something or putting the cap on the toothpaste or cleaning up something.

When I got that kind of feedback it was only natural for me to want to do more for her and of course thanking her also for all she gave to me. We also focus on gratitude which of course falls under thankfulness. We often go over a list of things for which we are grateful. I even learned to be grateful for every event in my life, not just the loving ones.

Each event reminds me that I am still here doing the best I can at every moment and being thankful for it all! Take time today to thank someone for just being who they are. They don't have to do anything to earn it. Then recall all of the things in life that you have created and be grateful for the experience. From my harmonious heart to yours, Thomas

Harmony in relationships begins with you! Try singing a tune to yourself even if it doesn't sound harmonious! Heartfelt laughter deepens any and all relationships!

November 14   Magical Sedona!

There are beautiful thunderstorms in Sedona during every monsoon season. This year is no exception. Sedona is one of the most unique places on Earth. Stunning red rock formations surround the area. Sedona attracts folks from all aspects of life. Many metaphysical, spiritual, wealthy, artists, wanderers and folks flock here looking for a complete change of their life and everything in between.

Dozens of people have come here just to visit, and quite a few are instantly motivated to move here. There is an energy present created by all the wonderful beings who show up that is contagious for a lot of us. Situated at 4500 feet in the high desert we get four seasons of weather including some hot summers, mostly short winters and gorgeous springs and autumns.

Lou Ann and I moved here in 1988 under guided circumstances. We were living in San Diego at the time and came to Sedona or actually the Village of Oak Creek for a seminar. The Sunday activity of the workshop was for the attendants to go for a walk in silence. As Lou Ann and I strolled up Verde Valley School road we stopped and looked at each other and broke the silence by exclaiming "why aren't we living here?" Ninety days later we arrived in March. Lou Ann got a job at a pharmacy and I was to search for housing. I looked at dozens of places with no luck. There were only two places left to see and I called Lou Ann to share with her the challenge of finding a place. She suggested since it was March 17th I should ask Saint Patrick for help in finding us a place.

I went to the last home and it was beautiful and vacant and closed up tight. When I went into the kitchen to look at the appliances and such and I saw the Irish blessing that begins with "May the road rise up to meet you, may the wind be always at your back". I called Lou Ann and we knew we were guided to have this home. From my heart to yours, Thomas

What magical events have happened for you!? The more you notice, the more they happen!

November 15   World Kindness Day

Life can be challenging in today's world. So many folks have to work more than one job to make ends meet. So many people don't have enough shelter, enough food, enough care, or enough love. Sometimes it feels overwhelming to find ways to make a positive difference in our society.

A simple way to make a difference is to be kind. Open a door for someone. Pay for someone's meal or coffee. Let others in traffic. Give out hugs. Let our smiles shine. Walk someone's dog. Mow someone's lawn. Rake someone's leaves. Shovel someone's snow. Give someone a ride to work. Cook someone a meal. Sing someone a song. Hold someone's hand. Empty someone's trash. Send someone an encouraging text. Send someone a love or heart Moji. Find someone and listen to their story.

Let us also be kind to ourselves. Give ourselves a treat of getting a massage, going to a movie, taking a walk, taking a nap, calling our family, reading a good book, enjoying a scrumptious dessert, ask for what we want, speak our truth, share our vision, take a hot bath, smile at ourselves in the mirror.

There are probably unlimited ways in which we can be kind to each other and ourselves. You will never regret being kind!

"People will forget what you said, people will forget what you did, but people will never forget how you made them feel." –Maya Angelou

Let us celebrate World Kindness day by finding ways to practice random acts of kindness. From my kind heart to your kind heart, Thomas

Today on World Kindness day and every day find ways to practice acts of kindness!

November 16   A Hobo's Sip of Wine

My very favorite John Denver song was written by him and Joe Henry. It is "The Wings That Fly Us Home."

Many of Denver's songs were created with verses and a chorus or two. This song was a message from the Universe; words channeled by Joe Henry and the music by John. One of my favorite lines is; "is a hero's blood more righteous than a hobo's sip of wine?" I don't think that it is! I believe that we all have the hero and the hobo within us.

We make choices in life that enhance or diminish us. Either way, they define us. However, they are not who we truly are. We are prophets in the meadow and we are mountains in the wind. We are the magnificent shining essence of Spirit in a human form. Here is the link: https://www.youtube.com/watch?v=2byV0zfl8Qg

Truly, love is seeing all the infinite as one! May we all begin to realize that we are a part of the spirit that fills the darkness of the heavens! May we all continue to spread our wings as they fly us home! From my hobo/hero heart to yours, Thomas

The light and the dark live within us – bless it all with deep compassion!

November 17   Life is Rich!

Early today, I had the privilege of working on our 'vegan forest', here on our property in Sedona. Our new beautiful friends, Ashley and Austin and their dog Sparky and our other wonderful friend, Mira worked on our greenhouse. We found a used greenhouse on Facebook a couple of hours away on Tuesday.

We are designing our property in a permaculture fashion. Permaculture is combining the best of natural landscaping and edible gardening. Permaculture systems sustain both themselves and their caregivers.

The ultimate purpose of permaculture—a word coined in the mid-1970s by two Australians, Bill Mollison, and David Holmgren—is to develop a site until it meets all the needs of its inhabitants, from food and shelter to fuel and entertainment.

We are also incorporating magical and mystical fountains and mandalas and soil formations to allow Mother Nature to flourish. The initial greenhouse will be about 450 square feet and provide lots of organic fresh produce for local folks who don't have enough to eat. We will also blend fruit and nut trees and other plants to compliment the overall natural design.

This evening we welcomed four guests into our vacation rental home, which is in our personal house. These lovely, happy, engaging folks are from India; a mom and dad and their two children, Krishna and Aparna.

In about thirty minutes, we fell madly in love with the whole family. We laughed more than we did anything else. They made a wonderful Indian dish which we loved! We felt like we had known them forever. Life is so rich! We are so blessed! From my totally abundant heart to yours, Thomas

Find what brings you joy and do that! Watch your life unfold into a rich one with promise and love!

November 18   Stay Young at Heart

Years ago, I was performing regularly in musicals. We would rehearse for about three months and then play several performances for audiences. During this long period of repeating the same music and lines over and over, I would have trouble keeping the songs out of my mind.

When I was up late and the lyrics kept repeating in my head, I would sing one particular song. I called it my "clearing" song. It is called Young at Heart. When I finished the song, I would fall asleep and be at *peace.*

Here is the YouTube link with a wonderful rendition by the inimitable Jimmy Durante:

https://www.youtube.com/watch?v=8ILE5Qfdy2E

I have had many impossible schemes and lots have fallen apart at their seams. Lou Ann and I have had our share of experiences that failed. However, it doesn't seem to deter us. We keep dreaming dreams, for ourselves and others. And life does get more exciting with each passing day.

I wish for all of you to follow your young heart. I encourage everyone to keep dreaming impossible dreams. This is what makes life so exciting. The promise of the song is, if you stay young at heart, life will be exciting, and worth every treasure on Earth. From my young heart to yours, Thomas

Let your young and happy heart fill you with magical dreams!

November 19 Heavenly Christmas All Year Long

By the time the official holidays are over you may be happy that I am over Christmas. But will I? Lou Ann and I watched a Hallmark movie titled Heavenly Christmas starring Kristin Davis, Shirley MacLaine and Eric McCormack of 'Will and Grace' fame.

The storyline is similar to a lot of the plots; an overachiever not having enough time for Christmas or family. Davis' character falls and dies and goes to heaven and meets an angel, played by MacLaine. She too is now an angel and is given an assignment of answering a nine-year-old girl's prayer. The girl's only Christmas wish is for her uncle, played by McCormack, to be happy.

Our new angel soon discovers all of the things she has missed in life, by being so focused on success. It brings to mind that perhaps many of us lose focus on what the most important things in life are. MacLaine's character shares "no one who has reached the other side has ever said," I wished I had worked more".

This holiday is going to be so busy for many of us that, we too, may miss the essence of the season. No, it is not Santa or that a savior was born. It is about giving and celebrating and loving each other and realizing all that we have been blessed to give and receive.

Maybe we can slow down a little for the next 39 days. Maybe we can renew friendships. Maybe we can contact family members more. Maybe we can serve in a soup kitchen. Maybe we can open more doors for each other. Maybe we can put more money in the tip jar at our local eatery.

 Maybe we can stop on one of the corners, where an apparently homeless person is asking for help and put some bills in their worn out hands. Maybe we can go sing some Christmas carols at the nearest assistance home. Maybe we can clean out our garages and basements and give it all away to where it is most needed. Maybe we can adopt a pet or a lonely human being. If we do some of these things, it will truly be a Heavenly Christmas. From my holiday heart to yours, Thomas

Be in the 'now' place in our heart so that it can overflow from within to others!

November 20   Holiday Desiderata

This is a wonderful reminder from last year. This is a time of year that can remind us that amid holiday celebrations, we may fall in love again with life!!

"Go placidly amid the blaring Christmas carols and hastening shoppers, and remember what peace there may be in the season. As far as possible without surrender, be on good terms with other shoppers and sales clerks. Share your needs quietly and clearly; and listen to others, especially the hurried and distressed; they too have their story. Avoid critical or demanding persons; they can kill the Christmas spirit.

If you compare your efforts with what others do, you may become prideful or envious; for always there will be richer and poorer persons than yourself. Enjoy your own achievements and holiday plans.

Keep interested in your own celebration, however humble; and remember that family and friends are the real possessions in the changing fortunes of time. Exercise caution in your buying, for the stores are full of tempting merchandise.

But let this not blind you to the virtues of the season; many persons give generously of their time and fortunes, and everywhere you can find stories of heroism and happiness. Be yourself.

Especially, do not give gifts without love. And do not be cynical about gifts you receive; for in the face of all commercialism, love still permeates this holiday.

Enjoy the maturity of your years, but do not be afraid to recall the pleasures of Christmases past. Nurture a spirit of joy to shield you from the negative aspects of the holiday. And do not distress yourself by imagining that you can achieve a "perfect" Christmas; that way lies fatigue and unhappiness.

Make your holiday plans, but take it in stride if events don't follow your plans. You are a child again at Christmas, no less than the youngsters in your family; you have a right to enjoy yourself.

And even if your plans get muddled, no doubt the holiday still will be a joyous one for all concerned.

Therefore, relax and enjoy the season, in whatever way is most meaningful to you, and don't lose sight of what's most important to you in all the hustle and bustle.

With all its stress, hectic schedule and occasional disappointment, it is still a marvelous time of the year. Hold tight to the true meaning of the holiday, and strive to inject a bit of happiness into every day throughout the season."

I couldn't have said it better. Let's relax and take a deep breath and know that everything we do this holiday season is in Divine order! Happy holidays to all and to all a good season! From my holiday heart to yours, Thomas

Reread that last paragraph while taking a relaxing deep breath!

November 21   Soul Love

Sounds like a 1960's TV show! We are love. We came from love, we return to love, we will always be love. Our limited ego doesn't know this. It often lives in fear. It has been brainwashed, indoctrinated, and otherwise completely filled with limitation and ignorance.

We get to learn to allow the ego to surrender its hold on illusion. We are eternal, limitless, beings of light and love. Our souls know this. The soul is patient. It will literally wait forever for us to get a clue.

One way to create a soul reunion is to learn to be silent. When we spend moments in a peaceful state and suspend our mind chatter, it is easier to reconnect with that eternal part of us. When we learn Yoga or meditation or some other form of mindfulness, we return home.

As we move through these busy days of work and play and holiday celebrations, let us remember who we are. We are One. From my soul to yours, Thomas

As you live a few moments in the silence, hear the birds singing their song; the wind swaying the trees; the rain or snow falling; let these sweet sounds nurture your soul.

November 22 Gratitude

Most of us who read this post are so blessed. We live in relative freedom. We are able to make choices about our life. We have family and friends whom we love and who love us. If we have good health, we are very blessed. If we are doing what we love to do, we are so fortunate. We have a warm house, comfortable beds. We get to watch or participate in entertainment. We make enough money to enjoy life.

What more could we ask? Perhaps peace on Earth? Perhaps no more wars? Perhaps a healthy climate for ourselves and our children and their children? Perhaps everyone on Earth having enough shelter, food, and warmth of heart and hearth. We are in the minority of the people of the world. While we take these moments to give thanks for all we have, it is also a time to recommit to all of the beings of the planet to live in safety and prosperity.

Let us be grateful for the opportunity to make a difference in the lives of others. Let us find ways to have everyone not only have enough but to thrive! I encourage us all to get involved in the simplest ways to spread the gift of love on our fragile spaceship. From my grateful heart to yours, Thomas

Find a group in your community who are giving to others and bring your big loving heart into their fold!

November 23 Thanks

When I graduated from the sixth grade at Hyde Park Elementary School in Cincinnati Ohio, the graduating class learned the iconic Bob Hope song "Thanks for the Memories." We substituted different lyrics to celebrate the school faculty and how they had served us. I remember crying a lot. It was the first time that I was aware of bittersweet tears. I was happy to be going to junior high school and was sad at leaving new found friends.

This was the school that I had my first metaphysical experience. A year prior, I was living in Hollywood California attending the only school I ever knew. I was a straight-A student and had earned favors from the school that had given me a healthy sense of self-worth. Then my mother announced we were moving back to Ohio. I was born there and we came to Hollywood when I was 1. I felt like my heart was being ripped from my chest. No, I wanted to shouted, how can you do this to me?

In the ensuing weeks, I had a dream. I dreamt that I was in a new school with the students and the homeroom teacher. Fast forward to September 1951, the first day of school in Cincinnati; my grandpa drove us to the school and I was full of fear. We turned the corner and suddenly I saw the school building of my dreams. I began to relax a little. Gramps let us out and as we walked to the front door, I was familiar with the entire place. We entered and went to homeroom. When we went into the room, my cousin was about to tell me the teacher's name. I interrupted him and said her name before he did. His eyes got huge! How did you.......? I then told him the names of several of our classmates.

Perhaps some of the aforementioned tears were full of the connection that my heart knew it had experienced. All I know is that I was thankful for that moment in time and I really felt it at a deep level.

On this day, when those of us in the United States celebrate being thankful, may you remember a time in your life when your soul and your angels and your heart teamed up to give you peace! From my thankful heart to yours, Thomas

If you gather today with others, share what you have been grateful for from your past or present and listen to others share their experiences too!

November 24   Noel

Lou Ann and I and our house-mates Austin and Ashley watched a movie tonight titled 'Noel'. It was a story of many different lonely people. The film weaves their complex life stories into a tapestry of caring, that arises out of a deep need to be loved. There is a young man whose favorite Christmas was when he was 14 and got to spend the night at a hospital. There is a woman whose mom is in the later stages of

Alzheimer disease. There is a couple and the man is a cop who is jealous of his wife's beauty. There is an elderly man whose wife was killed long ago and claims that she has reincarnated in other people. There is an ex-priest who after twenty years in the clergy has lost his faith. You will have to watch the movie sometime, to see how it turns out.

As I was watching it, my mind went to the words of a wonderful song by the singing group America called "Lonely people" that goes like this:

https://www.youtube.com/watch?v=4bSU_VtPgBo

All of us can feel lonely and sometimes it can overwhelm us. The song encourages us to never give up until we drink from the silver cup. The silver cup is the chalice that predates the cup of Christ; the silver highway is the silver astral cord leading from this life to that which comes next. She "will never take you down or never give you up" is a reference of how the Wiccans refer to the Goddess.

If you are feeling lonely this holiday season, please know that there are others who care deeply about you. Life has so much to offer each of us if we try. Let us be aware of one another and hold each other close, so we know we are loved and not alone. From my never quitting heart to yours, Thomas

Feel the aliveness in you and share it with others whenever you can today!

November 25 Fifty Burgers Please!

Doesn't sound like a to-go order for a vegan! My title tonight is a line from another Christmas movie to warm our hearts! We have watched the movie entitled "Christmas Angel" a few times. It is available in DVD from Netflix or on YouTube for free, here is the link: https://www.youtube.com/watch?v=YNYdKcn_IWg . I will try not to totally spoil watching the movie by my remarks.

The story shows a young woman who is having a tough time making it financially and emotionally. She tries to get employment and she lives in an apartment where the water runs out. She was a foster child in her younger years and passed from home to home. She has a defeated spirit about life. Her neighbor across the hall, in the apartment building where she lives, is a white-headed elderly man who uses a cane to walk.

Eventually, her neighbor lets her in on his secret—he is rich! He is also not very well physically. He decides to hire her to help him with his business. He anonymously donates money, food, clothing and gifts to others. He takes her out on the streets of Chicago and shows her many needy people whom he desires to help.

At one point, she goes into a restaurant with a friend and goes up to the counter and says "fifty burgers please"! They then take the food outside and give it away to the folks on the street. The film was produced in 2009 and has always been one of our favorite holiday flicks. The theme of it is what we try to do and would love to do more.

I invite all of you wonderful folks to join in the fun. Find some people this holiday season or any time of year and go out of your way to give them some food or anything that will make life better for them. Life is so much fun when we can be Secret Santa's or Christmas Angels! From my Secret Santa heart to yours, Thomas

Let's all find ways we can be Christmas Angels this season! Let it fill the giver and the receiver with pure delight!

November 26   Holiday Traditions

We watched a wonderful holiday movie on the Lifetime channel, which made us laugh a lot. There were two families, one Christian and one Jewish, whose son and daughter were engaged to be married. The film pointed out the holiday traditions of the two faiths.

It also showed how we can get so embedded in our own traditions that we miss out on the value of how other beliefs celebrate their Divinity. The movie is titled "Will You Merry Me?" and is worth the look, to see how it all works out!

While watching, I remembered my early exposure to the holidays at our home. I remember loving the romantic story of the Christ child. I loved the magical birth of the one being who was supposed to be Lord of all.

However, I grew up in Hollywood and I got a taste of secular celebrations that still stays with me today. The Judy Garland song from the "Meet Me in Saint Louis" movie "Have Yourself a Merry Little Christmas", was my favorite then and remains so to this day. The line in the song "through the years we all will be together if the fates allow" always touched my young heart at a deep level. I think I knew then, that the fates somehow had the upper hand.

In Hollywood, many of my friends were Jewish as well as many Eastern religions. I got a broad perspective on life at a tender age. As I grew older the holidays for me have always been about remembering that there is love in the air and it is ours to grab it, if we choose.

Even today, Lou Ann and I watch all these mostly corny and often tender films. My heart overflows as do my tears when I see people open their hearts to each other. Whatever your faith may be, please find the joy inside all of the activities and remember we are love! From my nostalgic heart to yours, Thomas

During this special season, celebrate the divine love within you and let it ripple out to others beyond the season!

November 27 Universal principle #18: The Universe Handles the Details

"The Universe handles the details of our lives in accordance with the beliefs we hold in consciousness. Our core belief is to supersede the Divine in how we live our lives. The sole purpose of that belief and all the others we have created is to give us a life opposite to our natural state. As we open the energy in our beliefs, we increase the flow of Divine Love into all aspects of our lives. We can then rest in the arms of the Divine and observe the details of our day and reflect the joy that the Love releases."

We think we are in control and we can figure it out. Often, that is not the case. As limitless spiritual beings playing a limited game we cannot possibly know all the possibilities of our life experience. It is good to take some time and go to a quiet place and just rest until the desire to do it all by our self passes by.

When we surrender to the magnificent beauty of who we are and let go then the magic can happen. Here is a message from Oneness: Dear human, you've got it all wrong. You didn't come here to master unconditional love. That is where you came from and where you'll return. You came here to learn personal love, Universal love, messy love, sweaty love, crazy love, broken love. Whole love Infused with Divinity, lived through the grace of stumbling; demonstrated through the beauty of messing up. Often!

You didn't come here to be perfect, you already are. You came here to be gorgeously human, flawed and fabulous; and then to rise again into remembering. Relax, don't try so hard. There is nothing you need to do to be more Divine than you already are! Go and gaze into a mirror and take a deep breath and then give yourself a wink! You've got this! From my heart to yours, Thomas

Rest in the arms of the Divine and surrender to the Universe as you play the game called life on the earth plane!

November 28   What Your Heart Desires

There is a biblical passage that says "For where your treasure is, there will your heart be also". We were watching another Hallmark Christmas movie tonight. Many have a recurring theme of two people who meet and are attracted to each other. Then the tension in the plot is usually a couple of twists. One is that they both have something in their past and they keep it a secret from each other.

Another theme is that one is either famous or wealthy and driven while the other is in a small town with old fashioned values. The successful person usually needs to learn balance in their life by stopping and smelling the roses. The more rural person often gets to have a breakthrough in risking and doing what they love.

Those concepts are probably alive in most of us. Many of us get into creating a career and making money and miss out on the humanity of hearth and home. Then a whole lot of us never realize our dreams because it is too risky and we don't want to fail.

It might be time for us to take stock and decide "where our treasure is". I don't necessarily mean physically, but what truly gives us joy and our life purpose and deep satisfaction. I have often said to folks that I am privileged to counsel "Follow your heart"! Perhaps the biblical aphorism could be said in reverse "For where your heart is, there will be your treasure also".

Make a list of the things in your life that you truly love. They can be anything; people, places, plants, pets, events, hobbies or whatever. Then visualize if money were no object what would you do for the rest of your life? With whom would you do it? Where would you do it? And finally when will you do it?

If you are already doing what you love with whom you love, where you love then congratulations! You are in a distinct minority of folks on our planet. If there is anything missing from your life experience right now, I urge you to follow your heart. When you do, Universe will do everything in its power to give you what your heart desires. From my encouraging heart to yours, Thomas

What is on your list? Begin bringing more of these things into your life!

November 29   Goodbye Christopher Robin

Lou Ann and I went to see the movie by the above name yesterday, here in Sedona. The movie is pretty emotional and has a lot of sadness running through it. It is the story of the creator of Winnie the Pooh, A. A. Milne. He was a writer and went off to serve in World War I. It was supposed to be the war to end all wars. Milne returns home and suffers from PTSD. His wife has a son to cheer him up but they are caught up in the stress of life instead of loving their son.

They hire a nanny whom Christopher loves dearly as she provides him with most of his nurturing and support. Milne leaves the luxury and frantic pace of London society for a place in the country. He decides to write about the horrors of war. He wants to make a difference and prevent another holocaust. The nanny leaves and he and Christopher spend time together and play in the woods with stuffed animals who become the famous Pooh, Tigger, Piglet, Eeyore and others.

The magic of the Hundred Acre Wood is that it takes something painfully fleeting and makes it stay forever. The tragedy of Milne's success is that it trapped a real child in that moment like a fly in amber and made it almost impossible for him to become that thing that every child wants to become – a grownup. Is there a threat more pathetic and painful than Christopher Robin's cry "We'll see how father likes it when I write poems about HIM"? Review by Roger Ebert.

The other part of my experience yesterday is that at our movie house there are six theaters of different size. The two largest were both showing action packed films with lots of violence and the smallest theater had Christopher Robin.

I always try to look at the positive side of life, however it makes me sad to see how much attention we give to carnage then we do to whimsy. I don't attend movies like Thor and they may be very entertaining. I do go to movies that allow me to dream and wonder and hope for all things good. Yes, I have admitted that I am a cockeyed optimist. I will continue to share with all of you the possibilities of the magnificence of the human spirit.

I wish for all of you to continue to discover your inner child. That place in your heart that still has magic and discovery and will never stop dreaming. From my hopeful heart to yours, Thomas

As often as you can, bring out your inner child and nurture and support its natural sense of joy, love and laughter!

November 30   I will never quit!

Some days it is so difficult for me to share this blog in light of what is happening on our planet. There is so much polarization of ideas and values that create an atmosphere of us against them. And for me there will never be an 'us' against them.

We are one incredibly flawed, amazingly talented, human race. There is almost nothing we can't do when we put our whole heart and soul into something. The problem is so many broken hearts.

We have broken each other's hearts by our choices, which we have made out of fear. Our fears have divided us. We are often in so much pain that we lash out against others. Those in the deepest pain seem to make the most horrible violent choices.

We keep trying to remedy the situation with laws and building armies, they both will never work. The only thing that will ever work is when we love each other enough that most of the broken hearts are healed.

And it probably can only work one on one. We get to forgive each other's brokenhearted choices. We get to know that we are all the same. There is only one human race. It has developed over the centuries of shared living on this fragile spacecraft. And if we are ever going to come into a safe landing; we get to find out how to love, to get us all home.

Most of the people in our life, that we love, already know it. They may not know how much but they can feel it deep inside. The other people in our lives that don't know we love them, get to find out!

Let's let everyone know how much we care. Perhaps if we do this more than we have done; the estranged folks might feel included. Then perhaps there will be less anger and more hugging. Then maybe tomorrow's headlines might read: Today there was a group of people arrested for mass hugging in a public place!

I refuse to give in to the painful choices we have made as a society. I will continue to find ways to have others feel they are loved and cared for. Please join me! From my never quitting heart to yours, Thomas

The wounding in our hearts is where the light can flow in, let it fill us with so much light that we can let go of the pain and be in alliance wholeheartedly with all beings!

December 1   Illuminate the World

Lou Ann and I just had the privilege of being a part of a brainstorming session for the Illuminate Film Festival. The fifth year of the festival is scheduled for May 31 to Jun 4 next year. It includes a couple of dozen films, healing seminars, virtual reality, hands on healing village and dozens of people who are in the conscious film making business.

Our programming team is working on a mission statement about the festival. There were many excellent ideas exchanged. There was a general consensus that the festival is a vehicle that does several important things.

Conscious cinema encourages people to become deeply inspired in a personal, local and global way. Life affirming films also create transformation by shifting millions of people to take action and make the world a better place.

You can be part of this amazing organization too! You can volunteer to be on the team and take an active role in creating life changing cinema. You can also join and become a member and lend your support and receive some wonderful benefits for being part of this amazing life changing festival. You can live anywhere and be a part of the team.

I have been sharing with you that our society needs to do something to create the planet we all desire. Here is a way we can all get involved and make a positive difference. Go to illuminatefilmfestival.com and find out how you might be part of the fun! Our world will be the kind of place we all want for our children and grandchildren when you and I get involved! From my illuminated heart to yours, Thomas

Find what you feel passionate about and do that!

December 2 She's got a way about her

She curls her toes under as she sits and records her dreams from the night before. I fall in love all over again when I see her in the kitchen baking a pie. I love life when I wake up in the morning and see her smiling face and eyes that can light up my darkness. I love how she gets so excited when she is going to the Sedona Charter School to teach little ones Yoga.

I love how she holds my hand when we watch a Christmas movie together and then we both have tears in our eyes. I love how we both celebrate the Christmas season beginning around Halloween. I love how she encourages me to continue to write this blog every day. I love how she sees perfect strangers, no matter where we are in the world and says "I think I know that person!" The truth is there are hardly any strangers to her.

I love how she sits at the computer and does her Daily Challenge, a Facebook healthy, social contact program. She has been doing it every day for the past 2295 days (Sad to say the Daily Challenge is no longer active). I love how my heart does a flip flop when I see her; even if we have only been a couple of hours apart. I love how she arranges her closet in the rainbow color spectrum and wears clothes in that order to match the days of the week.

I love how she reaches out in bed with her feet and touches mine in such a tender way. I love how she tells me every day that "she loves me so much! I love how she loves all the little people, the Menehune, Leprechauns and fairies. She has a connection to all of nature.

I love how she is a "bull dog" about important things in life. She has taught me how to not quit. When she starts out to do something, she just keeps going until it is complete. I love how much she loves to dance and teach Zumba. When we are out somewhere and there is music playing in the background, her body is rocking to the rhythm. I love how she says a protection mantra when we go somewhere in our car and she blesses everyone else who is on the road too. We have been together thirty eight years. Our anniversary is New Year Eve. I can't imagine loving anyone more. I am so blessed to be with my best friend, life partner, loving wife and my personal guru! The way she lives life has made me a better person. I am so grateful to have found Lou Ann and I will treasure every moment with her the rest of my life!

I apologize for this being so personal. I wanted you to know the Lou Ann I know. And to know why and what keeps me so positive and happy! From my totally thankful heart to yours, Thomas

When you find what brings you joy, love and laughter, treasure it!

December 3   Saving the Earth

Lou Ann and I went to our local, monthly Inspiration of Sedona meeting tonight. Thank you Pash and Marty for these events! There were a couple of short films; one on small farming and the other on composting.

Both of these activities are vital to the survival of our planet! I know I am often hyperbolic about this subject. If you check out information about climate change, you too may become as fervent an advocate as Lou Ann and I are.

The first film is titled Small-Scale Farmers Cool the Planet. The theme is about how small scale farming is combating climate change through regenerative organic agriculture, and reversing global warming. We all can help by home gardening, including composting. The second film titled SOS-Save Our Soil, which is done by restoring the top soil of our land.

There is also a book which I highly recommend, titled Drawdown: "The most comprehensive plan ever proposed to reverse global warming." It is a book which should be in every home. You and your family can do many of the suggestions in the book, written brilliantly by author Paul Hawken. Many are simple and inexpensive and together we can all make a huge difference in creating the healthy Earth most would love to live in.

Also attending the meeting was Darcy Hitchcock who is the founder of the Sustainability Alliance. They have a survey that anyone can take and see how sustainable you are living. Businesses can get a sustainability rating and use it as an advertising item that will let customers know that they care. If you are in the Sedona area; you can get your business on local TV by taking the survey of sustainability.

I wish you all a marvelous life. Please help out Mother Nature and all the beings on planet Earth by getting involved in combating climate change. Your children and grandchildren will thank you for it! From my Earth saving heart to yours, Thomas

Show your love for planet earth by doing something special for her every day!

December 4   Barking to the Choir

We listen to NPR (National Public Radio) as much as we can while we travel, whenever we can. We often listen to Terry Gross on her show Fresh Air that has been on the radio for more than forty years. She produces and hosts the program and what makes it work is her knowledge of her guests. Gross asks probing questions that allow her guests to open up and share from an honest and candid place.

Tonight, on the road back from Los Angeles, we tuned in to hear her interview a Jesuit priest Father Gregory Boyle. He is the founder of Homeboy Industries in Los Angeles, the largest gang-intervention, rehabilitation, and reentry program in the world. He has just written a new book titled Barking to the Choir: The power of radical kinship.

Homeboy Industries provides hope, training, and support to formerly gang-involved and previously incarcerated men and women allowing them to redirect their lives and become contributing members of their community.

Each year over 10,000 former gang members from across Los Angeles come through Homeboy Industries' doors in an effort to make a positive change. They are welcomed into a community of mutual kinship, love, and a wide variety of services ranging from tattoo removal to anger management and parenting classes.

Full-time employment is offered for more than 200 men and women at a time through an 18-month program that helps them re-identify who they are in the world. Job training is also offered so they can move on from

Homeboy Industries and become contributing members of the community – knowing they count!

Thomas Wolfe in his book "You Can't Go Home Again" writes "To lose the Earth you know, for greater knowing; to lose the life you have, for greater living; to leave the friends you loved, for greater loving; to find a land more kind than home; more large than Earth" Sometimes it takes radical loving action for us to find our way home.

Father Boyle does Buddhist meditation twice a day and has a daily mantra that helps him stay clear. When Lou Ann and I hear a program like this it encourages us to be more and do more about our planet and our local community.

It would be great if many of us found a new and powerful way to lose our lives for greater living. I invite you to find your local NPR station and listen to programs like Fresh Air and perhaps we can all live greater living. From my renewed heart to yours, Thomas

If there is a way for you to support a program like Father Gregory Boyle in your area, go for it! If there isn't one similar, create it!

December 5   So much Healing Available

We have been sourcing movies and entering them into our screening queue for Illuminate Film Festival. Most will not make our festival, however they still have value. I was watching a movie on healing today. It was a beautiful meditative holistic experience. Most of the people to be healed have cancer. And almost all of them are overweight.

Many have gone through the traditional ways to combat cancer. This film showed many alternative ways to augment their traditional therapy. These therapies and disciplines included: Yoga, Meditation, Acupuncture, Cranial-Sacral, Reflexology, herbs, spices, Zentangle (meditative art), exercise, activism and advocacy.

The patients discovered that healing comes from connecting with your heart and soul and spirit. The therapists were all in their hearts and just their presence helped people move toward healing. One of the most important lessons that the patients learned was that their disease reconnected them with their life. It seems we get unconscious and then an event, often a frightening one, wakes us up to what life is really about. We are not here just to work and have careers or many of the other aspects of life. We are here to stop and notice our relationship with All That Is. When we truly find it, we are often overjoyed and we take a different direction in life.

It is then we often find a closer relationship with our families and friends. We even find a way to heal old relationship wounds. Life works in a powerful way when we come face to face with our mortality and use it to find our joy.

Every success and failure is essential to bringing us to this moment in our journey. May we all find a way to appreciate the journey and celebrate our humanity and our divinity! From my healing heart to yours, Thomas

While healing your body, heal your heart too! Why not?!

December 6 Now

We are a society that mostly spends a lot of mental time in the past and in the future and not enough time in the now. Whenever we are reliving the past or thinking of what might occur we miss most of the juice of life. Our minds are helpful in a lot of ways. They organize our thoughts and days and schedules. It might be pretty chaotic without them. However, we give them too much power.

Our minds are limited by our thoughts and our thoughts are often formed from misinformation. When we take time in our day to simply sit and be quiet and take some deep breaths there is an opportunity for freedom. When we get silent and listen to our breath and tune into our inner world, we can get in touch with eternity. From this place, all the possibilities of life are available to us.

This quiet place is also the platform for unlimited creativity. It might be helpful to get into a relaxed space and allow our feelings to take us on a journey of beauty and magic. Ask the question "If money were no object, what would I be doing now?" If I had the freedom to choose anything I desire what would that be?

It is important to let yourself feel the feelings of what your life could be; even more so, then the what, of the previous two questions. We all want to feel loved, happy, abundant, needed and that we matter. Then without making any plans, consulting any experts, taking any lessons; let your positive affirming feelings guide you. Surrender and know that there are no wrong paths to take. Be here now! From my present heart to yours, Thomas

Taking gentle full breaths helps us be in the now, the only time there is! When we feel the feelings we want to create, magic happens!

December 7   Universal principle #19: What You Focus on Expands

"The flow of Divine Power (Love) through the beliefs you hold in consciousness manifest as limitations in your physical reality. Focusing on the physical brings you more of the limitations your existing beliefs are creating. Focus on releasing beliefs and surrendering to all possibility frees the flow of Divine Power to manifest more richness, beauty and joy in your life."

We had a friend that used to sing a mantra to the tune of twinkle, twinkle little star. It goes: what you focus on expands; your life is in your own hands. So true! We are the creators of these amazing lifetimes. Everyone else is a co-star, extra or bit player. We are also the directors and producers of this life script.

What a powerful literal metaphor. No one else has power over us. Not the government, our families, ex-spouses, IRS, in laws, outlaws! We get to choose in every moment exactly how we want our lives to be. Now sometimes this seems limited because we have already made choices that perhaps limit the options we now have. Never the less, we have set it all in motion and now we get to play it out.

If you desire your life to be different, now is the time. Don't wait for the perfect moment. Do it now! Be specific down to the last detail. If you want more love in your life, describe exactly how it will look and feel.

If you want the best relationships, best career, write it down and make it totally the way you desire. Don't do it for someone else. Do it just for you and you will be truly happy. From my heart to yours, Thomas

This completes the Universal principles as presented by Arnold Patent. Lou Ann and I started using these back in 1982 and they have been a major factor in creating the life we desired. Once again, do something good for yourself and go to arnoldpatent.com and connect with Arnold. Your life will never be the same!

This is so important to remember: what we focus on expands; our life IS in our own hands!

December 8   I Want to Live Forever

Today I went into Whole Foods which I always enjoy. When I exited, I walked by a mom and her tow-headed baby. Its hair was sticking up kind of like Harry Potter's and mine for that matter. I immediately got a lump in my throat and tears in my eyes. I took a deep breath and felt thankful for such a beautiful sight. I also thought that I would like to live forever so I could see that child be president. Or come back in another life time and see their inauguration.

I don't know for sure what is after this lifetime. I know Lou Ann feels strongly that her predecessors might be in some heavenly place. I am not sure. I believe that life is forever. I just don't know if that is true of personality. As I have matured, I have come to have more self-regard. I can see that I made a lot of choices that didn't serve me; and yet I also feel they were always on purpose.

I enjoy most of life so much! It truly is a Wonderful Life! I love people, food, sex, vacation, and laughter, sports, communication, hugging, sunshine, dark chocolate, nature, starlight, exercising, watching movies, massage, Christmas, Thanksgiving and licorice. Life is juicy in many ways.

I love to travel to different cultures and experience their differences and sameness. I love sharing this with you.

I get sad when I feel I am closer to the end of this lifetime. I wish it could go on forever. When I was younger, I used to get out of bed early; so excited to see the day. Now I stay in bed longer because I have Lou Ann beside me. Who wouldn't?

If there is an afterlife that consists of a conscious awareness of who I am; I can hardly believe it would be better than this one. I am so thankful for every second of my life; the joyous ones and the painful ones. I wouldn't trade it for anything. I wish for everyone to have as much joy, passion, abundance, love and yes more dark chocolate! From my eternally grateful heart to yours, Thomas

Treasure every moment in your life, especially this one!

December 9 What Love Feels Like

When I play tennis, a lot of the guys and gals exchange good natured barbs. It is a form of sarcasm. Most of it seems to be light hearted and not meant to hurt. I can tell when we cross over the line however. There is an energy present that feels like an old hurt still attached to someone's damaged heart!

Overall it feels like there is too much sarcasm being expressed these days and perhaps it always has.

After all, when you come right down to it, sarcasm is a subtle form of bullying and most bullies are angry, insecure, people who have a lot of personal pain. Alternatively, when a person stops voicing negative comments, especially sarcastic and critical ones, he or she soon starts to feel happier and more self-confident.

If you want to be happier and improve your relationships, cut out sarcasm since sarcasm is actually hostility disguised as humor. Despite smiling outwardly, most people who receive sarcastic comments, feel put down and usually think the sarcastic person is unkind.

I also thought about teasing. This can feel good natured as well and yet, once again for me, there feels like a hidden message of personal hurt. To tease someone means to laugh at them or make jokes about them in order to embarrass, annoy, or upset them.(Webster definition).

Lou Ann and I don't tease each other or speak with sarcasm. We had enough of that kind of banter growing up and it didn't feel good. We go out of the way to have the other person feel loved and nurtured and supported. We find ways to compliment and encourage. We look for the value in what the other person does while giving some alternative suggestions that might improve their effort.

There seems to be a movement to discourage political correctness. It is pictured as a weakness. I believe that when we stay centered in our joy and compassion for all life, it is okay to say things that love and support, rather than to denigrate and criticize.

It is also a choice for love to stand up and defend humanity, against those that are intent on creating chaos and mayhem and destroying our planet by their insecure and unloving choices. For me, when we come from our heart and not our bias or unhealed pain it feels more like love. From my loving heart to yours, Thomas

Notice sarcasm and teasing in your life, if it doesn't feel good, try changing the subject.

December 10   I Wonder

It is an understatement to say the film "Wonder" is wonderful. It is based on a true story of a little boy who was born severely disfigured and had some twenty seven operations to survive. He has very loving parents who eventually take him to a middle school prep school. He is brilliant, but his features are challenging for many of his schoolmates. He gets to figure out how to navigate his way through all the rejection. It is by far the best movie of this season. I believe your life will be better for viewing it!

I was discussing with Lou Ann my enjoyment of evaluating films. I have always felt the term movie critic was self-determining. The word itself defines the role of the person looking at the movie and describing it for potential viewers. And I have never been fond of these reviewers telling movie goers whether they should watch a film or not, based on their ideas.

I would like to propose a new term. I am a movie advocate. I only share with you movies that inspire and make a difference in my life. We also went to see Daddy's Home II. While not as inspiring as Wonder it still has its moments. Of course it has lots of slapstick comedy and a large cast of talented actors. This film depicts two fathers sharing the raising of their children. The plot allows the unfolding of the characters genuine love for each other. You probably will laugh your gluteus maximus off. The film ends with the wonderful song: "Do They Know Its Christmas?" It was performed in November of 1984 at the Band Aid concert to raise money for the starving people of Ethiopia. Here are the lyrics: https://www.youtube.com/results?search_query=do+they+know+it%27s+christmas

For Lou Ann and I it is the most wonderful time of the year. My wish for you is for you to enjoy it as well! From my holiday heart to yours, Thomas

Have a wondrous and loving holiday! Share that joy with others!

December 11 Beautiful night in paradise

We are at home this evening enjoying more Christmas movies that inspire us. We had a wonderful couple join us at our vacation rental part of the home. They were very sweet and friendly and kind.

Lou Ann gave a gift to our neighbor who watched our home a couple of weeks ago. I went for a walk in the beautiful sunshine. It is a normal day at our home and we are full of joy and thankful for all of our blessings. It occurred to me as I write this that it isn't necessary to have blockbuster events to have an exciting life. I am excited to be alive and to be present to all the beauty around me and Lou Ann.

I think sometimes we get trapped into thinking we must do something really important to be of value. When just holding a door open for someone or asking the name of your server at a restaurant is a rich treasure. I am going to make it my goal to do a random act of kindness for someone every day this coming week. They may be aware of it or not, it doesn't matter

Most of us in what we call the Western world live in paradise. However the majority of the world lives in poverty. While we are living in unparalleled luxury and safety, let us give back by finding others who are not so fortunate.

Please join us in sharing random acts of kindness and unspeakable beauty. If a few of us did this every day, we might make a difference! From my very fortunate heart to yours, Thomas

Set a goal to do random acts of kindness as frequently as you can today and throughout the holiday season. Then branch out even further!

December 12   The Soul of the Season

Tonight we watched a move titled "The Sons of Mistletoe." It is a wonderful story about a small town that has a home where wayward boys end up. There is a director of the home, who was stranded at the home when he was young. He grew up to be the kindred soul who loves these young lads unconditionally. It is a wonderful movie and I encourage you to see it if you can.

This movie is the kind of film that touches your heart in a tender way. The plot feels much more like real life. The kids and the hero and others have the kinds of challenges many of us have faced. The love that they discover when they support and care for each other is a true treasure.

This is what the season is all about. Yes, it is fun to give and receive presents. It is a joy to go to holiday functions and concerts and all of the rest. And of course, it is only for some five weeks at the end of the year. The soul of the season is being present for each other in a significant way that changes our lives. It is our gift to the Universe! From my deeply thankful heart to yours, Thomas

Be present as much as you can in your heart, it's the place to go to celebrate being alive!

December 13   Heal

Lou Ann and I went to another showing of the movie titled "Heal". It is a wonderful documentary about our own amazing ability to heal ourselves. The film was the winner at the Maui film festival and it was premiered at our own Illuminate Film Festival as well. I The movie shows several patients who have mostly chronic diseases.

A variety of experts are in the film to share what they have discovered about healing and how they use it. It is clear that stress is the number one killer on the planet. You can probably trace almost all forms of illness and disease to stress in some form. The challenge is that for most of us, we do not realize how much stress is occurring in our lives and the damaging and deadly accumulation of it.

HEAL takes us on a scientific and spiritual journey where we discover that our thoughts, beliefs, and emotions have a huge impact on our health and ability to heal. The latest science reveals that we are not victims of unchangeable genes, nor should we buy into a scary prognosis. The fact is, we have more control over our health and life, than we have been taught to believe.

This film will empower you with a new understanding of the miraculous nature of the human body and the extraordinary healer within us all. Healing can be extremely complex and deeply personal, but it can also happen spontaneously in a moment.

At the movie tonight, we had one of the healing practitioners in the film share his expertise in person. His name is Dr. Jefferey Thompson and he is located in San Diego. Dr. Thompson uses sound to help you heal yourself.

He discovered that the different levels of sound relate to different parts of the body and can be used specifically for that area. Everyone is different, so Dr. Thompson uses a system that measures each person's exact levels of energy. So each of us can get our own sounds that will help us heal! From my healing heart to yours, Thomas

Let yourself be aware of stress in any part of your body, like your shoulders, and relax them with a gentle and big breath!

December 14   Finding Your Jolly

There is a cute film titled "Finding Santa". There is a man who trains others to be Santa Claus' helpers. His mantra for this business is Finding Your Jolly. The movie depicts men and women who hold onto their emotional position of being right.

Many years ago, Lou Ann and I attended a very confrontational personal training. The process of the weekend was for each of us to release our beliefs and actions that did not serve us. There were thirty people in the room and when one person began their own processing; the rest of the group encouraged them to have a breakthrough.

It sounds more pleasant in the way I am depicting it. It was very painful to give up beliefs that I held on to so tight. I can remember when it came my turn and I was totally resisting the process; passionate women who were swearing at me and were very angry at my resistance. At the same time, I don't know of a time when I have felt more love from others. I can still remember that anger in their voices and the love in their eyes.

Another observation of the weekend was that women gave up their position more readily. They seem to be more in their hearts then the guys. Lots of men like to conquer. They learn how to use their will to get what they want. And many times, let nothing stand in their way.

However, when they finally come to the point in their life that those actions didn't create all they desire, something has to give. I noticed on that weekend that when I and other men finally spoke the truth, something magnificent happened.

We shared our fears and our beliefs and finally let go. The energy in the room was electric! Many of us hold on so fiercely that when we finally let go, it feels like a choir of heavenly angels just entered the room! Then the other twenty nine people all held this tender soul in their arms and loved them through the process of letting go and finding themselves.

My wish for everyone today is to find your jolly. What is it that really gives you joy? Not what is expected of us? Perhaps not what your education or life experience is about. What is it that truly lights up your eyes and gives you goosebumps? Without blowing up your whole life, go out and find it. Find your reason for joy and when you do, the world will light up! From my jolly heart to yours, Thomas

Start with feeling inner peace without any external circumstance creating it, and then go from there to discover more joy!

December 15   Atta Boy Clarence!

The title is the last line of the great Christmas movie "It's a Wonderful Life". Lou Ann and I have probably seen it at least fifty times or more. I weep openly when the movie ends. It is such an important message for all of us. We matter. We are all connected. We have touched so many lives. Not all of us are like George Bailey with such a huge giving heart. However, we shouldn't underestimate our value to each other.

From time to time I will reconnect with someone who was in our Spirit church family. I haven't spoken to them in years. Then, they will share with me that something I said in one of my talks changed their life forever. It may be why this movie affects me so deeply.

In the final scene of the movie there is an inscription from George's guardian angel, Clarence. It says "no man is a failure who has friends". It is so true. I think there should be a bumper sticker that says "those who die with the most friends, win!" I just want to remind all of you of the value that you give our planet.

I am so grateful that all of you showed up in my lifetime to demonstrate how to live powerful, loving lives! You make life a treasure. Together, we can all create a society where friendship and love, not money and things are valued above all. Then our guardian angels can get their wings. And we can get ours too when we fly home. From my angelic heart to yours, Thomas

Treasure your friends and angels in your life!

December 16   When You Care Enough!

We just watched the Christmas Train movie on Hallmark. It is adapted from a book written by David Baldacci.

Disillusioned journalist Tom Langdon must get from Washington to LA in time for Christmas. Forced to take the train across the country because of a slight 'misunderstanding' at airport security, he begins a journey of self-discovery and rude awakenings, mysterious goings-on and thrilling adventures, screwball escapades and holiday magic.

He has no idea that the locomotive pulling him across America will actually take him into the rugged terrain of his own heart, where he will rediscover people's essential goodness and someone very special he believed he had lost.

The Hallmark tag line has for a long time been "When you care enough to send the very best" The commercials on these wonderful films depict real life people making a difference in the world.   One is about a wonderful teacher who enrolls her students in being Secret Kindness Agents. Her name is Karolyn Roby and she is an instructional facilitator at the Skinner Magnet Center.

Every child must come up with their own acts of kindness and each must have a Secret Agent name. Some of the names are Agent Puppy Paws, Agent Chocolate Covered Caramel Donuts and Agent Kitty. These wonderful children practice acts of kindness all over the school.

Now the Hallmark tag line is "When you care enough.....followed by words like you can change the world or you can make a difference or to lead by example."

When we care enough, wonderful, magical, loving things happen. *And we can make the world a better place for you and for me and the entire human race...*thank you Michael Jackson. From my always amazed heart to yours, Thomas

Let us all be Secret Kindness agents – what a place the world will be when we do!

December 17 Angels We Have Heard on High

When I write about angels, I am writing about all of us! We are all divine. We are all love. We are Oneness. Sometimes we forget about our divinity and can't find our wings. Somewhere deep inside is the connection.

It is fun to incarnate on places like planet Earth and take on this human form. When we get caught up in believing in limitation we create circumstances that appear real and they are not. Our limitless energy is real. Our bodies are not real. Our jobs are not real. In fact most everything we can observe is only temporary. You and I are not temporary.

We agreed a trillion years ago to come here and support each other in creating what we desire. We knew then, it was all a dance. Somehow we turned the dance into conflict and limitation. That is not real. What is real is the love that we feel and share.

We are the angels we knew would come. It is time for all of us to spread our wings and fly together in a beautiful heart formation. Then our sisters and brothers who still can't find their wings will remember who they are. Once we all remember, there will be peace on Earth. I invite all of us to shine even brighter than before. From my angelic heart to yours. Thomas

There is a song that goes like this: You're an angel, you're a being of light! It's a song about you and me! Remember who we all are!

December 18   The Best Day of your Life

We watched another Christmas movie and a couple asked each other what was the best day of your life? They ended up creating their best day together.

I think it would be nearly impossible to choose only one day as the best day. Life is full of days that might fall in the top ten though. For me, the best days of my life were the days that each of my children were born, Michael, December 7th, Deborah, January 7th, Chris, December 20th and Jim, June 12th.

Then there is the day I met Lou Ann for the first time and instantly liked her even though we would not get together for three more years. Then New Year's Eve, 1982 we were married in Scottsdale AZ with our children present. I also got to perform weddings for my son Michael and his bride Pearl and for Lou Ann's daughter Uma who married Dave on a beach in Hawaii.

There have also been the worst days of my life, mixed in with the best. I won't go into the details of many of those. In retrospect though, some of the worst days have turned out to also be some of the best. I guess that might be true for most of us.

As I look back upon my life I remember the deaths of loved ones, business losses, loss of homes in Virginia. They pale in comparison to all the joy and wonder and magic of all the other days which would be most days! I remember too, I was blessed to be the pastor of a church here in Sedona for about three and a half years. There were about fifty folks who would show up on Sunday and we would laugh and cry and celebrate life in a wonderful way. Those Sundays were also some of the best days of my life.

I invite you to take some time after reading this post to reminisce about your life and see what your best days were. And perhaps like me, discover what might have been a worst day when it happened, that turned out to be a best day. I wish for you that all the days of your life from now on will be exactly what your heart desires them to be! From my thankful heart to yours, Thomas

Cherish the best days of your life and every day of your life as they are precious too!

December 19   Positive Place

There is a movie titled "Memories are like a bridge between the heart and the mind". It reminded me of something I used to share about the distance to travel from unconscious to conscious is only eighteen inches, the distance between your heart and your mind. That physical short journey is actually one that will have us feel more alive than we have ever felt before. We so often get stuck in our activities and plans and trying to succeed that we miss the heart and soul of being alive!

There was another line in the movie that was an Emily Dickinson quote "Possible's slow fuse is lit by the imagination". We truly do not know what is possible. We live lives of limitation, often because we have been told to and so we believe that there are limits to our human expression. And it is just not true. Countless times throughout history, people have been told certain "facts" that turned out to not be true. The Earth does revolve around the sun, and it is round!

In our personal lives, we have given away our imagination, power and passion and played it safe. It is never too late to take the journey from our minds to our hearts and discover our limitless abilities. No matter our age, education, experience or beliefs, today can be the day that we connect with our purpose for being and our joy of living! From my positive heart to yours, Thomas

When we take the trip from our mind to our hearts, magical things can happen! I'm positive about it!

December 20   Yearly checkup

As I look back upon this year there are some things that I know about all of you.

You are perfect the way you are.

You don't need fixing.

You are always on purpose.

You have unlimited ability.

You are an eternal spirit.

You always do the best you can do.

You are magnificent.

You are love.

You are loved.

You are here for a reason.

The reason is love.

You are a celebration of life.

From my heart to yours, Thomas

Change the word 'you' to 'I' in each of the above sentences and feel your confident feelings grow! Pick a few of these each day and let them speak to you about the truth of your being!

December 21   Believe

Lou Ann and I were headed back from Prescott Costco this afternoon; singing carols and songs all the way. At one point, the wonderful song "Believe" by Josh Groban was playing. Lou Ann and I were honored to perform it Christmas 2 years ago, as a duo here in Sedona during the Canyon Singers Concert. The song was featured in Disney's Polar Express, which I highly recommend. Here are the lyrics:
https://www.youtube.com/watch?v=Gr_skHRt6tM

The music was written for a Christmas movie. For me, it is so much more than that. Many of us, not so long ago, were dreamers. And sometimes the dreams slip away. We don't have to wait for Christmas or any other occasion to rekindle them. The admonition is to believe in what your heart is saying. I urge everyone to do that.

Your heart always knows the way. And the song also tells us to do it right away. "There's no time to waste". And finally, "you have everything you need, if you just believe" Then our dreams will have wings to fly! I encourage everyone to follow their hearts and then our dreams can become a reality. From my winged heart to yours, Thomas

Listen to the song on YouTube to remind you to believe in yourself and your dreams!

December 22 When You Wish Upon a Star

Yesterday was the winter solstice in the northern hemisphere and the summer solstice in the southern hemisphere. The winter solstice, also known as midwinter, is the shortest day of the year and the longest night of the year.

It occurs when the sun appears at its most southerly position. The earliest people on Earth built monuments to follow the sun's yearly progress, for example, Stonehenge in England. At sunrise at Stonehenge on the longest day of the year, the rising sun appears behind one of the main stones, creating the illusion that the sun is balancing on the stone.

I was fortunate to visit Stonehenge in 1978. While there I had an amazing spiritual experience where I could see back to the past and saw visions of people who were gathered there at different times.

I shared this information with a few who were with me at the time. They took pictures of me when I said these things but none of their pictures came out. Those particular pictures or slides were blank in their rolls of film although all their other pictures developed!

This year, we also get the treat of a full moon and some Ursid meteor showers as well. Quite a celebration for all of us! It is as if the heavens are celebrating something that is occurring on our planet and perhaps in our hearts. Take some time to experience these celestial events. It may give you some insight into something you have been wishing for!

In 1940, my birth year the Academy Award winning song was "When you Wish upon a Star". https://www.youtube.com/watch?v=pguMUFyJ3_U YouTube link.

If our hearts are in our dreams, no request is too extreme is the key for me. We all have dreams and sometimes it feels like they won't or can't come true. We can be the creators of those dreams when we really put our heart and soul into them. And when we do that and never let go of our dreams our wishes will come true. I wish for all of you that your dreams come true and that your heart is filled with a secret longing and that it gets fulfilled! From my wishing heart to yours, Thomas

Even Morning Star wishes can come true according to the song: 'The Rainbow Connection' – so make a wish, feel as though it has already happened, be grateful for it and take some steps toward it!

December 23   Connection

Every day, seven per cent of our body leaves us while another seven per cent replaces it. The breath you are taking now was on the other side of the planet four or five days ago. Part of us today will be in some living plants tomorrow.

There are more than one hundred thousand galaxies bumping into each other and they help create the iron that is in our blood. When each of us thinks a thought it is felt across the world. We are not only not alone, we are inseparable. So, what we think, say and do affects our lives, our close friends and families and people all over the Earth.

This is how we wanted it. We are Oneness, creating in our infinite ability to do so. That brings with it a responsibility to do our very best to think, speak and take actions that support all of us, all the time.

Right now on December twenty third, I encourage all of us to take some time to see, if what we are doing is supportive of the whole. It is a great time to repair relationships that have not gone so well. It is a wonderful time to let go of our judgments. It is a perfect time to celebrate each other and send loving thoughts to all. It's the time of year when the world could fall in love! From my connected heart to yours, Thomas

Be in the Oneness of love and gratitude in your conscious awareness – aren't we all amazing?!

December 24   Christmas Eve

Lou Ann and I are at the Hilton Woodland Hills, north of Los Angeles. Six of us will be sleeping in one room. It is almost like no room at the inn; in this case, no room to walk around. We are here with Lou Ann's daughter Uma, her grandson Ganapatiye, her grandson Alu (formally known as Bhima) and his girlfriend Sophie. Uma flew in from Hawaii, Alu and friend rode a bus for twenty six hours from Seattle, Ganapatiye lives here and of course we just drove in from Sedona.

Lou Ann made them all chocolate chip cookies with real butter and eggs. I made a loaf of German Stolen for each of the three of them. Where there is a Christmas will, there is a way! We will be here for three or four days.

We will be staying at the Hari Krishna center for a couple of nights down in Los Angeles. Over my lifetime, I have had some unusual Christmas experiences. A few years ago, we ended up eating Chinese food in a run-down restaurant in Warrenton Virginia. We laughed a lot!

I have found though, that it doesn't matter where or what the circumstances, it is always a merry Christmas. It may not look like a Hallmark Christmas, but the spirit and the love are the same as we celebrate the magic of the season.

I know many of you may not even celebrate Christmas. For me, this time of year is a time to connect with all that is good about life! So, I wish for you, all the love, joy and prosperity that your heart's desire. From my ho, ho, ho heart to yours, Thomas

*If the spirit of Christmas is in your heart, it doesn't matter where you are!
EnJOY!*

December 25   Merry Christmas

This was unlike any other Christmas, with five in our hotel room, stinky feet, coughing, snoring, and no fan in bathroom. But we were together. We exchanged some gifts then rehearsed some Christmas carols. We shared lots of hugs. Uma and I danced to Karen Carpenter's Merry Christmas darling.

I asked Universe to show me some sign that it was there and connected to me. I got a nail in my front left tire and Alu and I went out to change it. I got out the owner's manual and opened the four hundred page book to the exact page to change a tire on our Highlander. Message number one:

I received my daily message from the Universe to all of us; which I will share with you now.

"If it's not yet obvious to you, the real reason for this, and all seasons, is you, (your name). A more perfect child of the Universe has never lived. Until now, only celebrations cloaked in myth and mystery could hint at your divine heritage and sacred destiny. You are life's prayer of becoming and its answer. The first light at the dawn of eternity, drawn from the ether, so that I might know my own depth, discover new heights, and revel in seas of blessed emotion.

A pioneer into illusion, an adventurer into the unknown, and a lifter of veils. Courageous, heroic, and exalted by legions in the unseen.

To give beyond reason, to care beyond hope, to love without limit; to reach, stretch, and dream, in spite of your fears. These are the hallmarks of divinity – traits of the immortal – your badges of honor. May you wear them with a pride as great as what we feel for you!

Your light has illuminated darkened paths, your gaze has lifted broken spirits, and already your life has changed the course of history.

This is the time of year we celebrate (your name)

Bowing before Greatness, the Universe"

I encourage all of you to create your day, just like this and see what happens. It would be wonderful if you would get back to me and share your creations as well. Happy holidays! From my Universal heart to yours, Thomas

Have a joyous and happy day filled with happy surprises and wonder!

December 26   The day after

We are still in Los Angeles spending the day with Uma and grandsons. We tried to go to the Griffith Observatory but there were thousands of people visiting and we couldn't get in. The observatory is in the north part of Hollywood where I grew up. We traveled down many of the streets that I lived on as a child and it brought back many memories. I used to go all over the neighborhood and pick fresh fruit off the trees.

We went by the Hollywood Presbyterian Church where I used to roller skate on Wednesday evenings and eat spaghetti; I fell in love for the first time at 16. I have an urge to return sometime and take a few days to find many of the places that I lived and take some pictures and recall the memories. A magical place that will always stay embedded in my memory!

We are staying tonight down in Los Angeles at the Hari Krishna center. We had a wonderful vegan meal. The greater Hari Krishna world organization feeds over two million people for free daily all over the planet. This is the essence of spirituality! This is the Hindu religion that has been around for thousands of years. They are vegetarians. We are blessed to be able to be here tonight and then we will head home tomorrow.

The more I experience other philosophies of life the more I experience oneness. At our core, we citizens of Oneness create an amazing spectrum of beliefs and practices. However, when I talk with folks who honor Eastern religions it always feels like home to me.

They are more inclusive than many western religions, so it feels like family! I am so grateful for my early life in this incredible city of so many ideas, beliefs and activities. It is way too crowded for me now but it will always be home for me. From my all-inclusive heart to yours, Thomas

Feel the blessings of love in your heart and celebrate your Oneness with all of us!

December 27 Back home again

We just arrived back home after a nine hour trip from Los Angeles. It took us seven hours going there. Who knew that hundreds of thousands of folks had the same idea to leave at the same time? The first two hours of the return today, we only drove 78 miles!

I've written at length about being home and why it is important to so many of us. And, that home for us can be so many different things and places. Whoever said "home is where the heart is" hit it right on the nose. So, for me my home can be many places around the world that I have lived. It is also the place where my family is wherever that might be. However, my emotional physical place is Hollywood.

The place I would like to spend more time in is Virginia with my children and grandchildren.

Lou Ann and I planned our upcoming months as we drove along. We are really good at brainstorming around what we desire to create. They may not be New Year's resolutions, but they are things we definitely want to accomplish in the next year or eighteen months. We will let you in on our schemes and dreams as we go along.

What is up for you for the next phase of your life? Are you moving forward or feeling a little stuck? We love to help others create their dreams. If you have the desire to do what you love or just hang out, let us know, so that we can support you all. From my brainstorming heart to yours, Thomas

If you are feeling stuck, let it be okay for the moment and then breathe in and out to let your heart and soul move you into a harmonious place of taking tiny steps forward into loving yourself and others.

December 28 The Two Step

Some folks I know are having challenges with creating what they desire. They make plans and somehow they don't seem to finish them. Then they beat themselves up for not performing.

Our former mentor, Arnold Patent had a simple way of moving energy so we get what we want. It goes like this. *"If you create something that doesn't feel good; do not spend a lot of time figuring it out. Simply notice how you feel with the results; then without spending so much time in your mind about all the aspects of the result. Take step two. It is to feel how you want to feel now. Go within and find a feeling that gives you pleasure and stay with it. Our feelings are the connection to getting what we desire. Our minds will lead us on a not so merry chase. So, instead of focusing on what you want such as a great job, wonderful relationship, abundance or even world peace, spend time on how you want to feel and Universe will do all the rest!"*

Let's review. I encourage you to try the two-step. Remember, first notice how you feel about your creation. Then if it is not how you desire to feel, immediately let go of that energy. Then spend the most time in step two, in feeling fully how you really desire. You will be amazed at the results. From my dancing heart to yours, Thomas

A Holiday dance is always in order! Feel how you want to feel – this is where to linger in the 'two step'!

December 29   Christmas Carol

Lou Ann and I just watched the Muppet's Christmas Carol again. You all know the story of course. The unique telling of this one is the Muppets

gorgeous interpretation. It is a brilliant presentation with so much humor and tenderness. Then there is the music magnificently written by Paul Williams. If you have never seen this version, please find a copy and do so, you will not regret it. At one point there is a song entitled "Bless us all". Here is the YouTube link:
https://www.youtube.com/watch?v=vEtXQku79q0

The opening two stanzas that "life is full of sweet surprises and every day's a gift" could be a wonderful mantra for us all. Yes, there are surprises in life that are not so sweet and we all experience them. And each day, we get to have a brand new experience of seeing it as a gift.

Please read the lyrics and perhaps copy them or better yet go to Youtube.com and listen to the song if you can. And, as Tiny Tim once proclaimed "bless us all, everyone". May this coming year be filled with the richest of blessings for all of you. From my totally blessed heart to yours, Thomas

Repeat often today 'life is full of sweet surprises and every day's a gift'!

December 30   Mom

December was one of the best months of the year growing up in Hollywood. My dad was an alcoholic and had dozens of jobs he couldn't keep and so we struggled financially and emotionally. My mom worked at the local Sears Roebuck and company (as it was then named) to keep the family afloat. And she made the meals and tried to support her three sons in any way she could.

Somehow around Christmas time we would somehow get a fresh tree and decorate it. Gladys (mom), we also lovingly called her happy butt, and she loved it, would make Christmas Stolen. It is homemade bread, full of raisins, almonds and Citron, topped with powdered sugar. We would then have the huge turkey dinner with the gravy, mashed potatoes, sweet potatoes, cranberry sauce and of course pumpkin pie.

It was also the time of year when I would get clothes and shoes and things for school, which I appreciated so much. Then somehow on

Christmas morning there would be lots of presents under the tree. We listened to Christmas music on the radio and in later years watched "It's a Wonderful Life" and "White Christmas".

You can see how I came to love this time of the year. It was Gladys Naomi Bruck who was the anchor of sanity and bringer of joy that made it happen for the youngest of three boys. As the years went by, my mom and I were the closest to each other in heart and deed.

So now, Lou Ann and I give a lot of time and energy to the celebration of the season. We both love giving gifts and watching the corny, but lovable films that make us cry and remember our past. We continue to create new loving memories of this special time of year.

I wish for you all to have this kind of love and caring that I got from my mother. My mom helped me make it through some very difficult times and showed me how to be a compassionate caring person. I miss her each Christmas and I celebrate her holiday spirit which shone throughout the year! From my holiday heart to yours, Thomas

Hope there is someone in your life that you can celebrate during the whole year – if not, be it for yourself and someone else!

December 31   HAPPY NEW YEAR

It has been a year filled with all the things that make life rich. There were celebrations and parties and all that allows us to feel good. There were those who left us and went on to other adventures of their soul. There were newcomers who arrived and will be the ones that get to create a wonderful world for all of its inhabitants.

I wish for you the tastiest food, the liveliest dances, the mellowest path, the most abundance you have ever had. I hope you have more hugs, more kisses, more smiles, more laughs than ever before. I wish for you to know who you are, in the deepest part of your heart. I wish for you to find the job, hobby or activity that lights up your eyes and brings you tears of joy and allows you to leap out of bed!

I wish for you the health to do all you desire. I wish for you that you make choices from the center of your being and that you know they are divine. I wish for you quiet moments when you connect with Oneness. I wish for you a path that is filled with passion, treasure and completion.

I wish for you to find the place within that has wanted to be loved more. I wish for you to take your life to its highest possible expression of love and compassion and caring.

I wish for you, puppies to lick your face, babies to kiss your cheek, flowers that smell like heaven and words from fellow travelers that let you know how much you are loved. Have a wonderful new year from my joyful heart to yours, Thomas

Hope our wishes for you come true! We want you to know you are greatly loved!

Our Hearts Journey

We have shared a journey of exploring our Divine nature in a variety of ways. We have celebrated marches all over the world. We have discovered Universal Principles to guide us along the way. We have laughed and cried and had goosebumps. We have seen goodness shared all over our planet. We have been shown new ways to protect our environment. We have learned to trust our inner voice. We have learned to follow our hearts.

My deepest thanks go to my life partner and loving wife Lou Ann. Every day for the past few years she has edited this post. It would have been a mess without her. She has a sharp eye and a brilliant mind and she keeps me on track. Thanks for being with me all this time. For love is the light that shines from heart to heart. From my celebratory heart to yours, Thomas

Notice the italicized quotes at the end of each day and you will find a message from Lou Ann to you straight from her heart!

EnJOY!!

Author bio page

Thomas Bruck has been sharing Universal principles for over fifty years. He graduated from the National Spiritual Science University in 1975. He has spoken to thousands of folks around the world about living life from our hearts. He led a Spiritual Center in Sedona Arizona from 1993-1997. He developed a television show in 1997 called The Positive Place Television Talk Show that was endorsed by many celebrities including Mother Theresa. He currently is writing and producing a new television show with his wife Lou Ann, called Enriching Life Forever. He blogs on Facebook under his name and the blogs can be found on positiveplace.com.

Lou Ann Bruck has been a pharmacist for 40 plus years, Yoga and Zumba instructor last 20 years. Her leaning is toward holistic health and alternative medicine. She and Thomas met in 1979 at the A.R.E. Medical Clinic in Phoenix. A.R.E. stands for Association for Research and Enlightenment - based on Edgar Cayce's readings. There she did massage therapy for clients and dispensed pharmaceutical medications recommended by holistically oriented Medical Doctors. Also she helped patients with herbal products that Edgar Cayce had suggested. Lou Ann learned many mind, body and spirit modalities to help her and others with their growth. She continues to love and support in whatever capacity she can.

Besides sharing positive news they love to share Universal Principles of living life in every moment – filled with laughter, love and magic!

They are currently writing and producing television show segments called Enriching Life Forever. Two of these can be found on YouTube.

https://www.youtube.com/channel/UColxOBAIudg5IKwY384eoZg

They will be going across country to share this book and create videos of people making a difference in their community. Let them know if you or a friend has been helping others by sending an email to Thomas@positiveplace.com or louann@positiveplace.com

Made in the USA
Columbia, SC
17 July 2021